Socialist Entrepreneurs? Business Histories of the GDR and Yugoslavia

This book breaks new ground, taking business history where it has only reluctantly gone in the past. The introduction reviews the small, but growing, literature based on fresh archival materials, which investigates the history of business organisation in the Global East, or the Second World in the Cold War. It argues that there is already a great variety of approaches that go beyond the view of the Soviet-style firm as primarily a production function. Focusing on East Germany and Yugoslavia, seven chapters showcase new directions in the field, and demonstrate that the combination of business history with other historical and disciplinary approaches can help unpack the diversity of historical experiences, explain geographical variances, and offer new avenues for synthesis. The volume's exploration of different historical eras, including those of postwar reconstruction, through globalisation, to transformation, also shows that the Global East should not be treated as disconnected from the rest of the world, but as part of wider, global trends. As such, the volume makes a plea for the utility of studying the Global East to business history and the utility of business history to the study of the Global East.

The chapters in this book were originally published as a special issue of *Business History.*

Vladimir Unkovski-Korica is Senior Lecturer based in Central and East European Studies at the University of Glasgow. His first book *The Economic Struggle for Power in Tito's Yugoslavia: From World War II to Non-Alignment* was published by I.B. Tauris in 2016.

Saša Vejzagić earned a PhD in history and civilisation from the European University Institute in Florence in 2021. He is interested in economic, business, and social history of the 20th century in Yugoslavia. Currently he is a research associate at the Strossmayer Gallery of Old Masters, Croatian Academy of Sciences and Arts.

Socialist Entrepreneurs? Business Histories of the GDR and Yugoslavia

Edited by
Vladimir Unkovski-Korica and Saša Vejzagić

Routledge
Taylor & Francis Group
LONDON AND NEW YORK

First published 2025
by Routledge
4 Park Square, Milton Park, Abingdon, Oxon OX14 4RN

and by Routledge
605 Third Avenue, New York, NY 10158

Routledge is an imprint of the Taylor & Francis Group, an informa business

British Library Cataloguing in Publication Data
A catalogue record for this book is available from the British Library

ISBN13: 978-1-032-84522-7 (hbk)
ISBN13: 978-1-032-84524-1 (pbk)
ISBN13: 978-1-003-51362-9 (ebk)

DOI: 10.4324/9781003513629

Typeset in Myriad Pro
by Newgen Publishing UK

Publisher's Note
The publisher accepts responsibility for any inconsistencies that may have arisen during the conversion of this book from journal articles to book chapters, namely the inclusion of journal terminology.

Contents

Citation Information vi
Notes on Contributors viii

Introduction: Business history goes East 1
Vladimir Unkovski-Korica and Saša Vejzagić

1 Persistent centralisation of decision-making in the age of industrial atomisation and self-management on the case of construction company *Industrogradnja* Zagreb (1966–1980) 18
Saša Vejzagić

2 Tensions between plan and market in a political factory in socialist Kosovo 39
Pieter Troch

3 Management of technological innovation: High tech R&D in the GDR 57
Dolores L. Augustine

4 Workers against technocrats: The failed economic reform and the rise of consumer socialism in the German Democratic Republic 74
Eszter Bartha

5 Entrepreneurs as saviours of socialism? The complicated relationship between East German state socialism and entrepreneurship 89
Max Trecker

6 Losing the global: (Re)building a Bosnian enterprise across transition 106
Anna Calori

7 Varieties of capitalism or variegated state capitalism? East Germany and Yugoslavia in comparative perspective 122
Gareth Dale and Vladimir Unkovski-Korica

Index 155

Citation Information

The following chapters in this book were originally published in *Business History*, volume 65, issue 7 (2023). When citing this material, please use the original page numbering for each article, as follows:

Introduction

Business history goes East: An introduction
Vladimir Unkovski-Korica and Saša Vejzagić
Business History, volume 65, issue 7 (2023), pp. 1119–1136

Chapter 1

Persistent centralisation of decision-making in the age of industrial atomisation and self-management on the case of construction company Industrogradnja *Zagreb (1966–1980)*
Saša Vejzagić
Business History, volume 65, issue 7 (2023), pp. 1137–1157

Chapter 2

Tensions between plan and market in a political factory in socialist Kosovo
Pieter Troch
Business History, volume 65, issue 7 (2023), pp. 1158–1176

Chapter 3

Management of technological innovation: high tech R&D in the GDR
Dolores L. Augustine
Business History, volume 65, issue 7 (2023), pp. 1177–1193

Chapter 4

Workers against technocrats: The failed economic reform and the rise of consumer socialism in the German Democratic Republic
Eszter Bartha
Business History, volume 65, issue 7 (2023), pp. 1194–1208

Chapter 5

Entrepreneurs as saviours of socialism? The complicated relationship between East German state socialism and entrepreneurship
Max Trecker
Business History, volume 65, issue 7 (2023), pp. 1209–1225

Chapter 6

Losing the global: (Re)building a Bosnian enterprise across transition
Anna Calori
Business History, volume 65, issue 7 (2023), pp. 1226–1241

Chapter 7

Varieties of capitalism or variegated state capitalism? East Germany and Yugoslavia in comparative perspective
Gareth Dale and Vladimir Unkovski-Korica
Business History, volume 65, issue 7 (2023), pp. 1242–1274

Notes on Contributors

Dolores L. Augustine is Professor of History at St. John's University, Queens, New York. Her monograph *Taking on Technocracy: Nuclear Power in Germany, 1945 to the Present* has won the German Studies Association Book Prize.

Eszter Bartha is Associate Professor at Eötvös Loránd University (ELTE) of Budapest, Hungary (Department of Eastern and Central European History and Historical Russistics). Her main research field is the post-war social history of Eastern Europe, with an emphasis on labour and gender history. She has published extensively on the state socialist era and the working class including her book *Alienating Labour: Workers on the Road from Socialism to Capitalism in East Germany and Hungary* (2013) published by Berghahn. In 2023, she co-edited the volume *State Socialism in Eastern Europe: History, Theory, Anti-capitalist Alternatives* (Palgrave Macmillan).

Anna Calori is Lecturer in Contemporary Economic History at the University of Glasgow. Before joining Glasgow, she was a Marie-Curie COFUND postdoctoral research fellow at the University of Vienna. Anna is part of a collaborative research project titled: YU-ZAM: A Socialist Workplace in Postcolonial Africa , funded by the Austrian research fund.

Gareth Dale is Reader in political economy at Brunel University. His publications include books on Karl Polanyi, the GDR and Eastern Europe, revolutions in the present era, Green Growth, and international migration. His essays have appeared in *The Conversation, Open Democracy*, and *The Ecologist*.

Max Trecker is Visiting Associate Professor at University of Pittsburgh. His research deals with questions of privatization, theories and practices of foreign trade, and entrepreneurship, among others.

Pieter Troch is Assistant Professor in Southeast European Languages and Cultures at Ghent University. His first book Nationalism and Yugoslavia: Education, Yugoslavism and the Balkans before World War II was published by I.B. Tauris in 2015. His ongoing research concerns the social history of Kosovo since WWII. His publications on the topic include the photobook Layers of Time in the Urban Landscape: Visions of Socialist Modernity in Mitrovica, which came out with JOVIS Verlag in 2018.

Vladimir Unkovski-Korica is Senior Lecturer based in Central and East European Studies at the University of Glasgow. His first book *The Economic Struggle for Power in Tito's Yugoslavia: From World War II to Non-Alignment* was published by I.B. Tauris in 2016.

Saša Vejzagić earned a PhD in history and civilisation from the European University Institute in Florence in 2021. He is interested in economic, business, and social history of the 20th century in Yugoslavia. Currently he is a research associate at the Strossmayer Gallery of Old Masters, Croatian Academy of Sciences and Arts.

Introduction: Business history goes East

Vladimir Unkovski-Korica and Saša Vejzagić

ABSTRACT
This article introduces the special issue 'Socialist Entrepreneurs? Business Histories of the GDR and Yugoslavia'. It starts with a review of the growing literature on the history of business organisation in the Global East, or the Second World in the Cold War. It then argues that mainstream business history struggles to incorporate the findings of this emerging body of work, relying as it does on the traditional view of the Soviet-style firm as primarily a production function. We show that a more nuanced view, exploring a greater variety of experiences in the USSR and beyond it, has now developed, through the use of fresh archival evidence and the combination of business history with other historical and disciplinary approaches. Focusing on the GDR and Yugoslavia, the seven contributions in this special issue showcase new directions in the field and demonstrate how we gain innovative perspectives by taking business history 'eastwards'.

Introduction

Following the October Revolution in 1917, the nature and extent of the challenge posed to the capitalist system by the Soviet Union and various Soviet-style polities across the globe gradually became the subject of intense study and debate. The growth of the field of Soviet Studies in the years after the Second World War, which included many historians, pitched establishment critics of the Soviet system against scholars with broadly socialist sympathies (Engerman, 2011). Even taking into account the difficulty of access to primary materials during the Cold War, however, the sub-discipline of business history was comparatively slow to venture 'eastward'. Explaining why that was so is difficult. According to some critics (Scranton & Fridenson, 2013), the founders of the sub-discipline, from the 1950s to the 1970s, tended to take the US as the norm and as normative, which might have made an 'eastward' direction in research difficult. Critically, the most influential and extensive *oeuvre* of one of the sub-discipline's founding figures, Alfred Chandler (1918–2007), concentrated on the era of American big business (Chandler, 1962, 1977, 1993). It focused on the firm, was based on extensive empirical data, mostly from archives, as well as cross-country comparisons in the US and Western Europe, and explored themes such as technology, management, organisation and operation. The Chandlerian method was widely seen in its time as methodologically rigorous and open to discussion with other disciplines like economics and business management. Given the transnational spread of Fordism (Link, 2020), it would have been logical for the firm in Soviet-style economies to come under the scrutiny of Western scholars, and some, like the economist David Granick, extensively studied the Soviet and East European system of industrial management (Granick, 1954, 1960, 1975). Ironically, though, it was only after the end of the Cold War, when the West's great protagonist had been defeated, that business history began to more systematically engage with the Cold War's Second World.

This special issue showcases an emerging literature exploring and incorporating the business history of Soviet-style societies. It aims to demonstrate that going 'eastward' can contribute to current debates around the themes, boundaries and methods in the field of business history as a whole. While it is important to acknowledge that we are not starting from a *tabula rasa*, it is equally important to acknowledge that the field has become more lively and contested than in the past. Indeed, the contributors to the special issue would probably not share a common approach to defining or doing business history. How far there is an emerging business history literature on Soviet-style societies may itself be quite debateable. Valentina Fava and Volodymyr Kulikov, for instance, take issue with Martin Kragh when he claims that Russian (and, even more, Soviet) business history is a field 'in its infancy' (Kragh, 2013, p. 386) and instead offer a definition of it as 'a disciplinary hybrid' (Fava & Kulikov, 2022, p. 326). We find the latter characterisation to be a more accurate reflection of the variety of approaches, preoccupations and methods open to, and being employed in, the exploration of the business histories of Soviet-style or Soviet-derived systems in the decades following the end of the Cold War. According to many leading figures in the field, in fact, the Chandlerian period in business history came to an end in the 1990s, as researchers not just questioned particular findings in Chandler's works, but turned to small as well as big business, and explored business in a greater geographic variety, with increased interdisciplinary openness, and in relation to a wider areas of themes across politics, society and culture (Friedman, 2010).

Even though business history has opened up to going 'eastward', however, it is also the case that the field still grapples with how to include Soviet-style polities and firms, a problem that we modestly hope our special issue can help the field overcome. Few textbooks or handbooks on business history at the moment entertain Soviet-style systems as a topic worth exploring. A rare exception is the inclusion of Kragh's (2016) chapter 'Enterprise in the Soviet and Soviet-Type-Economies' in *The Routledge Companion to Business History* (Wilson et al., 2016). Despite its inclusion in the volume, though, the firm in Soviet-style polities is even here mainly discussed in light of how it stood in contrast with the firm in Western economic systems, which are taken as the norm. Kragh argues that, on account of their subordinated position in the totalitarian command-and-control system,

> enterprises do not possess any of the features we associate with normal corporate governance in market economies. Firms do not engage in strategic planning, spending decisions or marketing, nor do they fully control related activities such as logistics or personnel capabilities. (Kragh, 2016, p. 177)

Such an approach to the Soviet-style firm as defined by what it is not, or as simply a unit of production, seems very much to be an echo of past approaches. Indeed, it would be unsurprising to find that debates surrounding what is normal and normative still have identifiable roots in the Chandlerian era of business history, given that the side championing business won the Cold War. It is notable, for instance, that, two prominent neo-Chandlerians, Franco Amatori and Andrea Colli, still rely heavily on texts largely published before the collapse of the Soviet bloc in the chapter on the Soviet Union in their authoritative *Business History: Complexities and Comparisons* (Amatori & Colli, 2013). Despite the broadening of the original Chandlerian framework to deal with new preoccupations, like globalisation, entrepreneurship or the relationship between enterprise, society and culture, Amatori and Colli continue to frame the Soviet experience largely in contrast with Western experiences. They argue that the defining feature of the Soviet firm was that it was different from the Western firm because its freedom to function was severely delineated by the diktat of the plan; it was fundamentally just a unit of production. Citing Andrei Yudanov, a Russian economist who wrote the key relevant chapter in Chandler et al.'s (1997) *Big Business and the Wealth of Nations*, Amatori and Colli go on to explain that the Soviet command-and-control system scuppered the emergence of a business community, in which firms developed diverse, competitive strategies that normally provide 'solidity to the economic fabric of Western nations' (Amatori & Colli, 2013, p. 166).

An expanding, hybrid field

Following the brief triumphalism of the unipolar moment, however, it is also entirely to be expected that there would be more space for challenges to narratives which take the West as normative. Central to the departure from the (neo-)Chandlerian approach in much of the scholarship was the abandonment of the idea that firms in the USSR and Soviet-style societies were merely production units. As Fava (2016) explains, viewing what she calls 'socialist enterprises' as more than just subordinate production units shifts the focus from high management to a variety of other actors and factors, political and social, within and outside the enterprise. While partial and contested (Marks, 2020), the greater accessibility to Soviet-era archives in much of the region since the 1990s certainly made this easier for historians to make such a turn (Fitzpatrick, 2015). Fava and Kulikov (2022, pp. 334–337) actually argue that there is a developing literature discussing the overall and changing economic decision-making complex including the firm under Stalin (Yudanov, 1997), under Khrushchev (Kibita, 2013; Markevich & Zhuravskaya, 2011) and after (Feygin, 2017). They likewise posit that there is increasing interest and research in how relations between Soviet enterprises and Western counterparts were formative of Soviet practices (Millward, 2013), as were transfers of various knowledges and models from the West (Grachev & Rakitsky, 2013; Kravets & Sandıkçı, 2013; Shpotov, 2013), and also how informal practices and freedoms enjoyed by Soviet enterprises affected the post-Soviet transformation (Freris, 2018). Resting on new archival materials from many countries, Fava's own extensive work on the car industry has demonstrated the significant extent of West-East transfers, adaptations and transformations of technologies, knowledges and management practices, often in response to local pressures and circumstances across Eastern Europe during the Cold War (Fava, 2008a, 2008b, 2013, 2019; Fava & Gatejel, 2017).

A further spur to this growing business history scholarship came from the increasing attention drawn by the seemingly inexorable rise of the People's Republic of China in the twenty-first century. In a review essay on business history in China, Adam Frost (2022a) points out that a major innovation in our understanding of Chinese enterprise is precisely that

Soviet forms were not simply transplanted top-down by all-powerful elites. Rather, many historical legacies going back to the nineteenth century could be seen as important to the transformation of business under the Chinese Communist Party after its seizure of power in 1949 (Bian, 2005; Giersch, 2020). Furthermore, improvisation rather than ideological fervour on the part of the party elites and negotiation with the extant private sector characterised decision-making and institution-building in the 1950s (Cliver, 2015, 2021; Finnane, 2011; Li, 2006; Thai, 2018). The period from the Great Leap Forward in 1958 to the initiation of Deng Xiao Ping's market reform era from 1978, however, remains largely understudied from the perspective of business history. Frost (2022a, pp. 34–35) suggests that two major exceptions include Philip Scranton (whose work is discussed below in greater depth) and the wider debate caused by Karl Gerth's (2020) work on consumerism in China in this period, especially the debate that contained in a special issue of the *PRC History Review*. In the latter, much of the discussion revolves around how similar the Chinese experience was to that in Eastern Europe, and how far consumerism can be conflated with capitalism or be seen as (in)compatible with communism. Finally, like with the scholarship on the USSR, the persistence of informal practices across eras retains an important place for business historians (Feng, 2013; Frost, 2022b; He, 2010).

Quite what could be said to have been specifically socialist about enterprises in the USSR, Eastern Europe or China, though, remains elusive. Perhaps one way of approaching this problem would be to avoid system-building as a whole and purposively remain elusive. Such is the method chosen by a well-established historian of American business, and a critic of the Chandlerian method from an earlier era, Philip Scranton. In what constitutes a spin-off from his earlier work on jet-propulsion, Scranton's research into business history in Eastern Europe (first discussed in a special issue of *Enterprise and Society*, 2018; see also 2022) and China (2019) began with work on historical documents translated into English by the US Joint Publications Research Service (1957–1995). Rather than approaching the documents with the intention of system-building, akin to the Chandlerian method, Scranton begins with simple, open-ended questions (eg 'How did communist enterprises work?'), only to make broader comparisons later. In both his work on Eastern Europe and China, Scranton finds broad similarities or resonances in terms of the challenges managers faced (vulnerability to being sacked, responding to arbitrary rules, finding their formal training did not prepare them for the real tasks of management) and the tasks they performed (producing cheaply, providing services, remunerating employees, responding to unpredictable situations). This was 'despite communist and capitalist enterprises being responsible to polar [opposite] masters: the Market versus the Plan; the Board versus the Party; the shareholders versus the state' (Scranton, 2018a, p. 571). The comparisons Scranton draws suggest management went beyond simply implementing production decisions from above, and his comparisons are not reduced to those between firms in the West and the USSR. Instead, they represent a more de-centred view of business history, where comparisons can be made between peripheries, Eastern Europe and China, and not solely with reference to the more advanced capitalist states. Challenging teleological explanations of business development success as tied simply to Chinese adaptation of market reform, Scranton in fact argues that Chinese openness to experimentation with new methods of production and new technologies allowed for greater business capacity to match resources and needs than in Eastern Europe during the Cold War era and even before the advent of market reform (Scranton, 2019, p. 5).

A contrasting approach, but similarly empirically rich, has its grounding in global history, and challenges dominant notions that globalisation started in the 1970s with the rise of what is often termed neoliberalism. Containing more voices belatedly sympathetic to the Cold War's Second World, a literature has emerged in recent years which writes the Global East (Müller, 2020) into the business history picture. Spearheaded by historians such as Mark and Betts (2022), recent titles like *Socialism Goes Global: The Soviet Union and Eastern Europe in the Age of Decolonisation*, *Alternative Globalizations: Eastern Europe and the Postcolonial World* (Mark et al., 2020), and *1989: A Global History of Eastern Europe* (Mark et al., 2019) demonstrate that there were in actual fact different, competing projects of globalisation from the 1950s onwards. Rather than emphasising Euro-Atlantic visions of globalisation that later became dominant under their so-called neoliberal variant, these new histories aim to challenge conventional chronologies, re-discover alternative visions of globalisation often constituted by (self-defined) anti-imperialist internationalisms challenging deeper, structural inequalities in international affairs, and uncover more diverse agents involved in conceptualising and implementing different routes to development.

What does business history gain from this global turn and its attention to the Global East in particular? Where could the relatively micro study of business organisation and the macro study of global processes intersect? At the macro level, many of the new studies contend that the (geo-) economic and (geo-) political context in a wider sense shaped economic ideas, institutions, industries, and even individual firm strategies in the Global East. In *Markets in the Name of Socialism: The Left-Wing Origins of Neoliberalism*, for example, Johanna Bockman (2011) shows that the innovative ideas of various East European economists inadvertently contributed to the development of neoliberal ideas. Oscar Sanchez-Sibony's (2014) *The Political Economy of the Soviet Cold War from Stalin to Khrushchev* has been similarly influential in establishing the extent to which Soviet trade policies were shaped by the global economy. More recently, Alessandro Iandolo's (2022) *Arrested Development: The Soviet Union in Ghana, Guinea, and Mali, 1955–1968* explores the ways in which the Soviet Union's developmental agency in West Africa played a major part in the emergence and shaping of the import substitution industrialisation road to development, including at the level of economic enterprises. Moving onto the micro-level, much of the new global history scholarship emphasises the recovery of the agency of alternative actors in the Global East and South, including businesses, in the co-constitution of globalisation and its active contestation (Calori & Spaskovska, 2021). A concrete example is Irina Yányshev-Nésterova's (2020) investigation into the shaping of the Soviet fishing fleet Sovrybflot, its global reach, and consequently its role in forging 'Red Globalisation and Soviet efforts to construct global development by becoming a donor to developing states, importing food and raw materials, gaining access to, and exploiting fishing resources, exporting industrial plants, and providing low-rate credit' (Yányshev-Nésterova, 2020, p. 2). Meanwhile, Spaskovska and Calori (2021) show how deeply embedded some Yugoslav industrial giants were in global economic networks, West, East and South.

The business history of the Global East has also gained from attention by historians of European integration. On both sides of the Iron Curtain, Western and Eastern European elites at various levels sought to create spaces for cooperation and trade beyond the control of the superpowers (Autio-Sarasmo & Miklóssy, 2011; Cain, 2013; Dobson, 2012; Stone, 1996). This percolated to the level of business. In the most relevant findings, Angela Romano and Federico Romero spearheaded several co-edited publications (Romano & Romero, 2014,

2021) that showcase work done in this direction and the creation of what Romano calls 'Pan-Europe' as a space for continental cooperation at multiple levels (Romano, 2021, pp. 31–49). In the first of these publications, particular note should go to the article of Pavel Szobi (2014), who explores contacts between East German, Czechoslovak and West European companies in the 1970s and 1980s. He argues that the resulting

> economic co-operation was an important means of filling gaps in the supply of goods, as well as prolonging the life of the crumbling Communist regimes…[but that] the choice of relying on Western means – whether technology or credits – revealed the inadequacy of the socialist system to cope with modernisation and global competition. (Szobi, 2014, p. 264)

In a further contribution in the same special issue, Pál Germuska (2014) argues that Hungarian economic elites in the late 1970s began to look 'westward'. Meanwhile, in the later publication, Benedetto Zaccaria shows that Slovene and Croatian business elites lobbied for closer Yugoslav relations with West Germany and Italy in the 1960s and 1970s (Zaccaria, 2021, p. 226), in a rare documented direct example of business elites trying to shape foreign policy in Eastern Europe. Such work shows, however, that there are major possibilities for studying the economic integration of Europe across the Iron Curtain before and after 1989 through the prism of business history.

Indeed, if we take the notion of the business history of the Global East as a hybrid seriously, we may find it fruitful to cursorily map here recent histories of the Global East in sub-fields adjacent to business history or with potential elective affinities with it to illustrate the potential for cross-fertilisation. Economic history and the history of development are obvious such fields, which have seen significant expansion in recent years (Berend, 2009; Berghoff & Balbeir, 2013; Gatrell, 2006; Kalinovsky, 2018; Lorenzini, 2019; Steiner, 2010; Varga, 2020). Traditionally, technology is a field of interest to business historians, and the histories of technology specifically related to the Global East have indeed been popular (Augustine, 2007, 2018; Miljković, 2021; Petrov, 2023; Stokes, 1997, 2000). Recently, historians have also fruitfully turned their attention to the role of money in the USSR and Eastern Europe (Ironside, 2021; Zatlin, 2009). Issues from industrial policy across Europe (Grabas & Nützenadel, 2014) to industrial relations specifically in the countries formerly ruled by the communists (Archer & Music, 2020; Bartha, 2013; Bonfiglioli, 2019; Musić, 2021; Ost, 2018; Pittaway, 2012), from joint ventures between Western and Eastern companies (Ironside, 2023) to the advertising industry and marketing in former communist-run states (Papushina, 2020; Patterson, 2012), have much to contribute to the writing of business history. Such a list is far from systematic or exhaustive, but serves to illustrate the potential breadth of the literatures that business historians could make use of when travelling 'eastward'.

Altogether, the sheer diversity of business history approaches outlined above, and possibilities for business history research to be undertaken, indicates a strong sense of the multiplicity of business experiences in the Global East. This may lead to the question of whether it is possible to speak not just of 'Varieties of Capitalism' but of 'Varieties of Socialism'. Certainly, with the publication of David Soskice and Peter A. Hall's *Varieties of Capitalism: The Institutional Foundations of Comparative Advantage* (Hall & Soskice, 2001), the Varieties of Capitalism (VoC) paradigm rose to prominence in terms of explaining different transformational pathways in Russia and Central and Eastern Europe from the 1990s onwards, as well as to China since the market reforms of the late 1970s (King & Szelényi, 2005; Lane & Myant, 2007; Myant & Drahokoupil, 2010; Offe, 1996). Could we read backwards from that? An important question within that vast literature has been how far the legacies of the past affected the transformation processes of different states. There are, as we have intimated, different ways of viewing these societies and their legacies. At one end, it is possible to claim that some of them still have not yet even developed a capitalist economy (Williams et al., 2011), while on the other it has also been argued that they had never been socialist at all, but had always been a form of capitalism (Dale, 2011). Both history and theory clearly matter here, and how socialist enterprise is defined and how business history is done has implications for our understanding of the period since the end of the Cold War. Moreover, it has implications for the broader calls business history to develop an impact agenda outside academia on policy and practice (Wilson et al., 2022, pp. 84–93), which it can here do by discussing the importance of the legacies of the past to the successes and failures of the transformation process since 1989.

Nevertheless, let us go back to the possibility and utility to business history of developing an agenda that could help map the 'Varieties of Socialism'. Business historians have indeed attempted to make use of the VoC literature, even while criticising its ahistorical model-building approach (Marx & Reitmayer, 2019). Any attempt at building models akin to the liberal market economy (LME) vs coordinated market economy (CME) paradigms for a 'Variety of Socialisms' approach could learn from these ventures. Although we do not make any such systematic attempt with this issue as a whole, it is obvious that comparing the businesses histories of a more statist country like the GDR and a more marketised country like Yugoslavia may generate empirical findings that could help develop such an approach. In fact, one of the two editors of the special issue makes an explicit call for a 'Variety of Socialisms' agenda in his own contribution (Saša Vejzagić, see below), while the other editor's co-authored contribution does indeed undertake a systematic comparison of the GDR and Yugoslavia, but polemicises with both the notions of 'varieties' and 'socialism', preferring to define these states as capitalist and to emphasise differences *within* capitalism rather than *between* capitalisms (Gareth Dale and Vladimir Unkovski-Korica, see below).

Business history goes East: towards the special issue

As a matter of fact, this special issue of *Business History* arises from the two editors' initial discussions on the nature and extent of the idiosyncrasy of the Yugoslav business world. Given Yugoslavia's early exit from the Soviet bloc in 1948, following the Tito-Stalin split, and the introduction soon after that of workers' councils in Yugoslav industry (Unkovski-Korica, 2014), the Yugoslav industrial enterprise looked different to the image prevailing in the rest of the Soviet bloc. With the deepening of decentralisation and market reforms in the 1960s and then of the re-organisation of Yugoslav industry to create workers' councils at lower and lower levels in the latter 1970s and 1980s, obvious questions arise, among them: the extent to which Yugoslav enterprise managements differed from their Western or Eastern counterparts; how far enterprise structures evolved in new directions; what role workers' councils and workers themselves played in enterprise functioning in reality; in what ways enterprises related to the (local) state and (global) market; how much more or less dynamic they became in terms of acquiring and adapting technology from abroad or spurring technological innovation; how they were shaped through their interaction with the local unevenness in Yugoslavia (including the existence of the private sector in land and elsewhere) and global unevenness (including Yugoslavia's non-aligned position in the Cold War, with economic links in the West, East and South); what different functions enterprises fulfilled, from making profits to providing welfare or shoring up defence compared with counterparts elsewhere; how they adapted to consumer demands and pressures; what kind of role they played in gendering social citizenship in Yugoslavia compared; and how Yugoslavia's international economic and political position affected many of these questions.

We resolved to organise a workshop to explore a subset of these questions, and the use of comparison as an initial method to test the nature and extent of the idiosyncrasy of the Yugoslav business world struck us as poignant. To quote Jürgen Kocka, quite simply, 'comparison helps to distance oneself a bit from the case one knows best…[and] can have a de-provincializing, a liberating, an eye opening effect…' (Kocka, 2003, p. 41). We decided on the Democratic Republic of Germany (GDR) as a comparator. The choice of the comparison between Yugoslavia and the GDR was initially fortuitous. It arose from conversation the two editors of this special issue had while were both based at the University of Glasgow. Saša Vejzagić was a visiting doctoral fellow from the European University Institute exploring Yugoslav business organisation during the market reform era, and Vladimir Unkovski-Korica an early career lecturer in Central and East European Studies and author of *The Economic Struggle for Power in Tito's Yugoslavia: From World War II to Non-alignment* (2016). While doing research related to his doctoral thesis in the library, Vejzagić found that Yugoslavia and the GDR drew a brief comparison in Raymond Bentley's (1984) *Technological Change in the German Democratic Republic*. Vejzagić and Unkovski-Korica were intrigued by that comparison, and found an interested, supportive and sharp interlocutor in Professor Ray Stokes, Chair in Business History, Director of the Centre for Business History in Scotland at the University of Glasgow, and author of *Constructing Socialism: Technology and Change in East Germany, 1945-1990* (Stokes, 2000). Combining our joint research agendas to ask how (dis) similar the business worlds of two very different states of the Global East were made for an intriguing set of possibilities.

As we tried to justify and develop the comparison, however, both the advantages and disadvantages associated with comparative history soon became obvious. Let us start with some of the advantages. Using the case-oriented comparative research could test how definite phenomena worked themselves out in several nations, how particular institutions developed diverging forms in different societies, and how certain macro-causal conjunctures produced significant historical outcomes (Skocpol & Somers, 1980). Certainly, asking questions like how far their shared socio-economic system was determinative of their business world and their broader fate, what common institutions they tried to build in differing contexts with diverging results, and how particular conjunctures in their short period of existence shaped the Yugoslav and East German trajectories all seemed to us fruitful. These two states also made sense as a comparative choice because they were arguably as well researched as any other potential comparator states in Eastern Europe, making it relatively easy to attempt a more systematic comparison in the first instance, which could be a classic methodological criticism of comparative approaches (Kocka, p. 41).

Yet we also had to contend with the inherent problems of potential traps of ahistorical approach and methodological nationalism in making comparisons, as well as questions related to the selection of the elements or parts of the totalities we were comparing (Kocka, pp. 41–22). In our mind, the differences between the two countries made for an intriguing contrast. Of the Eastern European states, the GDR was among the more statist; concentrated largely on the Comecon market at the high end of technological production; and dependent on the USSR for political support, given it was largely a product of Soviet occupation. By contrast, Yugoslavia was outside of the bloc, an outlier in terms of market reform; largely agrarian; linked to the EEC and Comecon as well as major Third World production chains and markets; and among the least dependent on the USSR for domestic legitimacy, given it was largely a product of a domestic revolution. These very differences obviously echoed some of the preoccupations of the VoC literature, like the CME (GDR?) vs LME (Yugoslavia?) divide, which could either set the agenda for a 'Variety of Socialisms' research paradigm, or at least for an interesting debate around such paradigm-building even when we disagreed with it and a challenge to offer a better alternative. Intriguingly, and in the spirit of much of global history, the comparison could moreover be said to de-centre the study of the global Cold War, by comparing not core states in the system, but, rather, two states removed from the core and entangled in particular geopolitical contexts in competition with the core. If we were to be provocative, we could be said to be comparing states in some important ways developmentally akin to the Global North (the GDR) and the Global South (Yugoslavia), a departure from more common core-core or East-West comparisons.

Nevertheless, some of the classic problems, particularly linked to identifying common approaches and cases to study, emerged. This became evident as the three of us, Stokes, Unkovski-Korica and Vejzagić, organised a workshop entitled 'The Second World Does Business? Enterprise in the GDR and Yugoslavia', at the University of Glasgow in late 2018. Following the keynote by Ray Stokes, there were eleven participants from all career stages presenting on five panels, interrogating the following problems: 1. The state as entrepreneur in 'state socialist' societies?; 2. Business organisation transformed?; 3. Technology transfer and adaptation?; 4. Business from below: what about the workers?; and 5. Transition/transformation compared. A round table of leading business historians fed into the discussion at the end. The sheer variety of perspectives on the questions at hand and the extreme unevenness in terms of the sources available revealed that any attempts at systematic comparison or paradigm building would not be possible in the short term. Still, there was also a general feeling that the field was more vibrant than any of us had anticipated and that bringing to light some of its major strands would strengthen the case both for more attention to business history in relation to histories of the Global East and for bringing the experiences of the Global East into mainstream business history.

Our contribution: showcasing different approaches

The resulting special issue brings together seven articles that draw on the workshop discussions. The first four articles by Vejzagić, Pieter Troch, Dolores Augustine and Ezster Bartha analyse the emergence of new management structures, elites, practices, priorities and cultures from a variety of complementary and contrasting viewpoints in Yugoslavia and the GDR. At the forefront of a new generation of historians looking into Yugoslav business history, Vejzagić reconstructs the pathway undertaken by Zagreb's *Industrogradnja* on its path to becoming a construction and engineering giant in the 1960s and 1970s. His focus is on the continuous and unresolved system clash between socialist and market principles as seen through the history of the growth of the company. While this is a familiar theme, Vejzagić's contribution is at the cutting edge of the scholarship in terms of mapping out the interaction between, on the one hand, the rise and fall of the market reform agenda and the accompanying institutional transformation of the socio-economic and political system, and, on the other hand, the evolution of a self-managed company. Relying on the company newspaper and oral history interviews, Vejzagić shows the company's management negotiating federal, republic and local governments, the powerful investment banking system that operated autonomously from political structures, and internal industrial relations as refracted through workers' self-management structures with the workers' councils at their core. His contribution therefore speaks directly to the emerging theme of linking business history to business power (Rollings, 2021). It also

> speaks of a fairly autonomous and authentic company modernisation, technological experimentation, and a strategically planned market expansion (and flexibility) in a business environment established within one of the twentieth century European socialist projects... enterprises and their managements in Yugoslavia went through an original experience, one that ultimately supports the idea of a variety of socialist projects. (pp. 16–17)

By contrast, Troch engages with similar themes and processes, especially the tension between state and market, but also power. Nevertheless, he does so, not from the standpoint of big business, but of a small company in a peripheral setting of Yugoslavia. He explores the history of an unsuccessful wood processing plant, *Kosmet Šper*, which emerged largely as a local government attempt at creating employment in an underdeveloped area, but on the eve of the market reform period and the federal move towards intensive growth and international trade in the 1960s. Despite several internal re-organisations and an ever more professional top management, the company struggled to perform on the market, largely because its original purpose clashed with its new function. It was not efficient enough to convince market-oriented actors like commercial banks to fund it long-term, and it was not big enough to gain subsidies from federal, redistributive bodies. Its all-South Slav top management had to rationalise a multinational, but majority Albanian, workforce. Moreover, it found itself permanently stuck between the need to increase wages to attract skilled workers from the countryside on the one hand and the need to raise sufficient income to cover these wage rises. Troch concludes that the management was faced with the difficult task of responding to the intersecting problems of function, ethnicity, and origin, a task in which it ultimately failed.

If the contrasting fates of these two different companies in Yugoslavia suggest the need to understand the diversity of businesses in order to gain a fuller appreciation of the role of business in the country's history, the next two articles in the special issue concentrate on the same East German company, Carl Zeiss Jena, but from divergent perspectives. Researching management culture in electronics and microelectronics R&D, Augustine traces changes from the 1950s to the 1980s. She argues that, for a complex set of reasons ranging from ideology to geopolitical pressures, the GDR cracked down on the professional ethos and relatively risk-friendly managerial style of top managers whose careers started in the Weimar or Nazi eras in the years leading up to Erich Honecker's coming to power. Their over-reliance on using the Stasi to literally copy Western technologies actually retarded innovation, roll-out of new technologies and the ability to raise foreign currency. By contrast, Bartha focuses more on industrial relations, and argues that the state-led 'scientific-technical revolution' and market-like reform of the 1960s failed amid struggles between management and workers. She demonstrates that the memory of the working class uprising of June 1953 and labour resistance to attempts at implementing Taylorism through the New Economic System (NES) after 1963 frustrated management. If this was symbolic of the power of the workers' moral economy, to which Honecker appealed, the socialist consumerism implemented in the 1970s slowly and unwittingly unravelled labour solidarity. That, ultimately, led to the collapse of the regime, as access to Western money and goods created cleavages in East German society.

Both of these articles rely heavily on factory archives, and explore the history of the Zeiss in a similar period, but the former's gaze on high management culture and the latter's on industrial relations lead the two authors to rather distinct and possibly conflicting conclusions about the reasons for the failure of the GDR. An intriguing contrast, worth more future research, between the findings of both these two articles on the GDR and the preceding two on Yugoslavia, relates to the apparent weakening of top management over time in the former, but not necessarily so in the latter, at least not in the case of *Industrogradnja*. This may speak to the theme of the two tales of the power of business and management in the two systems.

The following two articles by Max Trekker and Anna Calori, while very different in approach, both have in common their challenge to long-held assumptions in the scholarship, while also sharing a common preoccupation in the form of the transformation period in the 1990s. Trekker points out that while the GDR is often seen as the most reform-resistant of the Soviet bloc states, it was also the country that maintained its largest private sector until the early 1980s, usually smaller manager-owned companies supplying the larger state sector. Ironically, too, the GDR attempted to harness private entrepreneurs to reform and save the system in the late 1980s. Using archives and memoirs, Trekker shows that the reform wing of the SED leadership in 1990 still hoped to save the system by charting a middle road between what they called capitalism and Stalinism. The reform leadership sought to re-privatise the *Mittelstand* that had been nationalised during the Honnecker era in the early 1970s as part of an effort to create what they termed a social market economy. Yet their plans were vague, possibly deliberately so. They clearly did not wish to privatise the public sector as a whole. Furthermore, they were friendlier with the Hungarian than the Polish leadership, which was attempting shock therapy, and later referenced Yugoslav self-management and Israeli Kibbutzim as their inspiration. Nevertheless, Trekker finds no proof of any foreign inspiration in the documents of the time. In the event, too, the *Mittelstand* were the only economic survival of the reformed SED in power, but one that proved a failure quickly following the shock therapy imposed with reunification of the two Germanies.

If that is the story of a potential middle road not travelled, or of a failed transformation to a social market economy combining strong public and private sectors, Calori looks at transformation in Bosnia and Herzegovina through the prism of the rise and fall of *Energoinvest*, a Yugoslav-era engineering and power plants construction giant. Resting on archives and oral history interviews, she finds that '[f]rom the perspective of a small country in Europe's semi-periphery, the advantages of Bosnia's "in-betweenness" amongst Europe, the middle East, Africa and the rest of the Non-Aligned world, was lost on the post-communist country's path to economic transition (p. 11) The country's integration with the West after the end of the Bosnian War (1992–1995) ironically led not to the rising competitiveness of companies like *Energoinvest*, but their restructuring and privatisation as small and peripheral companies in a poorer setting. Horizons narrowed from the preceding era's globalist visions of development among the company managers and experts. What this story tells us, explains Calori, is that we need to reassess the world that disappeared in the amnesia of the era of Euro-Atlantic globalisation to re-open the horizons closed in the meantime, to help us imagine new understandings of development and globalisation. Further research cutting across business history, history of globalisation and histories of the Global East would therefore foster more dialogue and discussion of the past, present and future.

The final article in the special issue, co-written by Gareth Dale and Vladimir Unkovski-Korica, is in fact a comparative analysis of the business histories of the GDR and Yugoslavia conceptualised as countries implementing a form of state capitalism, rather than socialism, and is crafted as a contribution to comparative capitalism studies. Dale and Unkovski-Korica embark on an ambitious critique of the VoC literature, turning instead to the concept of variegation. The literature on variegated capitalism emphasises interconnectedness and hierarchies in the world economy which are most often left out of the VoC literature. Nevertheless, Dale and Unkovski-Korica argue that the literature on variegated capitalism increasingly tries to incorporate China in its approach, but without explaining how or when China turned capitalist. They therefore argue that the former communist world's participation in the world economy needs theorising and inserting into histories of global capitalism. Placing the former communist world into a broader context of statist late industrialisers, Dale and Unkovski-Korica posit the communist states as a state capitalist model of catch-up industrialisation. This approach still needs to account for differences within global capitalism, including down to the granular level of business units. Bringing in the concept of uneven and combined development, Dale and Unkovski-Korica extend, in time and space, the use of the concept of variegation. They argue that the state-capitalist societies were integral parts of a variegated global capitalist system, as was the state-capitalist firm. They then insert the GDR and Yugoslavia into three phases of post-war global capitalist development, explaining differences in their evolution according to the interaction of their global position and domestic circumstances. They conclude by calling on business historians to re-write global business history in the twentieth and twenty-first centuries by engaging more systematically with the experience of all the co-called 'communist' societies.

This special issue, taken as a whole, aims to help make the growing, hybrid literature on the business history of the Global East more relevant to, and a more integrated part of, business history as a whole. The diverse findings of the articles published here strongly challenge traditional views of the socialist firm as simply a unit of production. Furthermore, this special issue represents only the second special issue in the field to explore the business history of the Second World project during the Cold War. While the first, published in *Enterprise and Society*, centred on an article 'Managing Communist Enterprises: Poland, Hungry and Czechoslovakia, 1945-1970' by Philip Scranton (2018b), this special issue expands the geographical, thematic and temporal boundaries dealt with in the pioneering attempt. This current, second special issue breaks new ground by making comparisons between, and spurring the investigation of, business operation in two very different states, East Germany and Yugoslavia, respectively a Central European and a Balkan country. It therefore allows for a more refined understanding of the operation of the Second World project in regions with different levels of development and different degrees of integration with core countries of the global system, as well as different historical legacies and sources of legitimacy for the respective regimes. As such, the special issue is a stepping stone to including a greater variety of experiences of the Second World project both inside and outside its initial Eurasian location. In thematic terms, it goes beyond management practices to include wider economic, social, cultural and political factors in the operation of companies. It dissects business operation in both very unique complex, multinational settings and in terms of global entanglements and hierarchies of power. It poses questions surrounding both business power and power relations within business. It interrogates roads taken and not taken. In terms of pushing temporal boundaries, the articles contained within this special issue stretch the boundaries both backwards before the advent of communist party regimes in the wider Central and East European region and the Balkans, and forwards, to the transformation period of the 1990s and beyond. Overall, too, the articles in this special issue, while written by specialists of all career stages versed in both the languages and archives of the region, suggest not just that the writing of business history can travel 'eastward', but also that, in doing so, it will not leave the field of business history as a whole unchanged.

Acknowledgements

This special issue 'Socialist Entrepreneurs? Business Histories of the GDR and Yugoslavia' would have been impossible without the financial support of the Business History editors, the Centre for Business History in Scotland, and the Central and East European Studies (CEES) Research Incentivisation Fund, for a workshop held at the University of Glasgow in 2018 and entitled 'The Second World Does Business? Enterprise in the GDR and Yugoslavia'. Big thank you to all the participants, and particularly to Jeffrey Fear, Nataliya Kibita and Angela Romano for their comments at the final round table. We express our sincere gratitude to Sara Bernard, Valentina Fava, Phil Scranton and Ray Stokes for useful comments on this introduction. Ray Stokes was a pillar of support in the early days of the project and it would have been impossible without him. Neil Rollings kept us afloat at a critical time while acting as Ray's successor in the editorial team of the journal. Rebecca Kay was a supportive mentor in CEES. Last, but not least, our appreciation goes to our diligent managing editors, Andrea Colli and Susanna Fellmann, without whom this special issue would not have seen the light of day.

Disclosure statement

No potential conflict of interest was reported by the author(s).

References

Amatori, F., & Colli, A. (2013). *Business history: Complexities and comparisons*. Routledge.
Archer, R., & Musić, G. (2020). New perspectives on East European labor history: An introduction. *Labor, 17*(3), 19–29. https://doi.org/10.1215/15476715-8349332
Augustine, D. L. (2007). *Red Prometheus: Engineering and dictatorship in East Germany, 1945-1990*. MIT Press.
Augustine, D. L. (2018). *Taking on technocracy: Nuclear power in Germany, 1945 to the present* (Vol. 24). Berghahn Books.
Autio-Sarasmo, S., & Miklóssy, K. (Eds.). (2011). *Reassessing Cold War Europe* (p. 66). Routledge.
Bartha, E. (2013). *Alienating labour: Workers on the road from socialism to capitalism in East Germany and Hungary* (Vol. 22). Berghahn Books.
Bentley, R. (1984). *Technological Change in the German Democratic Republic*. Routledge.
Berend, T. I. (2009). *From the Soviet bloc to the European Union: The economic and social transformation of Central and Eastern Europe since 1973*. Cambridge University Press.
Berghoff, H., & Balbier, U. A. (Eds.). (2013). *The East German economy, 1945–2010: Falling behind or catching up?*. Cambridge University Press.
Bian, M. L. (2005). *The making of the state enterprise system in modern China: The dynamics of institutional change*. Harvard University Press.
Bockman, J. (2011). *Markets in the name of socialism: The left-wing origins of neoliberalism*. Stanford University Press.
Bonfiglioli, C. (2019). *Women and industry in the Balkans: The rise and fall of the Yugoslav textile sector* (Vol. 105). Bloomsbury Publishing.

Cain, F. (2013). *Economic statecraft during the cold war: European responses to the US trade embargo*. Routledge.

Calori, A., & Spaskovska, L. (2021). Reimagining the world: Decolonisation and the promise of development. *Contemporary European History, 30*(4), 613–620. https://doi.org/10.1017/S0960777321000539

Chandler, A. D. (1977). *The managerial revolution in American business*. Belknap Press.

Chandler, A. D. (1962). *Strategy and structure: Chapters in the history of the industrial empire*.

Chandler, A. D. (1993). *The visible hand*. Harvard University Press.

Chandler, A. D., Amatori, F., & Hikino, T. (1997). Historical and comparative contours of big business. In A. Chandler Jr., F. Amatori, & T. Hikino (Eds.), *Big business and the wealth of nations* (pp. 3–23). Cambridge University Press.

Cliver, R. K. (2015). Surviving socialism: Private industry and the transition to socialism in China, 1945–1958. *Cross-Currents: East Asian History and Culture Review, 4*(2), 694–722. https://doi.org/10.1353/ach.2015.0031

Cliver, R. K. (2021). *Red silk*. BRILL.

Dale, G. (2011). *First the transition, then the crash: Eastern Europe in the 2000s*. Pluto.

Dobson, A. P. (2012). *US economic statecraft for survival 1933–1991: Of embargoes, strategic embargoes, and economic warfare*. Routledge.

Engerman, D. C. (2011). The second world's third world. *Kritika: Explorations in Russian and Eurasian History, 12*(1), 183–211. https://doi.org/10.1353/kri.2011.a411667

Fava, V. (2008a). "Between American Fordism and "Soviet Fordism": The Czechoslovak way towards mass production." In B. Apor, P. Apor & E. A. Rees (Eds.). *The Sovietisation of Eastern Europe. New perspectives on the post-war period* (pp. 47–64). New Academia Publishing, LLC.

Fava, V. (2008b). COMECON integration and the automobile industry: The Czechoslovak case. *Jahrbuch Für Wirtschaftsgeschichte / Economic History Yearbook, 49*(2), 93–116. https://doi.org/10.1524/jbwg.2008.49.2.93

Fava, V. (2013). *The socialist people's car: Automobiles, shortages and consent in the Czechoslovak road to mass production*. Amsterdam University Press.

Fava, V. (2016). Produzione, impresa, socialismo. L'impresa (post) sovietica nella business history Europea. [Production, enteprise, socialism. The (post) Soviet enterprise in European Business History.] In L. Cerasi (Ed.)., *Le libertà del lavoro. Istituzioni, diritti, rappresentanza e protezione del lavoro tra Otto e Novecento* (Vol. 3, pp. 131–157). New Digital Frontiers srl.

Fava, V. (2019). Between business interests and ideological marketing: The USSR and the Cold War in Fiat corporate strategy, 1957–1972. *Journal of Cold War Studies, 20*(4), 26–64. https://doi.org/10.1162/jcws_a_00822

Fava, V., & Gatejel, L. (2017). East–West cooperation in the automotive industry: Enterprises, mobility, production. *The Journal of Transport History, 38*(1), 11–19. https://doi.org/10.1177/0022526617698157

Fava, V., & Kulikov, V. (2022). Recent trends in the business history of Russia: The blurry borders of the discipline. *Business History Review, 96*(2), 325–351. https://doi.org/10.1017/S0007680521000386

Feng, J. (2013). *Xinhua fuyin changyede shengmingshi*, PhD dissertation, Beijing Daxue.

Feygin, Y. (2017). *Reforming the Cold War State: Economic Thought, Internationalization, and the Politics of Soviet Reform, 1955–1985*, PhD dissertation, Philadelphia, PA, University of Pennsylvania.

Finnane, A. (2011). Tailors in 1950s Beijing: Private enterprise, career trajectories, and historical turning points in the early PRC. *Frontiers of History in China, 6*(1), 117–137. https://doi.org/10.1007/s11462-011-0123-2

Fitzpatrick, S. (2015). Impact of the opening of Soviet archives on Western scholarship on Soviet social history. *The Russian Review, 74*(3), 377–400. https://doi.org/10.1111/russ.12021

Freris, A. (2018). *The Soviet industrial enterprise: Theory and practice*. Routledge.

Friedman, W. (2010). *Business history, post-Chandler. New ways of history: Developments in historiography* (pp. 143–164). IB Tauris.

Frost, A. K. (2022a). Reframing Chinese business history. *Business History Review, 96*(2), 245–287. https://doi.org/10.1017/S0007680521000477

Frost, A. K. (2022b). [*Speculation and profiteering: The entrepreneurial transformation of socialist China*] PhD dissertation, Harvard University Graduate School of Arts and Sciences.

Gatrell, P. (2006). Feet of clay? The Soviet economic giant in recent historiography. *The Historical Journal, 49*(1), 299–315. https://doi.org/10.1017/S0018246X05005145

Germuska, P. (2014). Failed Eastern integration and a partly successful opening up to the West: The economic re-orientation of Hungary during the 1970s. *European Review of History: Revue Europeenne D'histoire, 21*(2), 271–291. https://doi.org/10.1080/13507486.2014.888703

Gerth, K. (2020). *Unending capitalism: How consumerism negated China's communist revolution.* Cambridge University Press.

Giersch, C. P. (2020). *Corporate conquests: Business, the state, and the origins of ethnic inequality in Southwest China.* Stanford University Press.

Grabas, C., & Nützenadel, A. (2014). *Industrial policy in Europe after 1945.* Palgrave Macmillan UK.

Grachev, M., & Rakitsky, B. (2013). Historic horizons of Frederick Taylor's scientific management. *Journal of Management History, 19*(4), 512–527. https://doi.org/10.1108/JMH-05-2012-0043

Granick, D. (1954). *Management of the industrial firm in the USSR.* Columbia University Press.

Granick, D. (1960). The red executive. *The International Executive, 2*(2), 9–10. https://doi.org/10.1002/tie.5060020204

Granick, D. (1975). *Enterprise guidance in Eastern Europe: A comparison of four socialist economies.* Princeton University Press.

Hall, P. A., & Soskice, D. (2001). *Varieties of capitalism: The institutional foundations of comparative advantage.* Oxford University Press.

He, Q. (2010). Between business and bureaucrats: Pingtan storytelling in Maoist and post-Maoist China. *Modern China, 36*(3), 243–268.

Iandolo, A. (2022). *Arrested development: The Soviet Union in Ghana, Guinea, and Mali. 1955–1968.* Cornell University Press.

Ironside, K. (2021). *A full-value Ruble: The promise of prosperity in the postwar Soviet Union* (Vol. 191). Harvard University Press.

Ironside, K. (2023). "Because of him, we have pizza hut!": Joint ventures and the opening up of the Soviet economy under Gorbachev. *Russian History, 49*(2-4), 238–263. https://doi.org/10.30965/18763316-12340049

Kalinovsky, A. M. (2018). *Laboratory of socialist development: Cold War politics and decolonization in Soviet Tajikistan.* Cornell University Press.

Kibita, N. (2013). *Soviet economic management under Khrushchev: The Sovnarkhoz reform.* Routledge.

King, L. P., & Szelényi, I. (2005). *Post-communist economic systems.* In N. J. Smelser & R. Swedberg, (Eds.). *The handbook of economic sociology* (pp. 205–229). Princeton University Press.

Kocka, J. (2003). Comparison and beyond. *History and Theory, 42*(1), 39–44. https://doi.org/10.1111/1468-2303.00228

Kragh, M. (2013). The Soviet enterprise: What have we learned from the archives? *Enterprise and Society, 14*(2), 360–394. https://doi.org/10.1093/es/kht001

Kragh, M. (2016). Enterprise in the Soviet and Soviet-type-economies. In J. Wilson, S. Toms, A. De Jong & E. Buchnea (Eds.). *The Routledge companion to business history* (pp. 187–200). Taylor & Francis.

Kravets, O., & Sandıkçı, Ö. (2013). Marketing for socialism: Soviet cosmetics in the 1930s. *Business History Review, 87*(3), 461–487. https://doi.org/10.1017/S000768051300072X

Lane, D., & Myant, M. R. (Eds.). (2007). *Varieties of capitalism in post-communist countries* (p. xiv). Palgrave Macmillan.

Li, H. Y. (2006). *Mao and the Economic Stalinization of China, 1948–1953.* Rowman & Littlefield Publishers.

Link, S. J. (2020). *Forging global Fordism: Nazi Germany, Soviet Russia, and the contest over the industrial order.* (Vol. 33). Princeton University Press.

Lorenzini, S. (2019). *Global development.* Princeton University Press.

Mark, J., & Betts, P. (Eds.). (2022). *Socialism goes global: The Soviet Union and Eastern Europe in the age of decolonisation.* Oxford University Press.

Mark, J., Iacob, B., Rupprecht, T., & Spaskovska, L. (2019). *1989: A global history of Eastern Europe.* Cambridge University Press.

Mark, J., Kalinovsky, A. M., & Marung, S. (2020). (Eds.). *Alternative globalizations: Eastern Europe and the postcolonial world.* Indiana University Press.

Markevich, A., & Zhuravskaya, E. (2011). M-form hierarchy with poorly-diversified divisions: A case of Khrushchev's reform in Soviet Russia. *Journal of Public Economics, 95*(11-12), 1550–1560. https://doi.org/10.1016/j.jpubeco.2011.06.003

Marks, S. (2020). What difference has the opening of the archives since 1991 made to the historiography of Communism and the Cold War?. In J. Reinisch & D. Brydan (Eds.), *Researching and teaching twentieth century history* (pp. 34–37). The Historical Association.

Marx, C., & Reitmayer, M. (2019). Introduction: Rhenish capitalism and business history. *Business History, 61*(5), 745–784. https://doi.org/10.1080/00076791.2019.1583211

Miljković, M. (2021). The Yugoslav 'Operation Paperclip': German Geologists in the Yugoslav Nuclear Program in the late 1940s and early 1950s. *Godišnjak za Društvenu Istoriju*, (3), 7–32.

Millward, R. (2013). *The state and business in the major powers: An economic history 1815-1939.* Routledge.

Müller, M. (2020). In search of the global east: Thinking between north and south. *Geopolitics, 25*(3), 734–755. https://doi.org/10.1080/14650045.2018.1477757

Musić, G. (2021). *Making and breaking the Yugoslav working class: The story of two self-managed factories.* Central European University Press.

Myant, M., & Drahokoupil, J. (2010). *Political Economy of Russia, Eastern Europe and Central Asia.* Wiley and Blackwell.

Offe, C. (1996). *Modernity and the state: East, West.* MIT Press.

Ost, D. (2018). *The defeat of solidarity.* Cornell University Press.

Papushina, I. O. (2020). Marketing in the late Soviet garment industry. *Journal of Historical Research in Marketing, 12*(4), 551–566. https://doi.org/10.1108/JHRM-10-2019-0036

Patterson, P. H. (2012). *Bought and sold: Living and losing the good life in socialist Yugoslavia.* Cornell University Press.

Petrov, V. (2023). *Balkan Cyberia: Cold War computing, Bulgarian modernization, and the Information Age behind the Iron Curtain.* National Geographic Books.

Pittaway, M. (2012). *The workers state: Industrial labor and the making of socialist Hungary, 1944–1958.* University of Pittsburgh Press.

Rollings, N. (2021). "The vast and unsolved enigma of power": Business history and business power. *Enterprise & Society, 22*(4), 893–920. https://doi.org/10.1017/eso.2021.53

Romano, A. (2021). Pan-Europe: A continental space for cooperation (s). In *European socialist regimes' fateful engagement with the West* (pp. 31–49). Routledge.

Romano, A., & Romero, F. (2014). European socialist regimes facing globalisation and European cooperation: Dilemmas and responses [Guest Editor]. *European Review of History: Revue Europeenne D'histoire, 21*(2), 157–164.

Romano, A., & Romero, F. (2021). *European socialist regimes' fateful engagement with the West: National strategies in the long 1970s* Routledge.

Sanchez-Sibony, O. (2014). *Red globalization: The political economy of the Soviet Cold War from Stalin to Khrushchev.* Cambridge University Press.

Skocpol, T., & Somers, M. (1980). The uses of comparative history in macrosocial inquiry. *Comparative Studies in Society and History, 22*(2), 174–197. https://doi.org/10.1017/S0010417500009282

Scranton, P. (2018a). Author's rejoinder to comments on managing communist enterprises: Poland, Hungary and Czechoslovakia, 1945–1970. *Enterprise & Society, 19*(3), 570–577. https://doi.org/10.1017/eso.2018.17

Scranton, P. (2018b). Managing communist enterprises: Poland, Hungary, and Czechoslovakia, 1945–1970. *Enterprise & Society, 19*(3), 492–537. https://doi.org/10.1017/eso.2018.13

Scranton, P. (2019). *Enterprise, organization, and technology in China: A socialist experiment, 1950–1971.* Palgrave Macmillan.

Scranton, P. (2022). *Business practice in socialist Hungary, volume 1: Creating the theft economy, 1945–1957.* Springer Nature.

Scranton, P., & Fridenson, P. (2013). *Reimaging business history.* John Hopkins University Press.

Shpotov, B. (2013). *Amerikanskii biznes i Sovetskii Soiuz, 1920–1930-e gody: Labirinty ekonomicheskogo sotrudnichestva* [*American business and the Soviet Union in the 1920s and 1930s: Labyrinths of economic cooperation*]. Librokom.

Spaskovska, L., & Calori, A. (2021). A nonaligned business world: The global socialist enterprise between self-management and transnational capitalism. *Nationalities Papers*, *49*(3), 413–427. https://doi.org/10.1017/nps.2020.27

Steiner, A. (2010). *The plans that failed: An economic history of the GDR* (E. Osers, Trans.) Berghahn Publishers.

Stokes, R. (1997). In search of the socialist artefact: Technology and ideology in East Germany, 1945–1962. *German History*, *15*(2), 221–239. https://doi.org/10.1093/gh/15.2.221

Stokes, R. (2000). *Constructing socialism: Technology and change in East Germany, 1945–1990*. Johns Hopkins University Press.

Stone, R. (1996). *Satellites and commissars: Strategy and conflict in the politics of soviet-bloc trade*. Princeton University Press.

Szobi, P. (2014). Between ideology and pragmatism: The ČSSR, the GDR and West European companies in the 1970s and 1980s. *European Review of History: Revue Européenne D'histoire*, *21*(2), 255–269. https://doi.org/10.1080/13507486.2014.888705

Thai, P. (2018). *China's war on smuggling: Law, economic life, and the making of the modern state, 1842–1965*. Columbia University Press.

Unkovski-Korica, V. (2014). Workers' councils in the service of the market: New archival evidence on the origins of self-management in Yugoslavia 1948–1950. *Europe-Asia Studies*, *66*(1), 108–134. https://doi.org/10.1080/09668136.2013.855020

Unkovski-Korica, V. (2016). *The economic struggle for power in Tito's Yugoslavia: From World War II to non-alignment*. Bloomsbury Publishing.

Varga, Z. (2020). *The Hungarian agricultural miracle?: Sovietization and Americanization in a communist country*. Lexington Books.

Williams, C. C., Nadin, S., & Rodgers, P. (2011). Beyond a "varieties of capitalism" approach in Central and Eastern Europe: Some lessons from Ukraine. *Employee Relations*, *33*(4), 413–427. https://doi.org/10.1108/01425451111142701

Wilson, J., Toms, S., De Jong, A., & Buchnea, E. (Eds.). (2016). *The Routledge companion to business history*. Taylor & Francis.

Wilson, J. F., Jones, I. G., Toms, S., Tilba, A., Buchnea, E., & Wong, N. (2022). *Business history: A research overview*. Routledge.

Yányshev-Nésterova, I. (2020). Soviet big business: The rise and fall of the state corporation Sovrybflot, 1965-1991. *Business History*, 1–24. https://doi.org/10.1080/00076791.2020.1856079

Yudanov, A. Y. (1997). USSR: Large enterprises in the USSR – The functional disorder. In A. ChandlerJr., F. Amatori, & T. Hikino (Eds.), *Big business and the wealth of nations* (pp. 397–432). Cambridge University Press.

Zaccaria, B. (2021). From liberalism to underdevelopment: The Yugoslav elites facing Western European economic integration in the "long 1970s. In A. Romano & F. Romero (Eds.). *European socialist regimes' fateful engagement with the West* (pp. 221–248). Routledge.

Zatlin, J. R. (2009). *The currency of socialism: Money and political culture in East Germany*. CamBridge University Press.

Persistent centralisation of decision-making in the age of industrial atomisation and self-management on the case of construction company *Industrogradnja* Zagreb (1966–1980)

Saša Vejzagić

ABSTRACT
The history of *Industrogradnja* between 1966 and 1980, although only a short, in medias res, segment in its biography, provides a complete overview of phases that Yugoslav companies underwent on their path to becoming a large industrial system. This article explores changes in management structure and application of new managerial practices during this period, which in turn led this construction and engineering company to the status of the leader in the housing industry in Zagreb. Apart from reconstruction of the company history, this article delves into two stages of complex structural changes the League of Communist of Yugoslavia implemented in the country's socio-economic system, and investigates how a hybrid of two value systems, socialist and market, affected Yugoslav business practices. The case of *Industrogradnja* and this article aim to contribute to the understanding of socialist projects in the twentieth century as a variety of socio-economic frameworks as well as business environments.

A few days before the end of 1976, *Indostrugradnja* organised a grandiose ceremony celebrating the thirtieth anniversary of its foundation, hosting many dignitaries from Croatian political and business realms. The spotlight was on Jakov Blažević, the Croatian Prime Minister, who arrived on behalf of Josip Broz Tito to award the company for its 'efficient investment in extended reproduction [fixed capital]' and achieving 'high profits' in preceding couple of years.[1] Indeed, for a decade, between 1966 and 1976, *Industrogradnja* maintained an explosive growth and evolved from a medium size contractor into a construction and engineering giant, making it into the club of the Yugoslav Top 100 industrial enterprises.[2] The majority of companies on that list were part of the same phenomenon and shared similar growth trajectories on account of the liberalisation and marketisation of the socio-economic framework, launched in the first half of the 1960s, to build country's export capacities and integrate with the global market. And yet, a few months before the anniversary ceremony in 1976, the government enforced the new Law on Associated Labour, among the most elaborate legal acts in the country's history, explicating extensive decentralisation and new self-management relations in all Yugoslav enterprises.

Large business structures, like *Industrogradnja*, were the primary target of the counter-liberalisation campaign in the 1970s, since they were perceived as one of the main sources of alienated economic and political power that were the direct result of market reform from the previous decade. That being said, business giants in practice were reluctant to either bend their structural integrity or abandon centralised decision-making, while using creative ways of preserving those prerogatives. In this sense, in the first two parts, the article investigates how *Industrogradnja* became a large industrial system during the time of limited market reform and how the management used those conditions to find the most lucrative position on the local, national and foreign markets. In the final part, the paper looks at the magnitude of the campaign against liberalisation and how the management utilised structural problems and already established blueprints or legal loopholes for circumventing the counter-reform tendencies to maintain their business organisation and model of operation.

Methodologically the article predominantly relies on the *Industrogradnja*'s workers' bulletin. Company papers are generally a challenging type of source for reconstructing any given individual case. Thanks to self-management and legal obligation for all companies in Yugoslavia to continuously inform their workers' collective with the most relevant business news, prospects of new projects or the progress of the existing ones, managements' deals with business partners, work conditions, versions of company charters, etc., most of the country's factory bulletins certainly provided enough insight for drawing a broader picture of the company's growth and performance. As a source supplement two interviews were conducted with former company members of middle management, engineers Mirko Orešković and Đuro Mirković, who were heads of two important departments during the 1970s. There are also few company books published for the occasion of *Industrogradnja*'s round anniversaries. Nevertheless, apart from certain chronological insights, as well as an understanding of the types of buildings the company manufactured, they provide limited information.

It is encouraging that the micro-historical analysis of large industrial systems in Yugoslavia is becoming a trend in the past decade and is already offering a variety of approaches. The self-management and the workers' dynamics, both on the shop-floor and in relation to other actors in the enterprise, have already been explored by Igor Stanić in the case of *Uljanik*, as well as Goran Musić in the cases of *TAM* and *IMR*.[3] Particularly, Musić's recent book made a formidable impact on the historiography dealing with the Yugoslav socialist project, as it re-evaluated the agency of the workers in the country's final decade, while identifying the nuanced relationships between the workers, management, and the state, both inside and outside of their companies. Moreover, Ljubica Spaskovska and Anna Calori in their joint article looked at the integration of two business giants, *Pelagonija* and *Energoinvest*, with the global market and, among other things, addressed an important question of how marketisation and self-management coexisted. They argued that the associated labour reform of the 1970s could be viewed as 'a genuine attempt at reconciling the market and socialism' in Yugoslavia.[4] Even though such understanding has certain validity in the broadest possible context, this account sees the associated labour as structural reaction to contradictions that surfaced with marketisation.

Business history has only recently, in the past two decades or so, gradually turned its focus on firms and business environments in twentieth century states, dedicated to the development of socialist societies. Many of those accounts often approached those geo-historical areas burdened with a market normative perspective and questions of success, efficiency, profitability, usually ignoring the structural circumstances and ideas behind socialist projects. In fact, similarly to that which Adam K. Frost rightfully recognised in the scholarship tackling Chinese experience.[5] Still, among them there are historians, such as Philip Scranton, who put in extra effort and thoroughly investigated the recently available translated sources on Chinese businesses.[6] Scranton not only recognised the existence of the business world in the Peoples' Republic of China in the 1950s and 1960s, but also identified the experimentative nature of Chinese enterprises as one of the key factors responsible for the longevity and success of Chinese businesses, as well as the point of divergence with the business experience in the Central European socialist projects. This article complements this argument and adds the Yugoslav business experience, with its structural and management peculiarities, to the diversity of socialist projects both in Europe and beyond. Primarily, the piece contributes to the discussion about business growth and the role of management practices and policies in a non-conventional framework. Indirectly, however, it adds to the debate on the approach historians should take when examining the fundamental business principles, within the economic frameworks established by the communist parties in this period. More precisely, on one hand, it brings political and ideological motives and programmes into the equations that question the efficiency, business performance and historical success of companies operating under the veil of socialist projects. On the other hand, it explores why those systems and their business actors struggled to adopt market policies and how the two value systems contradicted each other.

1. Marketisation and the birth of the large construction company

Established in 1946, *Industrogradnja* was a small construction enterprise,[7] with a collective of merely 37 workers, equipped with two mixers, one truck and seventeen carriages.[8] In this immediate post-war period, the company was mostly preoccupied with rebuilding what remained of Zagreb's industrial potential, which was ultimately the reason for assuming the name *Industro* (Industrial) *gradnja* (construction) in 1950.[9] The same year the enterprise elected its first delegates to the Workers' Council as the result of Yugoslavia's first endeavour into the new socio-economic system, known as self-management.[10] The framework inspired by direct democracy in industrial decision-making, however, remained in the experimental phase since in practice most of the workers' councils assumed an advisory role to otherwise hierarchically organised management. Managements, instead of being subjected to the new stakeholders, were at first accountable to the state directorates (1945–1952 during the time of soviet-like administrative economy) and later to respective local governments (1952–1965 on account of the political decentralisation in Yugoslavia).[11] Management loyalties changed again with emancipation of the business sector in the 1960s, but this will be elaborated in the second part of this article. In the 1950s, during the decade of rapid industrialisation the construction industry in general was not immensely favoured by the state that followed an autarkic model of development. Like in the most Soviet-like countries, import substitution configuration was set to first facilitate 'factories for production of factories',[12] or heavy industry that would supply manufacturing industry, and the construction industry was somewhere second or third in this modernisation line.

Indeed, during the first decade and a half of its history *Industrogradnja* had a slow pace of growth, yet, the company's initial steps were significant for rapid expansion in the 1960s. For instance, in 1951, the management expanded the company production capacity via horizontal integration with a small contractor, *Banija* from Sisak, making this industrial centre an important company outpost for later cooperation with the Sisak refinery and Sisak steelworks factory.[13] A close business relationship with the former eventually procured a sizable contract for participation in the construction of several hundred kilometres of long oil-pipeline in the 1970s.[14] In terms of strategic development, in 1954 *Industrogradnja*'s leadership acquired the company's very first 'Fiorentini' crane and it was immediately deployed to erect the first skyscraper in Zagreb, making it the company's first major landmark in the city.[15] When in the second half of 1950s Yugoslav policymakers finally cutback extensive military production and noticed the long-neglected standard of living, the shift of development focus also marked the start of a new era for various Yugoslav industries.[16] In turn, the overall economy recorded its most successful five-year plan in the country's history (1957–1961).[17] Favourable economic circumstances spread to all domains and both the social housing market and investments in fixed capital in general were flourishing. In this context, in 1959, *Indoustrogradnja* had to acquire three more cranes and immediately deployed them on the southern bank of the river Sava, to erect a whole neighbourhood consisting solely of high-rise apartment buildings, counting 1500 flats.[18] Arguably, this was the beginning of the company's specialisation for the industrial production of housing infrastructure in Zagreb and the overture to high-speed expansion that would occur in the second half of 1960s. Also, from henceforth, the enterprise practically earned the status of a key partner to the local government in the urbanisation of the southern riverbank, soon to be known as the New Zagreb.

The first sign of *Industrogradnja*'s development into a more complex business system landed in 1962 when *Industrogradnja* ventured into the expansion of internal capacities by opening a plant *Lomnica* for production of construction materials such as prefabricated and reinforced concrete.[19] Interestingly, this new factory was founded barely a year before the disastrous earthquake in Skopje that left over a thousand fatal casualties and destroyed close to 80 per cent of the city's buildings. In years after the tragic event in the Republic of Macedonia the Federal government decided to modernise the architectural standards and demanded that all new buildings were to be made of seismically more resistant material.[20] One of the essential products for fortified and safe construction at the time was reinforced concrete and *Industrogradnja* timely secured its own production capacities. *Lomnica* would become one of the bedrocks of the company's rapid expansion in the ensuing period and received the best part of *Industrogradnja*'s capital investments.

Immediately after the most successful five-year investment period, economic indexes started to reveal signs of decline. To avoid plummeting into severe recession, the government decided to abandon the autarkic model of development in favour of the pursuit for a solid presence on the global market with a pool of competitive companies. Since large industrial systems were at the time perceived as the most successful model of company organisation, in the first half of 1960s, the Party together with local governments and chambers of commerce, launched a cross-country campaign for systematic industrial consolidation.[21] The movement for vertical and horizontal integration, however, was only a part of a wider reform effort, aiming to 'marketise' the economic system. The main characteristic of the new model was gradual withering away of the state's influence on business and financial actors. The autonomy of banks and companies was certainly far from being comparable with their counterparts in capitalist countries, however, in juxtaposition with the administrative system from the 1940s and early 1950s, the difference was conspicuous.

With the desire to imbue the Yugoslav business world with values such as profitability or efficiency, the government transferred almost the entirety of its investment prerogatives and capital from centralised state/social funds into the hands of banks under the leadership of professional managers.[22] This major systemic change was complemented with hundreds of smaller measures, like the loosening of foreign trade restrictions, liberalisation of the price regime and the creation of other platforms and categories indispensable for the establishment of market relations.[23] That being said, marketisation was never fully achieved, for the state was still left with a significant degree of power to intervene, especially on the macro-economic level, which ultimately turned the Yugoslav economy into a form of a limping hybrid. The new socio-economic framework, Darko Suvin argues, was a 'market-administrative' environment, which was permanently in a state of contradiction, since neither of the two value systems could dominate the other one nor would be able to work together.[24]

Also, the market reform was poorly prepared and hastily implemented in a relatively short time span (1964–1965) or almost overnight, which for many companies probably seemed as if someone simply turned on the market switch after years of coordinated production.[25] This in turn caused widespread confusion among managements. For instance, at the start of 1966, the chief director of *Industrogradnja*, Nikola Krneta, complained of new circumstances that raised uncertainties in the construction market and the economy in general:

> The only thing I can affirm is that the next year will be even harsher in the whole construction sector due to the changes in the system of funding for housing construction – with the shift to commercial housing via permanent loans for working capital it is still unknown whether we are going to receive those loans, how big they will be, and who is going to give them to us. We only know that Zagreb's Fund for housing construction ceased to exist […].[26] Two novelties in the construction business surfaced with the reforms in the 1960s. First, as seen in Krneta's complaint, construction businesses were now dependent on investors (federal, state, or local government and their administrative bodies, as well as other businesses)[27] and their own working capital, now supported with bank loans.[28] Second, the notion of commercial housing was also introduced with dismantlement of investment funds. Now, apart from public housing, construction companies in Yugoslavia were allowed to use their budgets and take bank loans for investment into construction of 'apartments for the market',[29] and then sell those flats to either individual private owners or other Yugoslav companies looking to buy flats for their workers, which together immediately became a sizable portion of *Industrogradnja*'s business operations.[30]

In the new marketised environment, self-management or its workers' decision-making platform was supposed to act as the counterweight to the market or the watchdog overlooking its hazardous tendencies. Hence, while the entirety of short and most of the mid-term decision making was in the hands of management, workers' councils were entrusted with overlooking managements' affairs as well as deciding upon the company's long-term plans and arrangements.[31] The rationale behind this division of responsibility was to have professional managements coping with market forces, while relying on self-management to make sure that social property, workers' democracy, and socialist project in general were not to become endangered by business interactions under the veil of market. There was also a Party branch in every major industrial enterprise that was supposed to make sure this dynamic between managers and representatives of the collective (but also society) would not depart from the frame of socialist principles.

Nevertheless, by the time that the reform was launched, both watchdogs, the councils and Party outposts in factories, were often under the strong influence of the top management.[32] Negative aspects of the management's full control as well as hierarchical distribution of power were tackled and confronted in *Industrogradnja* at the beginning of 1966. Then, the chief company director, Nikola Krneta, together with his team and the president of the Workers' Council got accused of a series of corrupt deeds and abuses of power against the company's wellbeing and its collective:

> There are some unhealthy interpersonal relations between the director and his subordinates. [...] [H]e was taking advantage of female employees, driving them with the company vehicle to Plitvička jezera, Samobor, Tuheljske toplice, Klanjec [tourist destinations] during working hours [...] [H]e was using the service of workers who own a private car to drive him around and then paying them for overtime that they had never done. [...] [H]e is erecting a vacation house in Rovinj with our engineers from Sisak and a private house in Klanj [...] We are not holding a grudge just because he will build a house or had bought a car, but because he is using company material.[33]

Krneta tried to consolidate his ranks by demanding that his management staff ignore the issue, however, some of them rebelled and formed the company's Committee for internal investigation. The official inquiry confirmed evidence of 'inviolable concentration of power', involving corrupt misdeeds in collaboration with other members of the management, warehouse supervisors, chauffeurs, the president of the Workers' Council, the secretary of the Party branch and others.[34] Also, the Committee's statement revealed Krneta's firm influence on the company's self-management body, for he was 'arranging every single entry on the agendas for the Workers' Council sessions, while refusing any constructive comment or allowing discussion that would counter his arguments'.[35] In the end, Krneta was relieved of all his duties, while his collaborators either left the company or accepted other forms of punishment, most often demotions.

According to Suvin, the main goal of the reform was to have the market work in conjunction with self-management, so this marriage of the two could create the 'initiative from below'.[36] The entire project, however, failed on account of the already mentioned contradictory relations between the two value systems. Instead, this incompatibility rather immediately created vivid instabilities and caused major headaches for the state leadership, in the form of growing unemployment and inflation, as well as acute illiquidity in the business sector. The reform campaign was clandestinely abandoned in the late 1960s, although a large portion of implemented changes remained. Certainly, the most damaging of them was the control over the investment capital that stayed in the firm hands of the banking sector. Production companies also preserved their relative autonomy, but at the same time their performance was under the strong influence of the emancipated financial institutions. The Federal government never stopped to make corrections in the system. Their attempts came either in the form of the already-mentioned macro-interventions, or as a whole new bundle of structural reforms that attempted to pacify the overwhelming systemic contradictions. The latter will be addressed at greater length in the last of the three parts, but, before that, the article will explore how the management of *Industrogradnja* utilised the autonomy for the company expansion and positioning on the market.

2. Becoming a large industrial system

In months following the departure of the old management *Industrogradnja* had several empty offices to repopulate with fresh executives and supervisors. The new chief director, engineer Mate Čop, was among the very first to openly oppose Krneta and join the Committee for investigation, which altogether might have contributed to his appointment at the end of 1966.[37] That being said, at the time Čop claimed the head office, although only being 36 years old, he already had 14 years of experience in the construction business. From 1952, Čop was the head of the construction site on several major housing, industrial and infrastructural projects for smaller companies such as *GP Lika-Gospić* and *GP Vladimir Gortan*.[38] After ten years of 'field-work' he moved to *Industrogradnja* in 1962 and took over the Department for Planning, Analysis, and Development. Particularly his strong sense for strategising will become apparent throughout the entire thirty-year mandate behind the helm of *Industrogradnja*. In fact, Čop was among the representatives of the new generation of directors and his appointment coincided with the cross-country campaign for the modernisation of company leadership with professional managers and for the sake of better integration with the global market.[39] And while presence outside Yugoslav borders was far from being the core of the new *Industrogradnja*'s strategy, Čop's management in a matter of few years arranged the production process entrenched in the economy of scale and soon claimed the status of the leader on the Zagreb's largest construction market, the housing business.

The new management immediately launched a widespread administrative systematisation of all levels of management, aiming to make all offices and departments more disciplined and accountable for their plans and performance.[40] The spring cleaning in *Industrogradnja* was organised to repair the damage caused by years of negligence, but also as a response to challenging market conditions that the company faced at the time. Namely, the market reform period (1965–1969) was also the time of the government's measures set to tame local governments with a large appetite for capital investments bearing questionable economic logic or to shut down what were considered unprofitable enterprises, which ultimately squeezed the construction market and distorted prices of raw materials.[41] When prices of so called 'commercial apartments' [stanovi za tržište] rose in 1967 due to the increase of the costs of construction, the government, afraid of the social discontent on account of inflation, decided to 'transfer the burden of raising the standard of living on the construction businesses', by maintaining the low prices of apartments, while allowing the costs of raw materials to fluctuate.[42] According to Grga Jelinić, commercial flats were artificially maintained affordable, especially between 1966 and 1975, when the price of the square metre increased by 4.7 times while the average personal income was behind with an increase of 4.5 times, preserving the price of square metre below two monthly salaries.[43]

Čop and his new team resisted these pressures, by progressively industrialising *Industrogradnja*'s construction process via modernisation of products and services. For instance, in 1967, the company bought a state-of-the-art technology and technique, known as 'hydraulic sliding formwork'.[44] The new construction method, as its name suggests, involved sliding of the concrete blocks, one on top of the other, which substantially increased the pace of production, especially for industrial projects such as silos or factory funnels. The sliding framework, however, boosted the company's performance thanks to the ingenuity of *Industrogradnja*'s engineers. Namely, Vlado Despotović modified the technology and applied it for mass production of apartment buildings.[45] With the reconfigured sliding framework in 1969, the workers of *Industrogradnja* broke records in Zagreb by finishing the outer layer of three sixteen-story buildings in a little over two weeks per piece.[46] In this sense, the appearance of the new construction machinery was one of the management's keys for establishing a business model anchored in the economy of scale. Indeed, in the following period, *Industrogradnja* refocused its business orientation to housing industry, making high-rise apartment buildings their main product and Čop's business strategy was to acquire as many as possible of such projects.

Industrogradnja's achievements in the efficiency of housing production attracted the attention of the city government and in February 1969 brought the Zagreb mayor (Predsjednik skupštine), Jakov Kolar, to the construction site in Sopot where he publicly expressed his 'fascination' with *Industrogradnja*'s capabilities.[47] The same day Kolar also visited *Lomnica* and was equally happy with the growth of the company centre for production of finalised and semi-finalised concrete products. To make it official, the City recognised *Industrogradnja* as a business which 'in a short time-span adopted state-of-the-art technology for construction of all types of structures' and in April 1969 awarded it with 'Zagreb's economic award'.[48] The acknowledgment was a form of political watermark, important for potential future business partners, which certainly helped the company on its way to becoming 'the name' on the emerging housing market. At the end of the decade, Čop invited experienced architects and engineers to re-establish the Architectonic and project bureau, after the previous team of architects left the company.[49] The bureau was the last brick in creating the foundation of a vertically integrated industrial system that had consolidated standard three levels of production process.[50] In this case, instead of conventional integration of capacities for extraction of raw materials, manufacturing, and distribution, *Industrogradnja* had project design bureau on the bottom, production of cement and manufacturing of concrete in the middle, and construction and distribution as the final stage of the production process.

The housing market, although a fruitful business lane, was still far from being sufficient to maintain a steady income, especially during the precarious second half of the 1960s, and even less so enough for upholding company expansion. For this reason, Čop's management continued competing for infrastructural projects in this period and claimed various contracts, such as: electrification of the Belgrade-Zagreb railway and construction of the Istrian water supply system, building of an industrial refrigerator on three floors, warehouses, industrial silos, and large production halls.[51] Such flexibility was needed in order to fill the annual schedule and meet the planned income figures. Also, in 1967 the management signed a contract for its first project on foreign soil and took charge of erecting Gabe's school centre in Tunis.[52] The following year workers from Zagreb started their first assignments on two buildings in West Germany, Horetn's department store in Heilbronn and a distribution centre for postal packages in Hamburg, among the largest in Europe at the time.[53] In June 1972, the management decided to make a stronger presence in the West and opened a daughter company, *Industrogradnja GMBH,* which momentarily paid off since during that year it cashed in ten million DM of total revenue.[54]

The Yugoslav business world in the 1970s, although overall seemingly stable, was in fact ravaged with structural problems such as growing illiquidity and inflation as well as disturbances in the procurement of raw materials. The general context and the company's position in it are illustratively depicted in the management's financial report for 1972, where the performance was characterised as 'satisfying', despite the fact their expenses for raw materials increased as well as the pressure from their creditors on the account of the stack of unsold flats.[55] In fact, the company's liquidity was just positive and this was celebrated like a proper achievement at the end of each year with the same statement 'our bank accounts remained unblocked' for XY years in a row.[56] The same, however, could have not been said for a number of their partners. For instance, during 1972, the management of *Industrogradnja* had to settle on relieving most of the debt for one of the construction projects ordered by *Agrokombinat*.[57]

This Zagreb-based giant went bankrupt that same year and their creditors, including *Industrogradnja*, were forced to give up most of their claims.[58] *Industrogradnja* received 'compensation' in form of a brand-new headquarters tower in Zagreb (Savska street 66), the very same building the company erected for *Agrokombinat* and was demanding to be paid for.

Once again, the management combated adverse circumstances by insisting on 'upgrading the technology and development of a more efficient' production process.[59] The concrete plant *Lomnica* was enhanced in 1973 with new machinery, which significantly increased the rate of production as well as quality of blocks and models for sliding.[60] Also, the management yet again reorganised the company units and established the Concrete-sliding department.[61] The new unit reduced the production time of outer building layouts from two weeks (recorded in 1969) to six days.[62] All of the improvements contributed to the deal the management sealed with the Solidarity fund in 1973, for erecting an entire new neighbourhood of 1800 flats, out of which 1200 were designed to fit in a single building, 'Block 6' also known as *Mamutica* (the Mammut).[63] With multiple projects in emerging neighbourhoods of Travno, Voltino and Utrine, the company once again overcame the short-term crash of the housing construction market (1971) and became the top producer in Zagreb, delivering 1530 flats in 1973 alone.[64]

The management was able to sail through the mid-1970s despite unfavourable winds, by complementing its core production with industrial, tourist, and other projects for various Croatian companies. Alumina factory in Obrovac, as well as the thermal power plant, oil refinery, and ironworks factory in Sisak, like the rest of the Yugoslav business world at the time, continued heavily investing in fixed capital.[65] Also, *Industrogradnja* enriched Zagreb's tourist offer with the first 'super-comfortable' hotel, *Intercontinental*.[66] On top of that, the company continued expanding outside Yugoslav federal borders as the German branch signed to do masonry work on 32 university buildings in Bielefield.[67] *Industrogradnja* GMBH, however, was shut down by the summer 1974 due to 'general illiquidity on the Western construction market'.[68] Still, the most important foreign contract in this period was the first business deal sealed with the Soviets on 'Inturist' hotel in Yalta, which in turn opened the door for a number of future projects in the Soviet Union throughout the following decade and a half.[69]

Statistically, during the first half of the 1970s, although housing projects were still at the company's core orientation, *Inudstrogradnja* gradually started relaying on industrial and other non-housing projects outside Zagreb in order to maintain a stable financial balance (see Table 1).

Also, judging by the figures in the table, at the beginning of 1975 *Industrogradnja*'s Office for Planning and Development believed that the contraction of projects for the market (industrial and housing) would eventually achieve the same balance.

The economy, however, was more and more overtaken by the crisis and in response the same year the Federal government imposed a new tax on all industries, diminishing their investment capacities in the following period.[71] More importantly, by the mid-1970s the

Table 1. Structure of *Industrogradnja's* projects 1971–1975.

	1971	1972	1973	1974	1975	1976
Projects for the market	63%	57%	55%	57%	42%	87%
Projects for investors	37%	43%	45%	43%	58%	13%
Projects in Zagreb	76%	77%	76%	69%	52%	60%
Projects outside Zagreb	24%	23%	24%	31%	48%	40%

Values for 1976 were projected in 1975 by the Office for planning and development.[70]

Party's new reform platform, associated labour, was way under way and, among other things, it represented a structural solution to contradictions that escalated with the marketisation and liberalisation program deployed in the previous decade. Literally overnight the notion of commercial housing was abolished due to the unfavourable hike in prices and was replaced with the new category of 'Socially directed housing construction', managed by the 'Self-managing community of interest for housing' (SCIH).[72] The SCIH was supposed to be another democratising intervention in the Yugoslav associated society, and it truly was based on a humane initiative to involve all relevant actors into resolving housing needs of the society.[73] Nevertheless, petty local interests in time of crisis and clashes of power among delegates in the SCIH assemblies developed a state of ever lower productivity of housing projects between 1976 and 1979.[74] Only when the delegates from city governments took over executive positions in SCIH, did housing production once again relatively stabilise.

Industrogradnja's business plans and performance were affected by those changes since the company invested billions of dinars for the development of production capacities for the construction of high-rise apartment buildings in Zagreb and its vicinity. The company even strategically merged with *Jugomont*, another large Zagreb-based enterprise, specialised in housing projects.[75] Their share in *Industrogradnja*'s production in the eve of the 1980s, however, dropped to only 36% of all company business operations.[76] The global economic crisis at the beginning of the new decade hit the Yugoslav market much harder than the recession of 1973/74, and pushed the country towards unofficial bankruptcy. Industrial projects were also in decline as the country had to introduce harsh austerity measures to stabilise the economy. Even then *Industrogradnja* under Čop's direction was able to withstand external pressures and internal structural problems, often by utilising established political and business connections needed for overcoming the imposed restrictions. For instance, according to Orešković, he personally witnessed an unofficial meeting between Čop and the Prime minister of the Croatian government, Petar Fleković, in which they discussed the loopholes the company could utilise to circumvent the restrictions imposed by the Federal stabilisation programme.[77] On the one hand this example says a lot about the broader political context in Yugoslavia at the time, involving the clandestine collapse of economic and political unity, which in turn forbode the upcoming dissolution. On the other, their meeting represents a small piece of the puzzle, illustrating the regular business practices and inevitable links between large industries and the respective level of political elites.

3. The counter-reform and atomisation of the 1970s

With the end of 1969 the company papers were dismantled due to lack of staff which caused a relative gap in the sources until late 1972. During this three-year period, however, a great deal of political affairs culminated in Yugoslavia with direct repercussions for its business world. First, in 1969 the constitutional amendment XV started a controversial trend in companies, and allowed them, intentionally or not, to further centralise management and bypass democratic procedures of self-management.[78] In the meantime, the same process of liberalisation spread to the political realm through decentralisation of the Party and the arrival of younger generations of politicians at the forefronts of each state-level branch. It would not take long for the Croatian side of the Party family to openly criticise vivid signs of disharmony in the distribution of national wealth. Their public performances ultimately transformed into a political campaign for the restoration of the Yugoslavia's equilibrium that would be based on deeper administrative decentralisation and greater financial autonomy of the republics.[79] Their campaigning, however, sparked a mass movement known as the Croatian spring, which among other characteristics, also carried a nationalistic sentiment and, hence, represented a danger that could revive some of the old ethnic antagonisms. In response, Tito and the rest of the Party Politburo decided that both market reform and the Croatian Spring were seriously endangering the socialist project, including their political position, and, hence, smothered the movement to avoid further political destabilisation, but also to stop the advancement of liberalisation.

The social group that in the 1970s was most often associated with liberalism were directors of large companies, then pejoratively labelled as 'techno-managers'. Established directors in the business realm, Suvin argues, accumulated enough economic and political capital to become a 'rival monopoly' and threatened to claim the status of 'the first violin' in Yugoslav society, the one reserved for the Party and its leadership.[80] Also, those managers often took part in numerous public discussions during the reform period, when they felt free to more openly criticise self-management and even proclaim it 'redundant' in the market conditions.[81] For these intrusions the Party leadership believed it had enough reasons to label established directors as hazardous for the socialist project and ultimately start a purge. As a result, a noticeable number of managers were either demoted, expelled from the Party and fired, or even sentenced to prison-time.[82] Some of those rulings were questionable, however. A good proportion of the company leaders were in fact abusing their positions, as was the case with Čop's predecessor Nikola Krneta.[83] According to Orešković, there was an attempt to start a political process against Mate Čop and link him with the Croatian Spring. However, he was rescued by his colleague and the company's Party secretary, Mile Šumonja.[84] Allegedly, Šumonja refused to force political action challenging the general director and instead garnered him support among party members in *Industrogradnja*.

Dealing with the contradictions of 'market socialism' on the micro level was but the overture to the Party's counter-reform efforts throughout the 1970s, focussed on the business sector. Large industrial systems were recognised as 'epicentres of new forms of undemocratic social relations' where 'workers could not exercise their self-management rights in big units' and, hence, needed a structural solution.[85] Associated labour was developed as an enhanced version of self-management,[86] entrenched in the conviction that democratisation would be achieved through fragmentation of large structures. That being said, economic and political decentralisation, according to Dejan Jović, was not merely a reaction to rusting liberalisation, but a 'stage in the structural reforming of ideocratic state', since Yugoslav ideologists were faithful to the idea of withering away of the state.[87] Interestingly, the utilisation of associated labour to shrink the power of managements was somewhat similar to the phenomenon that occurred during the crisis of profitability at the end of 1970s in the United States. There, the corporate legislation was also changed to give more power to stake holders, which ultimately turned into even greater dominance of powerful CEOs.[88]

The new socio-economic framework envisaged atomisation of companies into clusters of smaller autonomous units, known as 'Basic organizations of associated labour' – BOALs (Osnovna organizacija udruženog rada – OOUR). In practice, every company department capable of independently producing a tradable product or service was now eligible to become a BOAL.[89] Once established, BOALs were organised to perform as independent legal entities, governed by their own workers' council, with prerogative to discuss and approve the most important business decisions. This in turn meant a substantial increase of administrative apparatus and decentralisation of management. At the same time, Čop's plans for *Industrogradnja* in the first half of the 1970s were almost diametrically opposite to the intentions of lawmakers and Party ideologists.[90] In this sense, he was a true representative of the new generation of technocratic managers, who often utilised loopholes in legislation to maintain control over decision-making.

For instance, during the first or transitional period, between 1971 and 1976, like most companies in the Yugoslav business realm at the time, *Industrogradnja* made just enough effort to satisfy the minimal legal requirements, by adopting the associated labour reform in the form of cosmetic changes to the company layout. Despite the decentralisation, a large proportion of manoeuvrable space was 'hidden' in the institution of the self-management agreement (SMA), which was supposed to define horizontal and vertical business, economic and financial relations between the BOALs, joint administration and top management. For instance, the signing of the SMA between twelve BOALs of *Industrogradnja* in 1973[91] seemed to represent a firm case of continuity of the old internal relations, only written in a new language of associated labour:

> BOALs will achieve their common goals of business policy with more success through associated labour, especially with joint appearance on the market, joint use of associated funds, through joint investment and mutual use of services. [...] BOALs signatories to this Agreement agree that the company continues to retain its existing legal status, i.e. that the legal entity is the company as a whole [...]. All BOALs except BOAL 'Komar' have agreed to assume joint responsibility for the obligations of the company created so far and for future joint obligations. [...] In order to better plan and monitor cash flows, perform transactions, solve illiquidity problems, and find a more favourable source of funding, BOALs agree that the company has a single giro account registered with the Social Accounting Service.[92] The authors of *Industrogradnja* SMA made sure to emphasise that the best way for BOALs to operate would be to remain in association with other units and have their business activities coordinated from the above. Needless to say, there was no evidence of any discussion suggesting a less centralised structure.

Indeed, professional managers often hesitated to approach the associated labour campaign wholeheartedly as it showed inconsistencies in company performance. For instance, the *Industrogradnja* leadership already in 1974 decided to lower the number of BOALs in *Industrogradnja* from twelve to nine, since some BOALs were 'exhausting themselves individually in order to reach higher [unit] income, instead of focusing on increasing [general] productivity'.[93] Like departments in complex business systems, BOALs also had unequal working conditions, which depended on their contribution to the entire production process. Since their input was measured through their share in the total income, some units decided to invest their time and energy on acquiring extra income by selling their products and services elsewhere, which was often done at the expense of collective performance. That being said, such manoeuvring around the intention of Constitutional legislation forced the Yugoslav government in 1976 to adopt, probably the most elaborate legal document in its history, the Associated Labour Act (also known as little or workers constitution for its size).

Following the new legal directive, in referendum held throughout November and December 1977, BOALs of *Industrogradnja* signed another SME and reconfigured once more. This time the restructuring had to be more than a simple cosmetic renaming of departments, since all constituent company units had to have an individual bank account,[94] and capacity to demonstrate independence in the decision-making process.[95] Now, on paper, the company looked more like a business confederation, than an integrated industrial system. Decentralisation and democratisation of the company, as well as simulation of bottom-up trajectory of decision making, in the late 1970s, are well illustrated in Figure 1, depicting the process of crafting of documents with mid-term or long-term effects, such as was a company's annual business plan.

In theory and practice, the director of a given BOAL had to initiate the creation of a plan and pass the initiative to a group of experts gathered into a committee to draft such proposal. This blueprint then reached the BOAL's delegates in its Workers' Council, who gave their comments and forwarded it to the Workers' Assembly to decide upon it via popular vote.[97] The ratified document was sent to the upper management, more precisely to the Office for Joint Planning, which used it to compose the overall business strategy and proposed it to the Central Workers' Council, the highest self-management body in *Industrogradnja,* to discuss and finally ratify the general plan. Following the confirmation, the general business plan was sent back to the BOAL management for its implementation. Overall, although the most inclusive and transparent road for crafting business plans, probably in the history of company organising, in the environment where the market and its logic of profit and competition was the main force moving all business actors involved, the associated labour was easily perceived as inefficient.

The company management was far from being amused with the new system but were eager to pretend yet again to follow the intentions of lawmakers. This can be read between the lines in Čop's short comment on the implementation of LAL at the end of 1977:

> Great efforts have been made to improve income relations between basic organizations of associated labour and labour organizations that perform certain tasks for BOALs. [...] We must not forget that our ultimate goal is to organize the application of LAL in the way that every worker in the BOAL participates in the distribution of funds for personal income according to the work invested as well as the value of the work invested, and in accordance with the realized income of BOAL and the company as a whole. [...] In this sense, compliance and unity in the

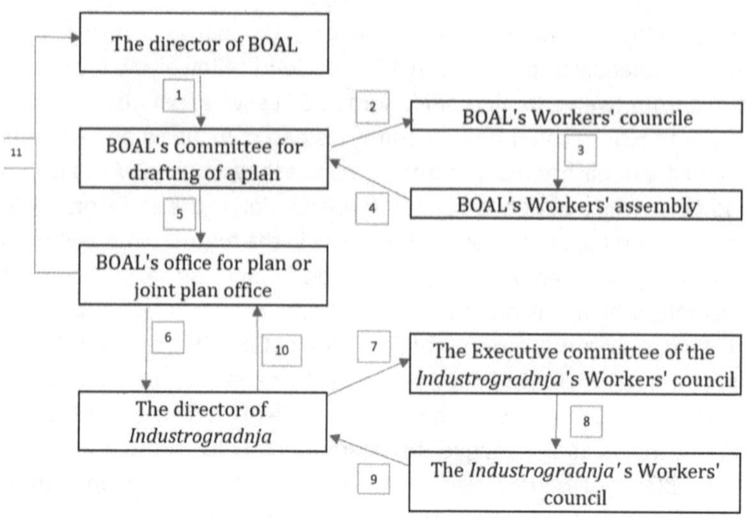

Figure 1. Crafting of an annual business plan in *Industrogradnja* Law on associated labour.[96]

market and in the production process come even more to the fore as the only possible way of operating, same as the fact that mutual obligations must be much more precise and specific with sanctions for those who do not fulfil their obligations.[98] In the first sentence the general director explains how much energy was invested to circumvent the financial autonomy of BOALs via elaborate administrative language in self-management agreements. In the second, Čop provides, to the least, a reductionist take on the entire idea of associate labour, making it all about fair measurement and distribution of personal income. Finally, the director reminds the company readership what *Industrogradnja* is all about and why each autonomous unit is operating under the joint umbrella.

Like before, lawmakers left enough tools for the management to manoeuvre around this hard organisational fragmentation of the system. For instance, in the field of finances, despite the appearance of separate bank accounts, SME was once again utilised to design a deal between *Industrogradnja*'s BOALs. They, according to the agreement, placed the funds for 'investments into fixed capital' as well as those for 'the working capital' and 'risk management' in the hands of the top management, leaving for themselves to decide upon the distribution of profits intended for the workers' income (salaries).[99] Basically, reducing associated labour exactly to what the company director wanted it to be in his comment. Apart from SME, the main role in the simulation of the bottom-up decision-making had the ever-widest company bureaucracy, processing and carrying out the paperwork for all the democratic processes in the company. One of the core tasks of this administrative hive was to calculate coefficients and norms for contracts with business partners that would then determine a just distribution of income and profits among the BOALs in the production cluster. And vice versa, the same administration would be there to calculate the share of profit each BOAL would have achieved to distribute it among its workers.

A simple comparison shows the rise in importance of administration needed to service numerous self-management procedures in this period. In late 1972, at the dawn of associated labour, *Industrogradnja* had almost four thousand workers (3940) in total, out of which only 180 worked in three administrative BOALs (joint services, sales and finances).[100] In other words, the administrative staff made around 5% of the entire company collective at the end of market reform era. Six years later, there were six out of total of twenty units, one BOAL and five so called Labour Communities (LC) [Radna zajednica],[101] in charge of variety of administrative work, and in 1978 together they employed 1140 out of total number of 7776 workers of *Industrogradnja.*[102] In other words, the company had at least one clerk for every six workers in production, or a 200% increase of bureaucratic staff. The force of white collars in labour-intensive industry was a necessity, but not so much one imposed by the lawmakers. Instead, it seems more for the sake of management to help it operate in the new socio-economic framework.

This respectable army of bureaucrats was, however, armed to combat complex routines of associated labour with the state-of-the-art technology. Computers became a standard in the Yugoslav business world during the 1970s and *Industrogradnja* had already acquired its own 'electronic data processing system' in 1973 from *Fujitsu Limited.*[103] For this reason, probably logistically the most important SME in 1977 for the *Industrogradnja* management was the one signed with the Labour community for informatics, development, and financial affairs.[104] The department had 270 white-collar workers tracing and processing almost the entirety of company non-productive processes: from development of new technologies, company investments, accounting and its coordination for all units, finances and associating of internal capital, payments and other transactions, calculation of basic income, all the way to keeping track of implementation of company policies.[105] This LC, therefore, represented the main processor of the company administration and was the leaver on which the management relied on the most for its day-to-day affairs. More importantly, this LC represented the cohesive matter gluing the company units together in the conditions of atomised company structure.

Still, despite the pressures of associated labour, the company kept growing and maintained stability well into the 1980s, when it was hit by the same crisis as the rest of the global business environment. That being said, large industrial systems, like *Industrogradnja*, were carrying the Yugoslav economy without the support of small-size enterprises (with hundred or less workers), for small companies made only 23% of total number of companies in 1965, unlike 73% in the UK or 91% in the US.[106] Maybe the greatest problem with having such a tiny share of small enterprises was the lack of innovation that would support the export appetites of the government. In fact, its campaign for industrial consolidation as the result of broader market reforms in the 1960s, Unkovski-Korica argues, was the reason Yugoslavia lost the status of a 'world leader in innovation' and became excessively dependant on foreign technology and licences.[107] Hence, hard atomisation of large business structures, apart from being a democratising process against concentration of power in large structures, could be understood as an attempt to create a clusters of smaller formations with more flexibility and creativity on the market, although without success due to poor state of self-management.

Associated labour, like self-management in the 1950s, was introduced by the political elite from above, instead of being a grassroots project developed by the labourers on shop floors, which usually meant there was a lack of necessary political awareness among the main protagonists. Also, the majority of those workers were usually lacking competences to take part in technical or business discussions. They were broadly discussing only the topics for which they felt proficient, i.e. their working conditions, while company business strategies or production process were tackled superficially without enough substance to make any major difference. In turn, these and similar business domains were necessarily left to 'experts' or the management to propose to the Workers' Council, which then accepted their propositions without much debate. On paper it seemed as if the majority of 'associated workers' were processing the entirety of business operations. In reality, however, automatised self-management bodies supported by large administrative apparatus were most often simply carrying out business ideas, plans and decisions prescribed by the management. One could argue that the management was elected by those same self-management bodies and was, hence, democratically mandated to provide services to its base. And yet, judging by the power relations between management and workers in companies, widely researched by sociologists in the 1960s and 1970s,[108] the former had not seemed to feel accountable to the latter.

4. Conclusion

The history of *Industrogradnja* between 1966 and 1980, although only a short, in medias res, segment in its biography, provides a complete overview of phases that Yugoslav companies underwent on their path to become large industrial systems. In this period, the Zagreb-based construction company, from legal perspective, was a piece of social property, governed by its delegates on behalf of the entire workforce (and Yugoslav society in general). At the same time, *Industrogradnja* was managed by the hierarchically structured management, whose main task was to expand its industrial capacities and increase production efficiency without limits. This task was fully embraced by Mate Čop, the new chief director (1966–1996), and his management team, whose technocratic methods of company administration – implementation of state-of-the-art construction methods and aggressive approach in the newly formed construction market – allowed the company to reach a high pace of growth and emerge in the early 1970s as one of the two largest construction enterprises in Zagreb.

Among the most important sources of the company's growth was Čop's orientation to the housing construction business. Namely, the management opportunely recognised the effects of rapid industrialisation and de-agrarianisation of the country, which naturally reproduced even faster urbanisation of large Yugoslav cities like Zagreb. For this reason, throughout the whole period and in the 1980s, the demand for apartments was permanently twice above Zagreb's supply level. In light of this context, the new management consistently heavily invested in the adjustment of existing production capacities and the development of new ones, solely for industrial production of high-rise buildings. For instance, by the end of 1969, the company labourers were capable of erecting skeletons of such buildings in a matter of two to three weeks, thanks solely to the new mechanisation and specialisation of the company's concrete plant *Lomnica* for production of prefabricated blocks. The efficiency of *Industrogradnja's* production was recognised by the local government in Zagreb, which in turn provided the company with significant number of new projects. *Industrogradnja*'s annual share of new buildings in totality of realised housing projects in Zagreb climbed to 40% by the middle of 1970s, which made it the largest producer of apartments in the city. This trend, however, changed overnight in the second half of the decade on account of the structural transformation of the socio-economic system and creeping economic crisis that was overwhelming the entire global and domestic business world.

Apart from the reconstruction of company history, this article delves into two stages of complex structural changes the League of Communist of Yugoslavia implemented into the country's socio-economic system. The first set of reforms (1965–1971) created conditions for the formation of a business world that was powered by certain market forces. The following period was characterised by the Party's campaign to counter the effects of liberalisation with an enhanced form of self-management, the associated labour, that ultimately led to partial recovery of administrative relations. Both phenomena significantly determined the outlines and internal dynamics of the Yugoslav socialist project, and arguably its faith. From the example of *Industrogradnja* and its internal structural problems it was clear that the two value systems, market principles and industrial democracy, were clashing and reproducing unresolving contradictions throughout the whole period. In the era of market reforms, the very appearance of the new technocratic company management and its solutions for achieving rapid growth was in collision with existing socialist principles.

Finally, this short episode in *Industrogradnja*'s history speaks of a fairly autonomous and authentic company modernisation, technological experimentation, and a strategically planned market expansion (and flexibility) in a business environment established within one of the twentieth century European socialist projects. As seen, the Yugoslav socio-economic model, similarly to that which Scranton noticed in the case of Chinese enterprises, was of a reformative or experimentative nature, from the 1960s continuously balancing between the two value systems, socialist and market. For this reason, I argue that enterprises and their managements in Yugoslavia went through an original experience, one that ultimately supports the idea of a variety of socialist projects. An idea that still needs to be further investigated, hopefully with adjusted research optics, according to the structural particularities in which business environments and their societies were operating.

Funding

This work has been fully supported by Croatian Science Foundation under the project HRZZ IP-01-2018-5394.

Notes

1. "Orden rada našem kolektivu," *Industrogradnja,* December 1976 (182–183), 2.
2. "200 Najvećih," *Ekonomska politika,* September 1974.
3. See: Goran Musić, *Making and Breaking the Yugoslav Working Class* (Budapest: CEU Press, 2021); Igor Stanić, "Što pokazuje praksa? Presjek samoupravljanja u brodogradilištu Uljanik 1961–1968. godine." Časopis za suvremenu povijest 46, br. 3 (2014): 453–474.
4. Ljubiva Spaskovska and Ann a Calori, "A Nonaligned Business World: The Global Socialist Enterprise between Self-Management and Transnational Capitalism," *Nationalities Papers* 49, no. 3 (2021): 413–27, 420.
5. Adam K. Frost, "Reframing Chinese Business History," *Business History Review* 96, no. 2 (2022): 245–87.
6. See: Phiip Scranton, *Enterprise, Organization, and Technology in China: A Socialist Experiment, 1950–1971* (London: Palgrave Macmillan, 2019).
7. The company was the result of nationalization of a pre-war workshop *Antun Res.* "Orden rada našem kolektivu, *Industrogradnja,*" December 1976 (182–183), 2.
8. Ibid.
9. Between 1946 and 1950 the company bore the name *Pionir.*
10. Yugoslav self-management became a globally popular phenomenon among scholars in the 1950s and 1960s.
11. See: Simo Đukić, *Direktor – pre i posle ZUR-a* (Belgrade: Privredapublik, 1988), 32–42; Josip Županov, *Samoupravljanje i Društvena moć* (Zagreb: Globus, 1985), 136–137.
12. Dušan Bilandžić, *Hrvatska moderna povijest* (Zagreb: Golden marketing 1999), 238.
13. From this moment on, the enterprise would usually grow and expand to non-Zagreb markets via integration with the smaller local construction businesses. Mario Bazina (ed.), *Industrogradnja 1945–1965* (Zagreb: Vjesnik, 1965), 2.
14. "Novogodišnji razgovor s generalnim direktorm Industrogradnje," December 1977 (209), 2.
15. Ivan Jugović (ed.), *Industrogradnja* (Ljubljana: ČGP Delo, 1976), 9.
16. Jakov Sirotković, *Ekonomski razvoj Jugoslavije, od prosperiteta do krize* (Zagreb: Narodne novine, 1990), 120.
17. Branko Horvat, *Jugoslavenska privreda 1965–1983 prijedlozi i rješenja* (Ljubljana: Cankrajeva založba Ljubljana, 1984), 15.
18. Jugović (1976, 9).
19. Ibid.
20. "Pravilnik o Privremenim tehničkim propisima za građenje u seizmičkim područjima," *Službeni list SFRJ* (39/64); "Zakon o tehničkim mjerama," *Službeni list SFRJ* (12/65). *aldad.*

21. David Dyker, *Yugoslavia: Socialism, Development and Debt* (London: Routledge, 1990), 138–139.
22. Dennison Rusinow, *The Yugoslav Experiment, 1948–1974* (London: C. Hurst & Co. for the Royal Institute of International Affairs, 1977), 110.
23. Bilandžić, 478.
24. Darko Suvin, *Samo jednom se ljubi: radiografija SFR Jugoslavije* (Belgrade, Rosa Luxemburg Stiftung, 2014), 240.
25. Renown ned economist Branko Horvat complained that it is madness that a structural intervention of such scale was generally prepared without the sufficient consultation with economists. Horvat (1984, 37–38).
26. "Na kraju godine," *Industrogradnja,* January 1966 (12), 2.
27. Milivoj Bosanac and Vasja Simić, *Građevinska regulativa* (Zagreb: Centar za informiranje i publicitet, 1971), 24.
28. Business budgets were able to expand and shrink, depending on the company's performance.
29. Ibid., 170–171.
30. Nikola Vukelić, "Stambena politika i arhitektura u socijalističkoj Jugoslaviji" (MA thesis, Juraj Dobrila University of Pula, 2019), 36.
31. See: Saša Vejzagić, "The Rise of the Business Class: The Role of Managerial Elites in Yugoslavia 1963–1978" (PhD diss., European University Institute, 2021), 77–81.
32. For more information on how managements spread their influence on workers councils in this period see: Ibid., 86–92.
33. "Odlučujuće pismo," *Industrogradnja,* April 1966 (2–3), 3.
34. "Nevjerojatno, ali istinito," *Industrogradnja,* April 1966 (2–3), 4–5.
35. Ibid.
36. Suvin (2014, 242).
37. "Članovi partijske komisije," *Industrogradnja,* April 1966 (2–3), 2.
38. Branko Nadilo, "Susretljivi i vitalni pradjed," *Građevinar,* LXVII (10), October 2015, 1026; Radošin Rajović, *Jugoslavenski savremenici - Ko je ko u Jugoslaviji* (Belgrade: Hronometar, 1970), 172; Dubravka Hrastovec, *Tko je tko u Hrvatskom gospodarstvu* (Zagreb: Goldedn marketing, 1996), 90.
39. The campaign was done through the self-management institution of re-election (Reizbornost), see: Jurij Fikfak, Jože Prinčič, and Jeffrey D. Turk, eds., *Biti direktor v času socializma: med idejami in praksami* (Ljubljana: Založb ZRC, ZRC SAZU, 2008), 68–79.
40. "Put k suvremenoj proizvodnji," *Inudstrogradnja,* January 1967, 6.
41. "Put do stranog tržišta," *Industrogradnja,* December 1966, 2.
42. "Koristi od porasta cijena stanova imaju isključivo učesnici u stambenoj izgradnji izvan građevinarstva," *Industrogradnja,* April–June 1969, VI (4–6), 8–9.
43. Grga Jelinić, *50 godina graditeljstva i stanovanja* (Zagreb: Studio Hrg d.o.o., 2012), 116.
44. "Novi pothvat u jugoslavenskom građevinarstvu," *Industrogradnja,* May–June 1968, 6–7.
45. Đuro Mirković (Former director of the *Industrogradnja*'s Project bureau) *in* conversation with the author (Zagreb, March 2022).
46. "Neboder samo za 24 dana," *Industrogradnja,* February–March 1969, 2.
47. "J. Kolar i M. Knežević posjetili Sopot i Lomnicu." *Industrogradnja,* February–March 1969, 1.
48. "Industrogradnja dobitnik Privredne nagrade Grada Zagreba za 1968," *Industrogradnja,* April–June 1969, VI (4–6), 1.
49. Mirković (2022).
50. Alfred Chandler, *Strategy and Structure: Chapters in the History of the American Industrial Enterprise* (Cambridge: MIT Press, 1963).
51. "Deset novih gradilišta," *Industrogradnja,* August 1967, 1; "Gradi se troetažna hladnjača u Petrinji," *Industrogradnja,* April–June 1969, 5.
52. Jugović (1976, 10).
53. "Od temelja do ključeva u ruke," *Industrogradnja*, March 1973 (94), 6.
54. Ibid.
55. "Zadovoljni smo rezultatima u 1972. godini," *Industrogradnja,* March 1973 (93), 1.
56. "Dosljedno primjenjivati stabilizacione mjere," *Industrogradnja,* January 1973 (90), 5.

57. "Osnovne smjernice plana za 1973. godinu," *Industrogradnja,* January 1973 (90), 1–3.
58. Vejzagić (2021, 236).
59. "Osnovne smjernice plana za 1973. godinu," *Industrogradnja,* January 1973 (90), 1–3.
60. "Lomnica pred modernizacijom," *Industrogradnja,* August 1973 (101), 5.
61. "Rekonstrukcija i modernizacija," *Industrogradnja,* September 1973 (104), 7.
62. Ibid.
63. Block 6 is still today the largest housing complex in Zagreb, accommodating over five thousand residents. "Grad u jednom objektu," *Industrogradnja*, September 1973 (104), 6–7.
64. The second largest producer was construction company *Novogradnja* with 1061 and *Tempo* with 1059 flats built in 1973. See in: "Izgradili smo najviše stanova," *Industrogradnja,* February 1974 (112).
65. Ibid.
66. "Hotel 'Zagreb' svečano otvoren," *Industrogradnja,* March 1975 (140), 1.
67. "Industrogradnja uspješno poslovala," *Industrogradnja,* January 1974 (111), 13.
68. "Što je s Južnim naseljem?," *Industrogradnja,* August 1974 (126), 2.
69. "Pohvale za izvedene radove," *Industrogradnja,* October 1974 (131), 1.
70. "Poslovni plan za 1975. godinu," *Industrogradnja,* January 1975 (136), 9; "Prijedlog plana za 1976 godinu" *Industrogradnja,* February 1976 (162), 7–8.
71. Ibid., 7–8.
72. Albert Antolović, *Samoupravna interesna zajednica u stambenoj oblasti* (Zagreb: NIU Pregled, 1974), 9.
73. SCIH was established in every municipality to plan and initiate housing projects as well as to organize maintenance of existing housing fund in municipalities. It gathered delegates from among all actors involved in housing industry: local governments, construction companies, residents, planners, architects, etc.
74. Vukelić (2019), 49.
75. Ibid.
76. "S novim izgledima u slijedeću godinu," *Industrogradnja,* December 1979 (257), 4.
77. Mirko Orešković (Former *Industrogradnja*'s director of engineering) in conversation with the author (Zagreb, March 2022).
78. For more details on controversy of the Amendment XV see: Vejzagić (2021), 93–96.
79. Music (2021), 53.
80. Suvin, 305.
81. "Ustavni amandman XV," *Direktor,* 11, I, November 1969, I–XXIV.
82. Latinka Perović, *Zatvaranje kruga. Ishod rascepa 1971–1972* (Sarajevo: Svjetlost, 1990), 453.
83. For more details on the question of purge of directors in Yugoslavia see: Vejzagić (2021, 198–202).
84. Orešković (2022).
85. Music (2021, 55).
86. Associated labour first appeared in constitutional amendments in 1970, however, it became an essence of the new constitution (1974) and was further developed in the Associated laobur act (1976).
87. Dejan Jović, *Jugoslavija, država koja odumrla: uspon, kriza i pad Četvrte Jugoslavije, 1974–1990* (Zagreb: Prometej, 2003), 104–105.
88. William Lazonick and Mary O'Sullivan, "Maximizing Shareholder Value: A New Ideology for Corporate Governance," *Economy and Society* 29, no. 1 (2000): 13–35.
89. *The Constitution of the Socialist Federal Republic of Yugoslavia* (Ljubljana: Delo, 1974).
90. Orešković (2022).
91. "Samoupravni sporazum o udruživanju OOUR u OUR Industrogradnja Građevno poduzeće Zagreb, Savska 66," *Industrogradnja,* March 1973 (93).
92. Ibid.
93. "Osnovne smjernice plana za 1974. godinu," *Industrogradnjai,* January 1974 (111), 8.
94. "Svaki OOUR poseban žiro-račun," *Industrogradnja,* March 1978 (215), 9.
95. "U toku 1977. godine u osnovi smo uskladili organizaciju i samoupravne opće akte prema ZUR-u i drugim sistemskim zakonima," *Industrogradnja*, February 1978, 4.

96. Ibid.
97. After 1976 the appearance of workers' assemblies in the process of decision-making (involving popular vote) represented yet another form of decentralization of the company governance and management.
98. "Novogodišnji razgovor s generalnim direktorom industrogradnje," *Industrogradnja,* December 1977 (209), 2.
99. "Svaki OOUR poseban žiro-račun," *Industrogradnja,* March 1978 (215), 9.
100. "Nova organizacija poduzeća," *Industrogradnja,* November 1972 (87), 2.
101. From 1976 Labour community was a type of a company unit strictly in charge of some form of administrative or coordinative joint affairs. For instance, *Industrogradnja* opened the LC for HR, legal and general affairs, the LC for informatics, development and financial affairs, two LCs for programming and coordination of production of constuction materials, and the one for international affairs.
102. "Manji broj zaposlenih – odraz dobrog planiranja," *Industrogradnja,* July 1978 (223), 4.
103. "Elektronska obrada podataka u industrogradnji," *Industrogradnja,* November 1973 (107), 5.
104. "Samoupravni sporazum o međusobnim pravima, obavezama i odgovornostima Radne zajednice za informatičke, razvojne i financijske poslove i OOUR-a korisnika usluga," *Industrogradnja,* December 1977 (208).
105. Ibid.
106. Suvin, 245.
107. Vladimir Unkovski-Korica, *The Economic Struggle for Power in Tito's Yugoslavia: From World War II to Non-Alignment* (London: I.B. Tauris, 2016), 43.
108. See: Županov (1985); Rudi Supek. "Protivurječnosti i nedorečenosti jugoslavenskog samoupravnog socijalizma," *Praxis,* 3–4 (1971), 347–371.

References

Antolović, A. (1974). *Samoupravna interesna zajednica u stambenoj oblasti.* NIU Pregled.

Bancetić, L. (2020). Zagrebačka stanogradnja u prijedlozima. *Časopis za suvremenu povijest,* (2), 389–418.

Bancetić, L., & Jurić, Z. (2021). Urbanistički program grada Zagreba iz 1965.: Nastanak, planirano i realizirano. *Časopis za suvremenu povijest,* (3), 1209–1247. https://doi.org/10.22586/csp.v53i3.17956

Bazina, M. (1965). *Industrogradnja 1945–1965.* Vjesnik.

Bilandžić, D. (1985). *Historija Socijalističke Fedrativne Republike Jugoslavije: Glavni procesi 1918–1985.* Školska knjiga.

Bockman, J. (2011). *Markets in the Name of Socialism: The Left-Wing Origins of Neoliberalism.* Stanford University Press.

Bosanac, M., & Simić, V. (1971). *Građevinska regulative.* Centar za informiranje i publicitet.

Chandler, A. D. (1963). *Strategy and structure: Chapters in the history of the american industrial enterprise.* MIT Press.

Dyker, D. (1990). *Yugoslavia: Socialism, development and debt.* Routledge.

Đukić, S. (1988). *Direktor – pre i posle ZUR-a.* Privredapublik.

Fikfak, J., J. Prinčič, & J. D. Turk (Eds.). (2008). *Biti direktor v času socializma: Med idejami in praksami.* Založb ZRC, ZRC SAZU.

Frost, A. K. (2022). Reframing Chinese business history. *Business History Review, 96*(2), 245–287. https://doi.org/10.1017/S0007680521000477

Hrastovec, D. (1996). *Tko je tko u Hrvatskom gospodarstvu.* Goldedn marketing.

Horvat, B. (1984). *Jugoslavenska privreda 1965–1983 prijedlozi i rješenja.* Cankrajeva založba.

Jelinić, G. (2012). *50 godina graditeljstva i stanovanja.* Studio Hrg d.o.o.

Jović, D. (2003). *Jugoslavija, država koja odumrla: Uspon, kriza i pad Četvrte Jugoslavije, 1974–1990.* Prometej.

Jugović, I. (1976). *Industrogradnja.* ČGP Delo.

Lazonick, W., & O'Sullivan, M. (2000). Maximizing shareholder value: A new ideology for corporate governance. *Economy and Society, 29*(1). https://doi.org/10.1080/030851400360541

Musić, G. (2021). *Making and breaking the Yugoslav working class*. CEU Press.
Nadilo, B. (2015, October). Susretljivi i vitalni pradjed. *Građevinar, LXVII*(10), 1023–1031.
Perović, L. (1990). *Zatvaranje kruga. Ishod rascepa 1971–1972*. Svjetlost.
Rajović, R. (1970). *Jugoslavenski savremenici - Ko je ko u Jugoslaviji*. Hronometar.
Rusinow, D. (1977). *The Yugoslav Experiment, 1948–1974*. C. Hurst & Co. for the Royal Institute of International Affairs.
Scranton, P. (2019). *Enterprise, organization, and technology in China: A socialist experiment, 1950–1971*. Palgrave Macmillan.
Sirotković, J. (1990). *Ekonomski razvoj Jugoslavije, od prosperiteta do krize*. Narodne novine.
Spaskovska, L., & Calori, A. (2021). A nonaligned business world: The global socialist enterprise between self-management and transnational capitalism. *Nationalities Papers, 49*(3), 413–427. https://doi.org/10.1017/nps.2020.27
Stanić, I. (2014). Što pokazuje praksa? Presjek samoupravljanja u brodogradilištu Uljanik 1961–1968. godine. *Časopis za suvremenu povijest, 46*(3), 453–474.
Supek, R. (1971). Protivurječnosti i nedorečenosti jugoslavenskog samoupravnog socijalizma. *Praxis, 3–4*, 347–371.
Suvin, D. (2014). *Samo jednom se ljubi: Radiografija SFR Jugoslavije*. Rosa Luxemburg Stiftung.
Unkovski-Korica, V. (2016). *The economic struggle for power in Tito's Yugoslavia: From World War II to non-alignment*. I.B. Tauris.
Vejzagić, S. (2011). *Godine liberalizacije u Jugoslaviji 1964.–1971* [MA thesis]. Juraj Dobrila University of Pula.
Vejzagić, S. (2021). *The rise of the business class: The role of managerial elites in Yugoslavia 1963–1978* [PhD diss.]. European University Institute.
Vukelić, N. (2019). *Stambena politika i arhitektura u socijalističkoj Jugoslaviji* [MA thesis]. Juraj Dobrila University of Pula.
Županov, J. (1985). *Samoupravljanje i Društvena moć*. Globus.

Periodicals

Ekonomska politika. (1973–1980).
Industrogradnja. (1966–1980).
Direktor. (1969).

Published sources

Statistički godišnjak Jugoslavije 1973. (1973). Savezni zavod za statistiku.
Statistički godišnjak Jugoslavije 1979. (1979). Savezni zavod za statistiku.
The constitution of the Socialist federal republic of Yugoslavia. (1974). Delo.

Tensions between plan and market in a political factory in socialist Kosovo

Pieter Troch

ABSTRACT
This article provides a business history of the medium-sized wood processing enterprise *Kosmet Šper*, established for local development purposes in weakly-developed socialist Kosovo. It explores business reorganisations undertaken by local political elites and management aimed to align the enterprise's continued operation with socialist Yugoslavia's market-oriented economic reforms of the 1960s. The first part of the article scrutinises these interventions and argues that the locus of ultimate political decision-making shifted to the units of the federal state. The second part of the article looks at the increasing authority transferred to professional managers in return for keeping the underperforming enterprise running. This led to a paternalistic style of management, but the legitimacy of the management remained subject to overlapping challenges of function, ethnicity, and origin. Part three explores the labour force fluctuations caused by the shift of responsibility for the performance of the enterprise to internal production failures.

Tensions between plan and market are a central feature of the socialist economies of East and Central Europe (Kochanowicz & Murgescu, 2017, pp. 101–12). Socialist Yugoslavia provides a particularly insightful case-study. Yugoslavia in the first post-war decade prioritised plan-oriented development through capital and labour input in industrial production. A series of market-oriented economic reforms in the late 1950s and especially 1960s shifted the balance to intensive growth and international trade, making the country a trendsetter of market socialism. Yugoslavia became a signatory of the General Agreement on Tariffs and Trade and opened to international markets. Prices were to a certain extent liberated. State-controlled investment funds were for the largest part abolished and transferred to commercial banks, although a federal investment fund for underdeveloped regions was put in place. Enterprises managed growing shares of their gross income and workers' self-management bodies gained increasing autonomy to determine wage rates, investment, and social consumption. Wage differentiation measures introduced parameters related to quality and skills and tied personal wages to production results. Regardless of these market-oriented reforms, however, the market did not replace the plan-oriented tenets of the socialist economy and ultimate strategic decision-making in business remained a political concern throughout

(Bićanić, 1973, pp. 108–10; 117–44, 181–91; Woodward, 1995, pp. 264–65). The resulting tensions between plan and market-oriented economic growth intersect with the question of development. Socio-economic conditions in the more developed republics and provinces in the north and northwest of the country fitted the market-oriented growth model, while conditions in the weakly developed republics and provinces to the south and east required extensive growth through political intervention and planned redistribution (Pleština, 1992, pp. 57–84; Woodward, 1995, pp. 282–98).

Yugoslavia's ideological and political exclusion from the Soviet Bloc and violent disintegration has led to overestimations of the singularity of its market-oriented economic reform agenda and decentralisation tactics. Socialist Yugoslavia was a pioneer and along with Hungary went furthest in decentralising its planned economy (including future-oriented development). Reforms to decentralise decision-making from the central state bureaucracy to (associations of) enterprises along with a shift from extensive and labour-intensive development to intensive growth, emphasis on consumption, and profit-based incentives to steer enterprise behaviour were, however, common to the economies of the Soviet Bloc in the 1960s. In addition, there was a widespread decentralisation drive to spread manufacturing capabilities to peripheral agricultural and mining districts in order to overcome rural poverty and even out gains from social investments (Swain & Swain, 2009, pp. 142–54). The Yugoslav case is thus illustrative of business operations under broader conditions of market reforms and regional development in socialist East and Central Europe.

Yugoslav business history focusses heavily on enterprises in the more developed parts of the country or high-priority heavy industry enterprises of federal political relevance, which were in a relatively favourable position to cope with the tensions between market and plan (see the introduction to this special issue). This article breaks new ground by analysing a medium-sized enterprise in Mitrovica in Kosovo, by all standards the least developed region of Yugoslavia. According to industrial branch and labour-intensity (wood processing), size (around 500 workers), and durability, *Kosmet Šper* is the opposite pole of the Chandlerian large enterprise (Chandler, Amatori & Hikino 1997).[1] It is also not a usual suspect in business histories of state-socialist East and Central Europe, which tend to focus on large employers in heavy industry, with continued access to subsidies that covered operating losses (Yudanov 1997).

The case-study is meaningful to business historians, however, because it provides insights in some particularities of doing business in an underprioritized setting under conditions of market socialism. *Kosmet Šper* was a typical product of regional development tactics to spread manufacturing and diversify industrial production in the underdeveloped regions and tackle rural poverty and overpopulation, but for which there was no clear economic rationale. In terms of branch, finance flows, and employment, *Kosmet Šper* was a secondary enterprise even at the local level, where it was in no position to compete for scarce resources with the big-system mining enterprise *Trepça/Trepča*. Throughout the 1960s, the enterprise struggled to strike a balance between reforms aiming to evaluate business on the basis of the market and the essentially political and social logic behind its very establishment, until it was ultimately liquidated in 1968. The article assesses how these conditions affected business processes, subscribing to recent pleas by Amatori (2009) and Scranton and Fridenson (2013) to study business in relation to society, bring the state in, and account for failure, improvisation, and uncertainty. The article is divided in three parts. Part one focusses on state–enterprise relations and tensions between market and plan, part two scrutinises the professionalisation of management, and part three explores labour force fluctuations. The study is based on an in-depth analysis of the enterprise archive, which is preserved in the local archives of Mitrovica.

The rise and fall of a political factory

Local governments were a crucial actor for political and economic decision-making in the development of Yugoslavia's self-management socialism in the 1950s. Although enterprises and production units formally served as the basic cells of workers' self-management, the municipality oversaw the internal work organisation and business cycles of enterprises. It established enterprises and set their market orientation, elected and dismissed enterprise directors, oversaw accounts, production planning, and income distribution, and guaranteed credit for investment. Municipalities also determined microeconomic planning and development, by allocating revenues from profit taxes on enterprises in its territory and federal investment funds through communal banks (Bilandžić, 1985, pp. 247–54, 310–11; Kežić, 2017, pp. 53–62, 67; Woodward, 1995, pp. 173–80).

Such localised investment policies led to fragmented and isolated markets. In the debates on Yugoslav economic policy in the 1960s, 'political factories' became paradigmatic of irrational local investments and the need to shift to market principles. The phenomenon was particularly widespread in weakly-developed localities, which made use of the financial and political means at their disposal to invest in extensive local development (Bićanić, 1973, p. 49; Comisso, 1979, pp. 48–50; Pleština, 1992, pp. 34, 49). The market reforms of 1965, which completed a series of reforms introduced in the late 1950s and early 1960s, tackled local political interference in business decisions. Financial investment means were transferred from municipalities to commercial banks at the republican or provincial level. These were supposed to evaluate enterprise performance on the basis of market indicators but quickly became powerful economic actors and vehicles for political interference from the republican or provincial level (Bićanić, 1973, pp. 123–30; Bilandžić, 1985, pp. 245–50, 305–19, 395–7; Kežić, 2017, pp. 64–71, 92–105; Suvin, 2016, pp. 166–79, 219–26; Woodward, 1995, pp. 264–75).[2]

The rise and fall of *Kosmet Šper* is situated against this background. Using the shift in Yugoslav federal investments to Kosovo, which was for the first time listed as an underdeveloped region in 1957, and to manufacturing industry, the local authorities in Mitrovica put forward a dual-sector model for growth. Local development plans invested in manufacturing and light industry to expand and diversify industrial production and transfer the unskilled labour surplus from agriculture into industry.[3] Wood processing was particularly suitable for this growth model, as it could employ unskilled and female workers. Microeconomic conditions were met, as raw materials were available in the region and basic timber production was among the rare industrial activities that were locally developed in the interwar period. In April 1958, the municipality established *Kosmet Šper*.[4] The enterprise originated from the merger of the existing plywood and veneer factory with the local sawmill and carpentry shop. Timber production was reoriented from unprofitable local construction to (semi-)final goods for a wider market.[5] The municipality used federal funds to invest in new halls and machinery to enable serial production.[6] Labour was steadily increased from 328 in 1958 to around 500 in 1960.[7] The workforce was overwhelmingly unskilled and directly absorbed from the rural labour surplus. In November 1958, 256 of the 414 workers were un- or semi-skilled.[8]

By the early 1960s, against the background of a first round of market-oriented economic reforms, which led to increased production costs, wages, and interest expenses, the enterprise faced a serious liquidity crisis and failed to pay minimum wages and pay back loans. There were macroeconomic issues. Supplies of raw material were irregular due to competition and inadequate transport infrastructure. Sales of plywood in particular were disappointing all over Yugoslavia, resulting in climbing inventories of unsold and low-quality finished goods.[9] According to the management and local authorities, however, the problem was not structural and the enterprise had prospects to function properly, provided that it addressed the lack of skilled labour and inadequate organisation of production and the partial and incomplete nature of investments under unfavourable loan conditions.[10] The financial difficulties at *Kosmet Šper* were by no means an exception. During the liquidity crisis of 1961, an estimated 10 to 30% of Yugoslav enterprises were on the brink of bankruptcy. However, as the municipality and not the individual enterprise was the main risk-taker for capital and labour investments, the political barriers to bankruptcy were enormous and local authorities resorted to a variety of alternative measures to stabilise loss-making enterprises (Tyson, 1977, pp. 284–91; Uvalić, 1992, pp. 106–15).

The municipality exempted the enterprise from taxes, covered part of the losses from the municipal reserve fund, and lobbied with provincial and republican banks—at this time still political vehicles for funds distribution rather than commercial creditors—for revisions of instalment terms, debt cancellation, and investments for further modernisation of infrastructure. In addition, the municipality started the reorganisation of production in the enterprise, dismissed 150 workers, and took measures to employ specialists.[11] After it found that the actual financial situation in the enterprise was much worse than previously thought, the municipality took *Kosmet Šper* into receivership (*prinudna uprava*). The primary task of the receivership was to establish the financial state of the enterprise and bring order to its accountancy, strengthen work discipline and improve work organisation, identify major shortcomings and needs in terms of infrastructure, and explore the prospects of the enterprise.[12]

In undertaking this exercise, local elites in the enterprise management, local Party organs, and municipality made a distinction between "objective" and "subjective" factors. Objective factors were related to macroeconomic matters (supplies, investments, and sales). Subjective factors referred to the organisation of work (norm-setting, technical oversight, production organisation) and work discipline (laxity, theft, absenteeism, late coming).[13] The argument was that the receivership would create favourable objective conditions for production through strategic decision-making. By the end of 1963, the municipality pulled the enterprise out of receivership and re-installed workers' self-management.[14] On the suggestion of an expert commission consisting of local political and economic decision-makers, the municipality agreed to cover the enterprise's debts through loans from the provincial reserve fund. The municipality also stood as a guarantee for further modernisation investments. The market orientation of the enterprise was shifted to packaging, while the carpentry shop was closed down. The municipality reached an agreement on guaranteed supplies with representatives of Kosovo's chamber of woodworking industry. At the same time, it reorganised labour to increase productivity, tackle the surplus of unskilled labour, and attract qualified specialists to manage the enterprise.[15]

The new management at the end of 1964 noted that the enterprise "was on the way to full recovery".[16] It was optimistic that the price liberation announced for 1965 would improve the position of the wood processing industry and allow the enterprise to pay higher wages and make necessary investments from its own funds.[17] It quickly turned out, however, that this optimism was unfounded. A municipal commission noted that the costs of supplies had gone up and that supplies were irregular, due to regional competition, while sales were insecure. The commission decided to revise the production plan for 1965 mid-way through the year, to "systematise" labour, and to reorient production to furniture and finished goods.[18] The plan for 1966 (again introduced half-way through the year) undid some of the measures introduced at the end of receivership: production in the new packaging shop was reduced, the carpentry shop was reopened, and a new veneer cutter machine was purchased to double the production of veneer, although there were serious quality complaints and a stagnation in demand.[19]

In early 1967, the municipality and the commercial bank issued a new report, which found that although the enterprise had considerably increased production volumes, it continued to operate on the verge of liquidation due to low productivity, climbing production costs, dropping prices for finished goods, and decreased demand.[20] Market-oriented investments turned out to have no prospects. Production in the packaging shop was stopped because of the dropping demand and the low quality of supplies.[21] The veneer shop did not realise the anticipated double production volumes, which was ascribed to weak quality of supplies, limited demand, and bottlenecks in the production process. Moreover, the demand for veneer was minimal.[22] Unlike five years earlier, commercial banks were no longer willing to bail out the enterprise's debts or approve new investments for modernisation without firm guarantees. The commercial banks in Mitrovica and Prishtina/Priština blocked the accounts of *Kosmet Šper* and started judicial procedures.[23] The municipal assembly found that "in the current conditions of full functioning of the economic reforms it is difficult and almost impossible to find economically justified reasons to cover the losses of the enterprise".[24] Supplies were irregular and of low quality, the significantly decreased production plan for 1967 was not realised, and debts were structural. There was no market for its products and sales dropped.[25] In a final attempt to avoid liquidation, the municipality ordered the enterprise to cut production and labour, close the carpentry shop, and engage outside experts for the reorganisation of production.[26] The enterprise consulted the Wood Institute in Zagreb, which found that there were prospects for specialised wood processing in Mitrovica if substantial modernisation investments were made.[27]

Regardless of lobbying provincial decision-makers with the external expert findings in hand, at the end of March 1968, the municipal assembly initiated the liquidation of *Kosmet Šper*. It noted that the municipality did not have the means to cover the debts of the enterprise and that it could not guarantee the repayment obligations for reconstruction loans. The municipal assembly added that there were no chances for regular supplies or market security and that the enterprise faced a lack of skilled labour and adequate production technology. It ordered other enterprises to give priority to former workers of *Kosmet Šper*.[28] In the early 1970s, wood-processing capacities in Kosovo were integrated into the combine *Kosovodrvo*, which had its seat in Peja/Peć and a number of sister factories in Ferizaj/Uroševac, Prishtina, and Istog/Istok (Abdyli, 1978, pp. 119–25). This was the end of wood working in Mitrovica.

The business history of *Kosmet Šper* boils down to a series of interventions aiming at establishing objective conditions for market performance. Three rounds of interventions can be identified: the establishment of the enterprise through merging of existing facilities in 1958, the receivership of 1962–63, and the internal reorganisation of 1965–66. In the first two rounds, the local political elite took the lead, while in the third round the new professional management carried out the interventions. Each of these rounds introduced extremely volatile measures aiming at guaranteeing supply, securing investment, and producing quality goods in high demand. These interventions, however, *could not* address broader market conditions, because of the fundamental collision with the primary non-market motive for the establishment of the enterprise, i.e., local development aiming to address rural poverty and diversify industrial production. As the third part of this article will show, each round of interventions was accompanied by a standard set of criticism about the subjective shortcomings within the enterprise. These were not inaccurate, but deflected serious research into and responsibility for the structural obstacles to the enterprise's success in market terms.

The case of *Kosmet Šper* shows that political structures remained essential for strategic decision-making in business in socialist Kosovo, even under conditions of self-management, market reforms, and liberalisation. The locus of political decision-making, however, shifted from local authorities to political, financial, and economic elites at the level of the province, republic, and federation (Uvalić, 1992, pp. 58–60). The case-study confirms that "the state is always in" (Scranton & Fridenson, 2013, pp. 16–22), but clarifies that state interference is dynamic and multifaceted. Local municipal authorities established the enterprise and ran its strategic business decisions, primarily aiming at extensive growth and employment. The reforms of 1965, however, undermined the local development rationale and reduced the weight of local authorities in the "superstructures" of socialist economic decision-making (Yudanov, 1997, p. 412). The rounds of political interference identified above should not be seen as leftovers of centralised political control over business. Local political elites (and after 1964 also the professional management of the enterprise) in fact defended local development strategies, which did not abide to a clear market logic, by superficially aligning them with the prevailing market context. As the case of wood processing in Kosovo illustrates, in the underdeveloped parts of Yugoslavia, the shifting locus of political decision-making turned economic development from a local affair into a "Yugoslav commitment" (Palairet, 1992, p. 902). Economic growth became increasingly reliant on capital investments from the federal fund for the underdeveloped regions, transmitted through gatekeepers at the provincial level. The distribution of this fund was notably inefficient and politicised and essentially subsidised chronically loss-making big-system, integrated enterprises in capital-intensive heavy industry (Comisso, 1979, pp. 99–103; Palairet, 1992, 1997; Pleština, 1992, pp. 71–78).

The professionalization of management

The section above already indicated that a new management of university-trained specialists played an increasingly important role in implementing market reforms in *Kosmet Šper*. This new management was put in place at the end of the receivership. Director Dimitrije Bulatović and Planning Manager Đorđe Vučićević were the outstanding figures. The relation between management and local political elites was ambiguous. On one hand, managers were appointed by the municipality. Many of the important business cycle or work organisation decisions were explicitly said to be talked through with local political elites before they were presented to the self-management organs for formal approval. On the other hand, top managers were not mere puppets of the local political leadership. In line with the broader professionalization of management in Yugoslav firms in the 1960s, the old style of managing, where political loyalty and connections prevailed, gave way to professional expertise (Adizes, 1971, pp. 198–213; Comisso, 1979, pp. 108–15; Županov, 1985, pp. 291–323). In the case of *Kosmet Šper*, the old management was dismissed on accusations of fraud and fake production reports.[29] "Expert cadres, capable of reorganising and reactivating the enterprise", replaced them.[30] The professionalization of management, however, led to "accountability without authority" (Scranton, 2018). Market-oriented reforms increased the responsibility of professional managers to make enterprises profitable. At the same time, reforms to strengthen workers' self-management formally deprived the management of the authority to implement decisions, while ultimate strategic decision-making remained a political concern. A new type of "contractual management" emerged (Adizes, 1971, p. 209). Specialist managers conditioned their employment and expertise on considerable concessions made by the enterprise in the form of salary bonuses, social benefits (primarily housing), and delegation of management authority (Adizes, 1971, pp. 209–13).

For *Kosmet Šper*, with its highly uncertain future and location in underdeveloped Kosovo, this caused extreme managerial uncertainty. Already by the end of 1966, General Director Bulatović gave up his position to become a sales representative in Belgrade.[31] The best-ranked candidate to succeed him came from Zaječar in eastern Serbia. He not only demanded an extravagant wage and a comfortable flat, but also conditioned his arrival on the attraction of specialists and exclusive decision-making authority for a five-month period to address the enterprise's crisis without interference from the self-management bodies.[32] In April 1967, the enterprise hired Sreten Aleksić, who received broad authority from the self-management bodies for "cleaning up" the enterprise.[33] As soon as he found that municipal authorities were not in the position to guarantee further investments and bailouts for modernisation, Aleksić withdrew, explicitly explaining to the workers' council that he would not jeopardise his career.[34] The enterprise also had difficulties in attracting badly needed specialists. It created two new positions for production engineers with relatively high wages, but never filled these positions, also because the enterprise could not offer flats.[35] In 1966, it took the enterprise almost a year to appoint a new chief production manager. Few candidates actually met the job requirements and those that did often demanded wages that were much higher than anticipated.[36]

In Kosovo and other weakly-developed regions, contractual management carried particular potentials for social divisions, as university-trained experts were typically attracted from outside the region. *Kosmet Šper*'s top management was not only from outside Kosovo but also exclusively South Slav, whereas the workforce was mostly Albanian.[37] In the 1960s, this situation changed as a result of the establishment for Albanian-language higher education and positive discrimination for Albanians in education and employment (Troch, 2019). *Kosmet Šper* provided a scholarship to the economics student Mazlum Novokazi, who in 1966 became the first local Albanian member of the top management. However, the dominance of big-system enterprises prevailed here as well. Less than a year after joining the enterprise and only a month after replacing Vučićević in the crucial position of planning manager (and receiving his flat), Novokazi left the enterprise for a more lucrative job in the mining giant Trepça.[38]

As noted above, against the background of the reduced weight of local authorities as the prime defenders of local development in the superstructures of economic decision-making, the professional management took over the task of aligning the enterprise with the new market-oriented context of the Yugoslav economy. Sessions of the workers' council of *Kosmet Šper* illustrate the degree of hope and responsibility that was invested into the professional management for the survival of the enterprise. This sets the context for a paternalistic style of management, in which the formally dominant bodies of workers' self-management delegate extensive authority to the professional management but demand continued operation in return. Although the workers' council was festively reinstalled as the highest decision-making body in the enterprise after the lifting of the receivership, the practice in *Kosmet Šper* confirms that ultimate decision-making authority lay with top management (Suvin, 2016, pp. 187–89). The management determined production planning, set norms, took measures to increase work discipline, and introduced wage differentiation, all with the ultimate aim to keep the political factory running. The role of the bodies of workers' self-management consisted of approving strategic business decisions taken by the management and local political elites. This does not imply that workers' self-management was entirely uneventful, however, for the inherent uncertainty in aligning a "political factory" with the market was deflected to so-called "subjective" factors discussed within the workers' council.

Labour relations under market conditions

The management and local political elites resorted to political authority and technical superiority to argue that the "objective" conditions for growth were secured and that the planning targets were technically correct. Such an evaluation shifted the ultimate responsibility for the performance of the enterprise to the so-called "subjective" production relations within the work collective.[39] As stated by Planning Manager Vučićević, "the realisation of the planned production volume depends on subjective factors, that is, man with his positive and negative sides".[40] Repeated failures to realise production targets were ascribed to a standard set of internal shortcomings in the production process: labour surplus, lack of skill, and limited responsibility in terms of quality and efficiency of production. The minutes of the workers' council read as a constant battle against "internal reserves": underutilised resources (material and human) that constrained production, reduced productivity, and hazarded profits.

As indicated in the first part of the article, however, supplies, investments, and sales were heavily volatile and "objective" reorganisations superficial. Production planning in fact was "a way of handling uncertainty" (Adizes, 1971, pp. 159–64, quotation on 160), which shifted accountability from external "objective" to internal "subjective" factors. While strategic business decisions were taken elsewhere, self-management organs searched for grounds for performance failures in the production relations within the enterprise. It is here that business history enters the traditional domain of labour history in socialist East and Central Europe, which has shown that market-oriented reforms were a source for major social conflict. Conflict was, however, depoliticised, individualised, and defused through informal bargaining, which was conservative by nature and reproduced social hierarchies based on skill and function (Filtzer, 1992; Grama, 2018; Heumos, 2005; Hübner, 1995, pp. 178–245; Pittaway, 2005).

Shifting understandings of skill

The careers of Budimir Antonijević and Xhafer Zhuri illustrate the shifting understandings of skill in *Kosmet Šper*. Antonijević had been director of the local carpentry shop before its merger into *Kosmet Šper*. He was appointed commercial manager of the new enterprise,[41] but the receivership demoted him to the position of carpentry shop manager. He was finally held accountable for the weak production results and discipline in his shop and dismissed on 9 January 1967.[42] Xhafer Zhuri was a highly-skilled foreman who was promoted to the position of shop manager in the important new packaging shop in 1964.[43] In 1966, he was transferred to the veneer shop, which was in a critical situation at the time.[44] In the course of 1967, he was a prominent voice in the workers' council and took the lead in lobbying for initiatives to assist the enterprise's rehabilitation.[45]

Shop managers supervised production in each workshop and were directly accountable for production results.[46] Measures to tie wages to monthly workshop production results further complicated the social position of shop managers. Given the arbitrary nature of production planning, such a policy was bound to create discord. In April 1964, when the top management introduced the first production plan after the lifting of the receivership, the shop managers strongly opposed the plan as unrealistic. The shop manager of the new packaging workshop estimated that his workshop could realise no more than 20% of the plan.[47] During the first month of production, the shop indeed realised only 27%.[48] In line with wage differentiation measures, Director Bulatović suggested that the sawmill and veneer workshops should receive bonuses for overfulfilling planned production, while the packaging and plywood workshop would receive reduced wages.[49] Shop managers strongly criticised such differentiation by workshop and three months later, the measure was abandoned.[50] The central management also revised the production plan, implicitly meeting the demands of the shop managers and recognising the uncertainty of production planning.[51]

In the ensuing internal discussions on failed production, however, the central management shifted accountability to the shop managers, thus redirecting a part of their "accountability without authority". At an open meeting of the workers' council before one hundred workers, discussants referred to lax work discipline, unrealistic production planning, worn out machinery, and technical failures. Bulatović shared the criticism of work discipline, but blamed the shop managers and foremen for the dramatic production results, arguing that they "do not participate in production as needed, but rather walk around and spend over 50% of their time in their offices".[52] He threatened strong measures and warned that the enterprise faced liquidation.[53] Two months later, noting that production results remained below plan regardless of reduced production targets, Bulatović repeated that "the skilled cadres in these workshops are stuck in their old ways and do not take care about the organisation and productivity of work".[54] Shop managers defended themselves by arguing that the problem lay with "objective" strategic decisions on supplies, production, and labour. Party-affiliated President of the Workers' Council Fazli Nimon backed the top management in putting the blame with the shop managers: "The workers are not guilty, you foremen and managers do not know or do not want to organise the production process and establish good human relations".[55] The workers' council accepted Bulatović's proposal to remove the shop managers without any discussion.[56]

A similar pattern occurred when the veneer shop in 1966 did not fulfil the anticipated production increase. Shop managers argued that the main problem was of an objective nature: the shortage of quality supplies, adequate infrastructure, and skilled labour. They also added that the plan itself was not realistic.[57] Bulatović ascribed the underfulfilment to low work discipline and "the lack of expertise of the managers in the workshop to organise the production process".[58] A disciplinary commission decided to remove the veneer shop manager.[59] The local newspaper explained that this harsh and extraordinary measure was justified because shop managers had failed to realise production plans regardless of "favourable conditions".[60]

The division between the new professional management and the shop managers is complex. Unlike the new managers, who were newcomers to the region, many of the shop managers had been part of the management of the local timber enterprises prior to the establishment of *Kosmet Šper*. They were thus rooted in the locality and the tradition of the enterprise and posed a potential challenge to the authority of the new management, particularly considering the market-oriented rationalisation the latter advocated (see also Hübner, 1995, pp. 197–205). The frequent references by shop managers to objective grounds for the enterprise's underperformance were particularly threatening to the legitimacy of the new management. The demotion of shop managers was thus part of a legitimation strategy by the new management to shift responsibility for the instability of the enterprise from "objective" to "subjective" factors, while drawing on anti-managerial tendencies among the workforce. Using the language of workers' self-management, the professional management discarded the shop managers as profiteers and opponents of the rights of production workers, who were to blame for production failures. In addition, the new professional management resorted to claims of professional superiority, which concurred with assessments by the local political elites that the old shop managers worked on the basis of experience rather than technical expertise, could not keep up with the fast development of the economy, and opposed the arrival of new specialists "out of personal interests".[61]

The demotion of old shop managers concurred with the promotion of a new group of skilled workers. Wage differentiation measures introduced by the new management in early 1964, "in agreement with the municipality", increased the starting wages of high-qualified workers.[62] The reforms of 1965 added momentum to these wage differentiation measures. In October 1965, the management revised an earlier decision by the workers' council to increase wages across the board, arguing that wage increases should favour the "carriers of production".[63] Commenting on "demonstrative" opposition against wage differentiation measures, Director Bulatović criticised that "many think that this still is a state enterprise and that they will receive wages exclusively on the basis of starting tariffs and not as a sort of participation in the distribution according to realised production."[64] After repeated criticism by the municipality against wage egalitarianism, the workers' council decided that the largest part of the 30% aggregate wage increase foreseen for 1966 would be used to increase the wages of skilled workers and experts.[65] In August 1967, when the crisis was immanent and parallel to lay-offs of unskilled workers, the management introduced wage increases for "certain workers at responsible and key positions (...) so that these would not leave the enterprise and it would not come to the dispersal of specialists".[66]

There are indicators that the all-South Slav central management aimed to assure Albanian ethnic solidarity among the workforce by promoting a group of Albanian skilled workers to the rank of 'carriers of production', including the abovementioned Xhafer Zhuri. A report of 1963 had noted that a group of workers and members of the League of Communists were openly critical about the labour cuts. There were talks in town that "only little care was taken for the national question" and that "especially skilled workers of the Albanian nationality had been fired".[67] The municipal committee of the League of Communists found that the criticism was without grounds, as a national filter was applied: Albanians, Serbs, and Montenegrins were dismissed in proportion to their shares of the work collective.[68] More relevant than the question whether or not nationalist motives were behind the labour cuts is the finding that Albanian skilled workers enjoyed sufficient social capital to cause social disturbance among the majority Albanian workforce and among the local political elites by activating the taboo issue of national discrimination. By promoting some of these skilled workers in the enterprise hierarchy, it seems that the central management aimed to defuse the potential ethnicisation of social conflict between production and management.

Because of the failure of the new professional management to secure political support for the continued operation of the underperforming enterprise, which was the essence of contractual management, the social settlement between management and skilled workers remained weak. At the meetings of the workers' council in the summer of 1967, Zhuri sharply criticised Director Aleksić for not delivering the expected results, "considering that he is an expert and that he made a lot of promises in the beginning but that it now turns out that nothing has come of that."[69] Another worker and fellow Albanian, Murat Bajram, had the impression that "some managers had the goal to place this enterprise in liquidation."[70] Zhuri and Bajram warned that there would be a revolt among the workers and demanded that Aleksić be held accountable for his failures.[71] Such open criticism of the professional management was accompanied by deteriorating "human and other relations in the enterprise", local parlance for social and national relations.[72] The workers' council increasingly lost its faith in the abilities of the professional management to lobby for the rehabilitation of the enterprise. In March 1968, the workers' council opposed the imminent liquidation of the enterprise and called on "the community" to grant financial means for modernisation. Instead of referring to market indicators, the workers' council returned to the political logic behind the establishment of *Kosmet Šper* and based its protest on the Yugoslav commitment to improve underdeveloped regions, stressing that the enterprise operated in an economically underdeveloped area, where the problem of unemployment was acute.[73] To increase pressure, some 150 workers went on strike, allegedly the first in socialist Kosovo (Höpken, 1984, pp. 246–47). The strike quickly ended after workers had a meeting with representatives of the municipality, at which they vaguely agreed that all actors would find the best solution to fix the situation in the enterprise.[74] Ten days later, however, the municipality initiated liquidation.

Attracting and repelling the peasant-worker

Market-oriented wage differentiation measures aiming to tie wages to performance, efficiency and skill, clashed with the dual-sector growth model behind the establishment of *Kosmet Šper*. While from a market perspective, wages could only increase on the condition that productivity or profit grew or in case an individual had made an extraordinary contribution to production or profit, from the perspective of extensive local growth, aggregate wage increases were a precondition to absorb labour from the agricultural sector into industry (Bićanić, 1973, pp. 110–11). Wage politics in *Kosmet Šper* constantly reflected this tension. On one hand, the municipality and management repeatedly expressed concerns that low aggregate wages in *Kosmet Šper*—even compared to less favoured branches such as trade and crafts—failed to absorb surplus rural labour. [75] In this line of argumentation, the municipality pushed for higher aggregate wages, financed from the municipal reserve fund and loans, along with labour cuts and production increases.[76] On the other hand, in aligning the political factory with the market, the local elites critically noted that the work collective "compellingly insisted on pay rises", although the enterprise never realised sufficient income to distribute full wages; it "made losses, and losses cannot be distributed".[77]

Under the market reforms of 1965, the inherent tensions became even more pronounced. The management resolved this tension by coupling wage increases to labour cuts and significant rises in production, which at least in the planning stage subscribed to the market logic.[78] Director Bulatović criticised the draft production plan for 1965, for example, for pushing up wages without measures to "reveal internal reserves, fight for the reduction of jobs, or increase production".[79] The reopening of the carpentry shop allowed for significant production increases, which rationalised wage increases in the logic of the market reforms.[80] In 1965, the enterprise followed the suggestion of the federal assembly to increase aggregate wages but at the same time appointed a commission to reveal labour surplus and introduced a third shift in the plywood shop to step up production.[81] Planned production increase and labour cuts for 1966 again allowed the enterprise to increase aggregate wages.[82]

The combination of labour cuts, pay rises, and increased production was characteristic of all the intervention rounds undertaken at the stage of planning to align Kosmet Šper with the market reforms. Constant production failure made clear, however, that wage increases determined production planning and not the other way around. In evaluating failed production, the management repeatedly noted that there was no "social justification" for pay rises as long as productivity did not go up.[83] The option to decrease wages in line with production results was, however, not possible because this undermined the primary local development logic behind the enterprise. Bulatović stated that "we have to be clear about these wages. If we cannot survive with these wages, we have to go in liquidation".[84] Evaluating the negative production results for 1966, the management recognised that aggregate wage increases were incomprehensible, as the production targets had not been reached. The top management warned that "decision-makers with full right could ask how come the personal incomes were increased when the enterprise was making losses".[85] Wage increases were, however, "useful and necessary, because we are dealing with over 2000 workers and their family members" and because the wages of a majority of the workers were below the absolute minimum.[86] Even in the crisis of 1967, the management insisted that an aggregate wage increase was necessary to increase productivity.[87] As acting Director Božidar Milačić put it, "with these personal incomes, which are the lowest in the municipality, we cannot continue."[88]

The constant tensions between market-oriented demands for labour rationalisations and skills differentiation on the one hand and the extensive growth model for absorbing rural labour surplus on the other singled out the category of the unskilled peasant-worker. Peasant-workers are a broader Southeast European phenomenon of new industrial workers who maintain residence and subsistence agriculture in the village (Brunnbauer, 2007, pp. 221–77; Petrescu, 2005). The local development plans of the late 1950s considered the large pool of unskilled rural labour an asset for expanding light, labour-intensive industrial production.[89] Reports of the 1960s, however, related the underperformance of *Kosmet Šper* to the lack of skilled workers, the labour surplus in the enterprise, and the huge absenteeism. This was linked to the fact that many workers lived in the village, "where they probably had other sources of income".[90] It was argued that these workers were not committed to the enterprise, preserved their "petty artisanal and rural instincts" on the shop floor, and were solely interested in social benefits associated with public-sector employment.[91] The failed production in the veneer shop in 1966, for example, was ascribed to the fact that 44 of the 54 workers commuted from surrounding villagers. Almost half of them had less than one year's experience in the enterprise.[92] Measures to rehabilitate the enterprise typically conditioned prospects for increased production and aggregate wage rises to labour cuts. In an intensive growth model focussing on skill and rationalisation, underqualified peasant-workers were evident targets for labour cuts and relative wage disadvantages. The measure was also presented as socially acceptable given that peasant-workers were not depending on their salaries: They were "with one leg in the enterprise and one leg on the land."[93]

Conclusions

This article has used the history of an unsuccessful and rather insignificant enterprise in Kosovo to explore the impact of the tensions between market and plan on business in socialist Yugoslavia. From the perspective of an unsuccessful, medium-sized, and labour-intensive enterprise in the Yugoslav periphery, the study has made three points of relevance for business history. First, it scrutinised the relation between enterprise and state in socialist Europe. Strategic decisions on supplies, production, and distribution were ultimately taken by political actors outside of the enterprise. Although it might appear that the market reforms were successful in driving an unsuccessful "political factory" under, the case of *Kosmet Šper* indicates how the locus of political decision-making shifted from local government to provincial political and financial elites. This led to the increasing monopoly in socialist development schemes of big-system enterprises depending on Yugoslav funding and bailouts. These were hardly more successful than medium-sized enterprises in market terms, but operated on a highly-visible economic and political scale, which granted access to political interference situated at the level of the federal units of socialist Yugoslavia.

Second, the article analysed management in the socialist enterprise. Management was professionalised but formal decision-making lay with workers. A type of contractual management emerged, in which technically-schooled managers conditioned their expertise to make an enterprise profitable on salary and non-financial benefits and delegation of management authority. This for its part led to a paternalistic style of management, which was particularly pronounced in political factories, where the new professional management was given exclusive authority and full responsibility to keep the factory running under market conditions. This deal remained vulnerable, however, because the ultimate decisions on business were taken by political actors and were not in the hands of the managers. The potential cleavage between workers and management overlapped with social divisions based on function, ethnicity, and origin.

Finally, the article studied the labour force fluctuations caused by attempts to align the political factory with market conditions. Each round of market-oriented interventions consisted of measures addressing "objective" and "subjective" factors. Because strategic decision-making could not address the fundamentally non-market logic behind the continued existence of the enterprise, accountability for production failures was transferred to the self-management bodies, which were disproportionally occupied with "internal reserves". These were not inaccurate, but deflected serious research and accountability for the structural obstacles to making the political factory performant under market conditions. Dynamic definitions of skill and the lack thereof were negotiated against this background.

Notes

1. A note on writing: I use the Serbian writing of the enterprise (*Kosmet Šper*), which was how it was registered and most often depicted in the sources. For names of places and enterprises in Kosovo, I give the Albanian and Serbian writing when first mentioning, and then use the Albanian writing throughout the text. In order to allow the reader to contextualise the unpublished archival sources, I provide the English translation from Serbian and Albanian.
2. Parallel to market reforms, the Yugoslav state was decentralised in the 1960s into republics and provinces with increasingly far-reaching competences. Kosovo was upgraded from an autonomous region to an autonomous province within the Republic of Serbia.
3. 'Odluka o društvenom planu sreza Kosovska Mitrovica' [Decision on the social plan for the district Kosovska Mitrovica], *Službeni list Autonomne kosovsko-metohiske oblasti* [Legal Gazette of the Autonomous Region Kosovo-Metohija] 12/19 (1957): 173–80; 'Društveni plan sreza Kosovska Mitrovica za 1958 godinu' [Social plan for the district Kosovska Mitrovica for the year 1958], *Službeni list Autonomne kosovsko-metohiske oblasti* 13/14 (1958): 132–41.
4. Regional Archives of Mitrovica, fond 88 (factory archive Kosmet Šper) / box 11 (hereafter RAM 88/11): Decision by the People's Municipal Council, 2 April 1958.
5. RAM 88/11: Workers' Council (hereafter WC), 1 July 1958.
6. RAM 88/11: Economic Office Belgrade, 'Investment programme for the construction of a veneer packaging shop in Kos. Mitrovica', 1959.
7. RAM 88/11: Unaccounted overview of the merger of *Kosmet Šper*, 1960.
8. RAM 88/11: District of Kosovska Mitrovica, 'Report from the commission for the revision of investment programmes on the evaluation of investment studies for the acquisition of machinery for Kosmet Šper', 12 November 1958.
9. RAM 88/21: People's Municipal Council Mitrovica, 'Information on business and results of the receivership over Kosmet Šper', September 1963.
10. RAM 88/21: People's Municipal Council Mitrovica, 'Information on the situation and a proposal for measures to solve the problems of the wood industry enterprise Kosmet Šper – Kos. Mitrovica', 4 April 1962; RAM 88/17: Report from Kosmet Šper to the People's Municipal Council Mitrovica on 'Situation and problems of some economic organisations – Kosmet Šper', June 1961; Nikola Pečić (Local Council of the League of Communists), 'Information of the impact of the new economic measures on the work of the wood industry enterprise Kosmet Šper', 5 June 1961.
11. RAM 88/17: People's Municipal Council Mitrovica to the Economic Bank of Serbia, 4 April 1962.
12. RAM 88/21: People's Municipal Council Mitrovica, 'Information on business and results of the receivership over Kosmet Šper', September 1963.
13. RAM 88/17: Nikola Pečić (Local Council of the League of Communists), 'Information of the influence of the new economic measures on the work of the wood industry enterprise Kosmet Šper', 5 June 1961.
14. RAM 88/23: Municipal Assembly Mitrovica, 'Decision on approval for the constitution of the wood industry enterprise Kosmet Šper in Kos. Mitrovica', 7 December 1963.
15. RAM 88/24: Municipal Assembly Mitrovica, 'Conclusion of the assembly of the municipality of Kos. Mitrovica on the lifting of receivership and other measures to solve the problems of the wood industry enterprise Kosmet Šper in Kos. Mitrovica', 6 December 1963.
16. RAM 88/33: Kosmet Šper (Accounting Department), 'Analysis of the financial results of the wood industry enterprise Kosmet Šper from Kosovska Mitrovica for the period January-September 1964', 20 September 1964.
17. RAM 88/40: Planning Manager Đorđe Vučićević to the WC, 23 August 1965.
18. RAM 88/41: Planning Manager Đorđe Vučićević to the management, 26 June 1965; RAM 88/41: Kosmet Šper and Municipal Assembly Mitrovica, 'Further work and development of Kosmet Šper: Analysis of supplies', 18 June 1965.

19. RAM 88/55: Kosmet Šper (Planning Department), 'Economic plan for 1966', May 1966.
20. RAM 88/56: Kosmet Šper (Planning Department) and Municipal Assembly Mitrovica (Council for Economy), 'Short review of the situation and prospects of Kosmet Šper in Kos. Mitrovica', 25 January 1967.
21. RAM 88/70: WC, 22 February 1967.
22. RAM 88/56: Kosmet Šper (Planning Department) and Municipal Assembly Mitrovica (Council for Economy), 'Short review of the situation and prospects of Kosmet Šper in Kos. Mitrovica', 25 January 1967.
23. RAM 6 (Fond Municipal Assembly) /1968–1: Municipal Assembly Mitrovica, 'Proposal for the opening of liquidation procedures for the wood industry enterprise Kosmet Šper in Mitrovica', 21 March 1968.
24. RAM 88/72: Municipal Assembly Mitrovica, 'The production and finance status of Kosmet Šper according to the balance sheet for the period January-June 1967', July 1967.
25. RAM 88/72: Municipal Assembly Mitrovica, 'The production and finance status of Kosmet Šper according to the balance sheet for the period January-June 1967', July 1967.
26. RAM 88/70: WC, 2 August 1967.
27. RAM 88/70: WC, 29 December 1967.
28. RAM 6/1968–1: Municipal Assembly Mitrovica, 'Proposal for the opening of liquidation procedures for the wood industry enterprise Kosmet Šper in Mitrovica', 21 March 1968.
29. RAM 6/1962–2: People's Municipal Council Mitrovica, 3 November 1962; RAM 88/21: People's Municipal Council Mitrovica, 'Information on the situation and a proposal for measures to solve the problems of the wood industry enterprise Kosmet Šper – Kos. Mitrovica', 4 April 1962; RAM 88/21: Decision by the District Court of Prishtina, December 1962.
30. RAM 88/24: Municipal Assembly Mitrovica, 'Conclusion of the assembly of the municipality of Kos. Mitrovica on the lifting of receivership and other measures to solve the problems of the wood industry enterprise Kosmet Šper in Kos. Mitrovica', 6 December 1963.
31. RAM 88/70: Management Board (hereafter MB), 1 June 1967. The management board was an advisory organ to the workers' council, consisting of delegates of the workers' council and the management. In practice, it was dominated by the management and determined the agenda of the workers' council.
32. RAM 88/53: Application file of Miodrag Kamenović, January 1967.
33. RAM 88/70: MB, 1 June 1967; RAM 88/70: WC, 22 March 1967.
34. RAM 88/70: WC, 4 August 1967.
35. RAM 88/52: MB, 29 March 1966.
36. RAM 88/52: MB, 20 January 1966.
37. In 1963, the total workforce comprised 320 Albanians, 180 Serbs, and 35 Montenegrins. There were 77 women and 453 men. In the accounting and planning & production departments, Serbs dominated (respectively, 14 Serbs to 4 Albanians and 2 Montenegrins and 4 to 1 and 2). RAM 88/33: Mitrovica Council of the League of Communists, 'Information on the termination of employment for workers of the work organisation', 26 March 1964.
38. RAM 88/70: MB, 12 February 1967.
39. Member of the local League of Communists and municipal assembly representative Mustafa Osmanagić, for example, assessed that "subjective" factors comprised two thirds of the enterprise's difficulties. RAM 6/1963–2: People's Municipal Council, 23 July 1963.
40. RAM 88/55: Kosmet Šper (Planning Department), 'Economic plan for 1966', May 1966, p. 11.
41. RAM 88/11: WC, 1 July 1958.
42. RAM 88/70: WC, 9 January 1967.
43. RAM 88/30: MB, 30 July 1964.
44. RAM 88/52: WC, 7 September 1966.
45. RAM 88/70: WC, 24 July 1967.
46. RAM 88/11: Kosmet Šper, 'Rulebook on the internal organisation and management of the wood industry enterprise Kosmet Šper in Kos. Mitrovica', 25 July 1958.
47. RAM 88/30: MB, 14 April 1964.
48. RAM 88/30: MB, 28 May 1964.

49. RAM 88/29: Kosmet Šper, 'Decision on the payment amount for wages in relation to the starting basis for the month May 1964'.
50. RAM 88/30: MB, 29 June 1964.
51. RAM 88/41: Planning Manager Đorđe Vučićević to the management, 26 June 1965; RAM 88/41: Kosmet Šper and Municipal Assembly Mitrovica, 'Further work and development of Kosmet Šper: Analysis of supplies', 18 June 1965.
52. RAM 88/30: WC, 20 April 1964.
53. RAM 88/30: WC, 20 April 1964.
54. RAM 88/30: MB, 28 July 1964.
55. RAM 88/30: WC, 29 July 1964.
56. RAM 88/30: WC, 29 July 1964.
57. RAM 88/52: WC, 23 April 1966; MB, 25 April 1966.
58. RAM 88/52: WC, 22 July 1966.
59. RAM 88/52: WC, 19 October 1966.
60. "Kažnjeni rukovodioci Kosmet-Špera: Prinudna uprava" [Managers of Kosmet Šper sanctioned: receivership], *Zvečan*, 13 August 1966, p. 3.
61. RAM 88/17: Nikola Pečić (Local Council of the League of Communists), 'Information of the influence of the new economic measures on the work of the wood industry enterprise Kosmet Šper', 5 June 1961.
62. RAM 88/32: Kosmet Šper (Planning Department), 'Economic plan for 1964', 13 October 1964, p. 32.
63. RAM 88/39: MB, 8 October 1965. Carriers of production was a sort of informal honorific title, along the lines of "heroes of socialist labour" but with a stronger focus on specialism and management capacities as opposed to production outputs. Beside the higher wages, the title came with material benefits (access to housing) and decision-making authority through leading positions in workers' councils. In the case of secondary enterprises like *Kosmet Šper*, however, the material benefits were insignificant (although informal shopfloor practices also mattered).
64. RAM 88/39: MB, 11 November 1965.
65. RAM 88/52: MB, 6 June 1966.
66. RAM 88/70: MB, 23 August 1967.
67. RAM 88/33: Mitrovica Council of the League of Communists, 'Information on the termination of employment for workers of the work organisation', 26 March 1964.
68. RAM 88/33: Mitrovica Council of the League of Communists, 'Information on the termination of employment for workers of the work organisation', 26 March 1964.
69. RAM 88/70: WC, 24 July 1967.
70. RAM 88/70: WC, 24 July 1967.
71. RAM 88/70: WC, 4 August 1967.
72. RAM 88/70: WC, 24 July 1967.
73. RAM 88/79: WC, 27 March 1968.
74. "Obustava rada u Kosmet Šperu" [Work stoppage in Kosmet Šper], *Politika Ekspres: Nedeljna Revija*, 21 April 1968, p. 2.
75. RAM 88/17: People's Municipal Council Mitrovica, 'Information on the situation, actions, phenomena, and problems related to the adoption of the internal distribution and development of wages', September 1961, pp. 21–22; RAM 6/1961–2: People's Municipal Council Mitrovica, 'Situation with regard to the formulation of rulebooks for the internal distribution in economic organisations', 9 October 1961; RAM 6/1963–2: Municipal Assembly Mitrovica, 23 July 1963.
76. RAM 6/1963–2: Municipal Assembly Mitrovica, 6 December 1963; RAM 88/24: Municipal Assembly Mitrovica, 'Conclusion of the assembly of the municipality of Kos. Mitrovica on the lifting of receivership and other measures to solve the problems of the wood industry enterprise Kosmet Šper in Kos. Mitrovica', 6 December 1963.
77. RAM 88/32: Kosmet Šper (Planning Department), 'Economic plan for 1964', 13 October 1964, pp. 44–46.
78. RAM 88/34: Kosmet Šper (Accounting Department), 'Balance sheet for 1964', 13 February 1965.
79. RAM 88/30: MB, 10 December 1964.

80. RAM 88/30: MB, 25 and 26 December 1964.
81. RAM 88/39: MB, 30 July, 4 August, 10 August 1965.
82. RAM 88/55: Kosmet Šper (Planning Department), 'Economic plan for 1966', May 1966.
83. RAM 88/30: Director Milorad Volić at WC of 10 April 1964.
84. RAM 88/39: WC, 12 November 1965.
85. RAM 88/52: WC, 22 July 1966.
86. RAM 88/56: Kosmet Šper (Accounting Department), 'Balance sheet for 1966', February 1967, p. 31.
87. RAM 88/56: Kosmet Šper (Accounting Department), 'Balance sheet for 1966', February 1967, pp. 31–32.
88. RAM 88/70: WC, 30 January 1967.
89. RAM 88/11: District of Kosovska Mitrovica, 'Report from the commission for the revision of investment programmes on the evaluation of investment studies for the acquisition of machinery for Kosmet Šper', 12 November 1958.
90. RAM 88/21: People's Municipal Council Mitrovica, 'Information on the situation and a proposal for measures to solve the problems of the wood industry enterprise Kosmet Šper – Kos. Mitrovica', 4 April 1962.
91. RAM 88/17: Nikola Pečić (Local Council of the League of Communists), 'Information of the influence of the new economic measures on the work of the wood industry enterprise Kosmet Šper', 5 June 1961.
92. RAM 88/56: WC, 30 September 1966.
93. "Hapat e pare te sherimit" [The First Steps To Recovery], *Zvečan*, 12 August 1967, p. 2.

Disclosure statement

No potential conflict of interest was reported by the author.

Funding

This article is the result of a research project funded by the European Union's Horizon 2020 research and innovation programme under the Marie Skłodowska-Curie grant agreement No 700759.

ORCID

Pieter Troch http://orcid.org/0000-0002-3009-7240

References

Abdyli, T. (1978). *Zhvillimi i industrisë në Kosovë [Industrial Development in Kosovo]*. Prishtina: Enti i historisë së Kosovës [Historical Department of Kosovo].

Adizes, I. (1971). *Industrial democracy: Yugoslav style. The effect of decentralization on organizational behaviour*. New York: The Free Press.

Amatori, F. (2009). Business history: State of the art and controversies. *Revista de Historia Industrial, 39*/(1), 17–35.

Bićanić, R. (1973). *Economic policy in socialist Yugoslavia*. London: Cambridge University Press.

Bilandžić, D. (1985). *Historija Socijalističke federativne republike Jugoslavije. Glavni procesi 1918–1985 [History of the Socialist Federal Republic of Yugoslavia. Main processes 1918–1985]*. Zagreb: Školska knjiga.

Brunnbauer, U. (2007). *"Die sozialistische Lebensweise". Ideologie, Gesellschaft, Familie und Politik in Bulgarien (1944–1989) ["The socialist way of life". Ideology, society, family and politics in Bulgaria (1944–1989)]*. Vienna: Böhlau.

Chandler, A., Jr., Amatori, F., & Hikino, T. (1997). Historical and comparative contours of big business. In A. ChandlerJr., F. Amatori, & T. Hikino (Eds.), *Big business and the wealth of nations* (pp. 3–23). New York: Cambridge University Press.

Comisso, E. T. (1979). *Workers' control under plan and market*. New Haven and London: Yale University Press.

Filtzer, D. (1992). *Soviet workers and de-stalinization: The consolidation of the modern system of Soviet production relations, 1953–1964*. Cambridge: Cambridge University Press.

Grama, A. (2018). *Laboring along: Industrial workers and the making of postwar Romania*. Berlin: De Gruyter Oldenbourg.

Heumos, P. (2005). State socialism, egalitarianism, collectivism: On the social context of socialist work movements in Czechoslovak industrial and mining enterprises, 1945–1965. *International Labor and Working-Class History, 68* (Fall), 47–74. doi:10.1017/S0147547905000190

Höpken, W. (1984). *Sozialismus und Pluralismus in Jugoslawien: Entwicklung und Demokratiepotential der Selbsverwaltungssystems [Socialism and pluralism in Yugoslavia: development and democratic potential of the self-management system]*. Munich: R. Oldenbourg.

Hübner, P. (1995). *Konsens, Konflikt und Kompromiß: Soziale Arbeiterinteressen und Sozialpolitik in der SBZ/DDR 1945–1970 [Consenus, conflict, and compromise: Social labour interests and social policy in the GDR 1945–1970]*. Berlin: Akademie Verlag.

Kežić, D. (2017). *Bauen für die Einheitsstaat. Die Eisenbahn Belgrad-Bar und die Desintegration des Wirtschaftssystems in Jugoslawien (1952–1976) [Building for the unitary state: The Belgrade-Bar railway and the disintegration of Yugoslavia's economic system (1952–1976)]*. Munich: De Gruyter Oldenbourg.

Kochanowicz, J., & Murgescu, B. (2017). Rural and urban worlds: Between economic modernization and persistent backwardness. In I. Livezeanu, & Á. von Klimó (Eds.), *The Routledge history of East Central Europe since 1700* (pp. 81–125). London/New York: Routledge.

Palairet, M. (1992). Ramiz Sadiku: A case study in the industrialisation of Kosovo. *Soviet Studies, 44* /(5), 897–912. doi:10.1080/09668139208412052

Palairet, M. (1997). Metallurgical Kombinat Smederevo 1960–1990: A case-study in the economic decline of Yugoslavia. *Europe-Asia Studies, 49* /(6), 1071–1101. doi:10.1080/09668139708412489

Petrescu, D. (2005). Workers and peasant-workers in a working class' paradise: Patterns of working-class protest in communist Romania. In P. Hübner, C. Kleßmann, & K. Tenfelde (Eds.), *Arbeiter im Staatssozialismus: Ideologischer Anspruch und soziale Wirklichkeit [Workers in state socialism: Ideological claim and social reality]* (pp. 119–140). Cologne: Böhlau.

Pittaway, M. (2005). Accommodation and the limits of economic reform: Industrial workers during the making and unmaking of Kadar's Hungary. In P. Hübner, C. Kleßmann, & K. Tenfelde (Eds.), *Arbeiter im Staatssozialismus: Ideologischer Anspruch und soziale Wirklichkeit [Workers in state socialism: Ideological claim and social reality]* (pp. 453–471). Cologne: Böhlau.

Pleština, D. (1992). *Regional development in communist Yugoslavia*. Boulder: Westview Press.

Scranton, P. (2018). Managing communist enterprises: Poland, Hungary, and Czechoslovakia, 1945–1970. *Enterprise & Society, 19*(3), 492–537. doi:10.1017/eso.2018.13

Scranton, P., & Fridenson, P. (2013). *Reimaging business history*. Baltimore: John Hopkins University Press.

Suvin, D. (2016). *Splendour, misery, and possibilities. An X-ray of socialist Yugoslavia*. Leiden: Brill.

Swain, G., & Swain, N. (2009). *Eastern Europe since 1945*. Basingstoke: Palgrave Macmillan.

Troch, P. (2019). Social dynamics and nationhood in employment politics in the Trepça mining complex in Socialist Kosovo (1960s). *Labor History, 60* /(3), 217–234. doi:10.1080/0023656X.2019.1533747

Tyson, L. D. (1977). Liquidity crises in the Yugoslav economy: An alternative to bankruptcy?*Soviet Studies, 29* /(2), 284–295. doi:10.1080/09668137708411123

Uvalić, M. (1992). *Investment and property rights in Yugoslavia: The long transition to a market economy*. Cambridge: Cambridge University Press.

Woodward, S. (1995). *Socialist unemployment: The political economy of Yugoslavia 1945–1990*. Princeton, NJ: Princeton University Press.

Yudanov, A. Y. (1997). USSR: Large enterprises in the USSR – The functional disorder. In A. ChandlerJr., F. Amatori, & T. Hikino (Eds.), *Big business and the wealth of nations* (pp. 397–432). New York: Cambridge University Press.

Županov, J. (1985). *Samoupravljanje i društvena moć [Self-management and social power]*. Zagreb: Globus.

Management of technological innovation: High tech R&D in the GDR

Dolores L. Augustine

ABSTRACT
Fundamental changes in the management of technological innovation took place over the course of the 40-year history of the German Democratic Republic. This article analyzes management culture in electronics and microelectronics R&D, as well as at Carl Zeiss Jena. R&D directors of the 1950s and 1960s, whose careers started in the Weimar or Nazi era, had a professional ethos and managerial style not rooted in state socialism. This article analyzes their approaches to management according to criteria such as reliance on authority and hierarchy, promotion of communication, and importance attached to political conformity. Developments in R&D management at Carl Zeiss are traced up into the 1980s. The role of the Stasi (secret police) in high tech R&D is discussed.

In what ways did enterprises operating under the state socialist system of the German Democratic Republic (GDR) function like Western enterprises?[1] Why did segments of the East German economy thrive for decades? Questions such as these bring a fresh perspective to the study of the East German economy. As the Cold War recedes ever further into history, it has become possible to see the state socialist economy, not as doomed from the start, but as subject to decline brought on by specific policies and changes in the structure and culture of state-owned industry.[2] Up until about 1970, some sectors of East German industry demonstrated a fair capacity for technological innovation. By the 1980s, however, the GDR was no longer competitive in many areas in which it had once been strong. This is particularly true of industries reliant on technoscience, which are the focus of this article.

What has often been overlooked in analysing this loss of vitality is the importance of managerial practices in the innovative process. Some have maintained that management is integral to Western capitalism but irrelevant to 'real socialism'.[3] This article, however, argues that the Western concept of 'management' is not only applicable to the GDR but is highly useful in understanding behaviours, processes, organisation, and aspects of enterprise culture that molded industrial research and development (R&D) and help account for its successes and failures. Under the planned economy, the state was supposed to largely take over managerial functions, such as the efficient supervision, allocation, and organisation of people and things, efforts to motivate employees, and planning for future growth and innovation. However, particularly during the first two decades of GDR history, those who oversaw R&D

in industries in technoscience fields were often experts who sought to keep up with world-wide developments in their respective fields and to compete internationally. This necessitated a certain degree of autonomy on the enterprise level, while not precluding close collaboration with the state. This model was rooted in personnel continuity with the Nazi and earlier periods, the survival of older enterprise cultures, and, ultimately, professional ethos. This article examines case studies from the semi-conductor, microelectronics, and precision instruments and optics industries. These were export industries and sectors that provided inputs for other economically important industries. Recent research helps to place our case studies in a larger context.

What do we know about innovation in the GDR?

As I argued in my 2007 study, *Red Prometheus: Engineering and Dictatorship in East Germany, 1945–1990*,[4] the relationship of the SED (Socialist Unity Party, de facto the East German Communist Party) to innovation was rife with contradictions. On the one hand, the economic system was productivist in nature, that is, geared to production goals set by the State Planning Commission. These were generally expressed in quantitative terms, leading to what many sarcastically called the 'ton ideology', i.e. an orientation favouring high output and heavy products. Not until the introduction of the New Economic System in 1963 was R&D accorded a place in economic planning. On the other hand, science and technology were viewed as a central motor of socialist change by SED leaders, a tenet rooted in Marxist-Leninist theory and practice. The Soviet Union was highly successful when resources were poured into particular projects, the best known of which are nuclear weaponry and Sputnik. East German leader Walter Ulbricht (in power 1949–1971) believed in the transformative power of technology, listened to technical and scientific experts, and allowed them to develop a certain amount of initiative in particular fields. High-visibility initiatives in areas such as plastics and chemicals were, at least theoretically, prioritised.

However, recent research has shown that innovation and innovative behaviour was much more widespread than that, encompassing a variety of industries as well as actors up and down the hierarchy.[5] The GDR was not in a position to become a major trailblazer in any field, but should have been capable of incremental innovation, involving improvement or adaptation of innovations developed elsewhere. However, what 'innovation' meant in different industries varied greatly. Similarly, the factors that impeded innovation were diverse. Ralf Ahrens points to policy decisions that were detrimental to innovation in the machine-building industry, notably the centralisation of R&D in socialist combines (a form of horizontal and vertical integration introduced mainly in the 1970s). This disrupted a major source of innovation: interactions with customers and adjustment of machinery to their needs.[6]

Ulrike Schulz and Thomas Welskopp found that Simson Suhl (*VEB Fahrzeug- und Gerätewerk Simson Suhl*), a manufacturer of motorcycles and mopeds, was able to negotiate with state planners and other enterprises in ways that allowed them to innovate. Simson Suhl had the advantage that it was operating in an industry in which innovations tended to be incremental and branding and design were important.[7] By contrast, new techniques developed by Kodak in the 1970s had a devastating impact on East German film manufacturer Filmfabrik Wolfen, according to a study by Silke Fengler. Unable to secure the resources needed to keep up with the West, Wolfen turned to trade with the Soviet Union, which kept it locked into the production of outdated products.[8]

Another line of inquiry involves the role of the Stasi (Ministry of State Security) in the innovative process. Kristie Macrakis concludes in *Seduced by Secrets* that industrial espionage conducted in the West by the Stasi allowed Robotron and other East German enterprises and socialist combines to make use of technological advances while saving on R&D expenditures.[9] A 2017 study by Erik Meyersson and Albrecht Glitz quantified this finding, calculating that in computing and electronics, espionage reduced the technology gap between the GDR and West Germany by 26%.[10] However, as Macrakis points out, the technologies socialist corporations reverse-engineered were outdated by the time they rolled them out. In addition, patent infringement—often obvious to potential Western customers—was an impediment to sales abroad.[11]

In a recent study, Mark Schiefer has shown that the importance of the chemical industry—specifically the chemical combines of Leuna and Buna—actually made them into the targets of counterproductive secret police interference. While state-owned industry had generally had greater independence under reforms[12] of the Ulbricht era, his successor, Erich Honecker (in power 1971–1989) brought about recentralization of economic decision-making. Growing East–West contacts heightened the risk of 'subversion'. The secret police had little understanding of the business world and the West, and they saw these Western contacts as highly suspicious. To contain the potential contagion, they investigated and persecuted key chemical industry personnel in charge of foreign trade and R&D. The Stasi was, however, surprisingly ineffectual, which greatly limited the harm they did. In addition, the chemical combines sought to protect their employees. Schiefer finds that the secret police did not play a constructive role in opening up lines of communication between enterprises and the SED, as some authors have argued. Rather, Ministry for State Security personnel saw themselves simply as enforcers of the economic plan and SED authority.[13]

What has not been properly examined in this literature, including in my own work, is the impact of managerial habits, practices, attitudes, and styles on the innovative process; how professional ethos helped mold management in this sense; and how changes in policies and practices of 'power trio' of state, SED, and Stasi—to use Kristie Macrakis's term[14]—expanded or (more likely) narrowed the ability of those in charge of industrial R&D to promote innovation. The results of this analysis will help evaluate the usefulness of applying the Western concept of management to the GDR.

Methodology and sources

A useful way to frame the analysis of management practices of the 1950s and 1960s can be found in a 1970 U.S. article by Knut Holt. He contrasts two styles of management and their suitability for the management of innovation. The first, deemed not very conducive to innovation, is hierarchical and 'mechanistic', with highly formalised rules and procedures, a high level of specialisation, and a hub-and-spokes organisation with little interaction between units. Employees are motivated by 'fear, threats, punishment, economical rewards'. Goals are established by 'orders from top' and are very specific. This starkly contrasts with an 'organic' management style much more conducive to innovation, characterised by a 'task oriented' structure, 'variable' division of work, relatively flat hierarchies, authority based on knowledge rather than on place in the hierarchy, a high level of interaction between units, encouragement of participation, an emphasis on 'initiative and creativity' as well as on communication, and motivating of employees through 'involvement' and 'satisfaction of psychological needs'.[15] More recent research seems to point in a similar direction.[16] In the GDR, the parameters of managerial practices were set by the state and the party, but within a complex historical context.

The history of professions and collective biography helps to elucidate this context. In the 1950s and 1960s, the generation of industrial scientists and engineers who had entered professional life before 1945 played leading roles in industrial R&D. Technoscience and high tech fields were dominated by experts who had worked for the Nazis and were deported to the Soviet Union in 1945–1946 to work on the Soviet atomic bomb program, rocketry, and many other projects.[17] Over time, the SED was able to mold the technical elite through systematic changes, involving targeted recruitment, higher education, and party membership. The GDR leadership was, to a greater extent than in other Eastern bloc countries, able to win support by offering educational and professional opportunities to young people from previously excluded strata of society.[18] However, it should not be assumed that older patterns of professional life and identity became entirely irrelevant to younger generations.

Carl Zeiss Jena and the semiconductor and early microelectronics industries provide good examples of the role of the pre-Communist technical elite in the GDR, and these make excellent case studies for other reasons as well. Zeiss was a major exporter, and electronic and microelectronic components were vital to other industries. The importance of microelectronics and lasers—produced by Zeiss—grew exponentially during the 1960s, and acquisition through importation was hardly feasible, due to the Western CoCom embargo in the case of microelectronics.[19] Compounding these difficulties was the low level of technical cooperation within the Eastern bloc. Hoping to preserve its dominant position in some areas, the Soviet Union was reluctant to share technologies with Eastern European countries, least of all the GDR.[20]

In addition, for the microelectronics industry, a truly unique source exists. The handwritten memoir of Werner Hartmann (1912–1988), who headed the Center for Molecular Electronics (*Arbeitsstelle für Molekularelektronik*, or AME) from its founding in 1961, is, to my knowledge, the only one of its kind: a frank, highly detailed insider account of what went on in one East German enterprise, from the perspective of someone overseeing R&D.[21] It provides unique insight into the motivations behind the management of technoscientific research in the industrial realm, presented against the backdrop of the author's professional life, going back to the Nazi era.[22] A wealth of other documentary evidence—secret police reports, as well as enterprise and state documents—allows for a critical appraisal of his account.

Available archival materials on other industries to be discussed here, notably the semiconductor industry and Carl Zeiss Jena (maker of precision instruments and optical devices) do not provide the kind of detailed insight into the inner workings of the workplace. However, much can be pieced together using other kinds of sources, such as state, enterprise, and Stasi records.

Professional ethos: historical roots

The professional ethos of four research directors discussed in this article—Hartmann, Matthias Falter (1908–1985), an important figure in the East German semi-conductor industry, and Paul Görlich (1905–1986) and Herbert Kortum (1907–1979) of Carl Zeiss Jena—was molded by experiences in Nazi Germany and in exile in the Soviet Union. All four participated in the 'self-mobilization' of science and technology during the Nazi regime.[23] Helmut Maier shows that within the military–industrial–technoscience complex, a cooperative relationship was forged that 'became deeply embedded in the collective consciousness of both the scientists and the military personnel'. The Nazi regime did much to promote a sense of common purpose, which evidently in many cases overrode any compunction about the crimes being committed.[24]

Looking back from the vantage point of the early 1980s, Werner Hartmann, who worked for Siemens and Fernseh-G.m.b.H. (a producer of early television technology and weapons guidance systems) during the Nazi period, described industrial research in the Nazi era as characterised by collegiality, flexibility, and relatively flat hierarchies:

> By today's standards, particularly in comparison with the overly bureaucratized and inflexible mode of operation in the GDR—whether in industry, universities, or other entities—such a flexible organization which is based on flexibility, honesty and trust, indeed must be based on those things, is a dream that appears unreachable and unrealistic. But it was reality.[25]

This quotation speaks volumes about the lack of guilt, sense of responsibility, or self-reflection of its author regarding his role in the Nazi period. This was not atypical. Historian Georg Wagner-Kyora found that in the chemical industry, industrial chemists and chemical engineers averted their eyes from crimes being committed around them, for example, in the treatment of slave labour. However, they held fast to a sense of identity based on 'higher values', such as a sense of duty and individual responsibility, loyalty to authority, nationalism, meritocratic values, and dedication to professionalism and science.[26]

German scientists and engineers who were forced to work on the Soviet atomic bomb project and other major technological projects in the Soviet Union after the war also thought of themselves as working in an apolitical bubble. Hartmann wrote of this period, 'I never during my professional life—neither earlier in Germany nor later in the GDR—was able to work with such concentration … in a congenial atmosphere that was never disturbed'.[27] What carried over into careers in the GDR was a professional ethos centered on science, collegial relationships, and loyalty to the state, but detached from political life.

Management of innovation in the building of the GDR's microelectronics program

Before embarking on an analysis of Hartmann's account of the establishment of the microelectronics, it is useful to examine an example of mismanagement in the field of electronics. In most countries, the microelectronics industry grew out of the semiconductor industry, but that was not the case in the GDR, due in part to the endemic problems of the GDR economy, but also due to problems in the areas of leadership and management. The invention of the transistor in the United States in 1947 set the stage for the development of semiconductors.[28] The GDR was rather advanced in solid-state physics, upon which semiconductor technology is based. Physicist Matthias Falter, who worked on semiconductors during a period as a captive scientist in the Soviet Union, was, in 1952, put in charge of the Works for Telecommunications Components (WBN) and later the Institute of Semiconductor Technology (IHT), which he led until 1964. By 1959, East German semiconductor R&D was five to six years behind world standards and unable to produce transistors that could be used in television sets, radios, and industrial equipment.[29] WBN and IHT faced two major problems. The first was that they were under the authority of an industrial ministry, which meant that they were treated like any other industrial enterprise, receiving very inadequate support for the complex and expensive plant and equipment they needed.[30] A second problem was the lack of communication and cooperation between industrial research on the one hand and the Academy of Sciences and university research on the other. WBN, along with an electronics production facility in Erfurt, remained mired in substandard practices, according to Werner Hartmann's account of visits there in the 1950s:

> Everywhere I went I encountered the good will of technical people. But what was almost completely lacking was scientifically grounded work, technological discipline and qualified personnel… People continued to use the 'formula of the master craftsman', who had been working this way since before the war.[31]

Hartmann did not think highly of Falter's organisational and managerial abilities, nor did the secret police.[32]

Hartmann's background prepared him well for the key role he was to play in the founding of the East German microelectronics industry. He was a student of physicists Gustav Hertz and Walter Schottky and an expert in solid-state physics and semiconductors. After his involuntary ten-year stay in the Soviet Union, he founded and headed the socialist enterprise *VEB Vakutronik*, which conducted R&D and produced equipment for nuclear physics, the East German nuclear power industry, and Soviet nuclear programs. The lack of success of the GDR's semiconductor industry was of great concern at *Vakutronik*, which needed high-performance electronic components for the devices it produced. Hartmann won the support of Erich Apel (1917–1965), a top economics minister, for an industrial research and scientific development enterprise that would develop the technical methods and the necessary equipment for microelectronics production. It was agreed that the equipment would be manufactured by a specialised machine-building enterprise, and the components themselves would be produced in the *VEB Halbleiterwerk Frankfurt an der Oder* (HWF). Hartmann became head of the Facility for Molecular Electronics (AME) with its creation on August 1, 1961.[33]

Hartmann characterised 'scientifically grounded work, technological discipline and qualified personnel' as the essential elements of success. His emphasis on scientific work was grounded in his own expertise. According to former AME employee Hans Becker, Hartmann foresaw the revolution that microelectronics would bring about before anyone else in the GDR.[34] He remained very professionally active during his years at AME, publishing frequently in technical journals and teaching at the Technical University of Dresden. He attended many conferences, was active in international professional organisations, maintained friendly ties with industrial scientists in the West, and visited microelectronics facilities in the West.[35]

As far as personnel is concerned, he personally interviewed everyone who applied for a position at AME and made the final hiring decisions, putting qualifications before SED membership. In doing so, he was encroaching on the power of his enterprise's 'cadre division', an SED-controlled personnel office. What he was looking for was ability, knowledge, 'technological discipline', professionalism, and a willingness to put in hard work.

Hartmann's leadership style cannot easily be classified as traditional or modern. Certainly, he was a figure of authority at AME. Despite the occasional reprimand, he commanded the respect and loyalty of his employees, according to interviews with two former employees.[36] There is strong evidence that he was admired, even 'idolized', in the words of a secret police report, by his employees.[37] He did not necessarily model himself on the pre-war university professor or industrial research head, who sat in a position of authority in a very hierarchical system. In his memoirs, he criticises the 'high and mighty' manner in which Manfred von Ardenne, a highly privileged atomic researcher, treated Vakutronik personnel when he visited.[38]

He viewed good communications and collegiality as of central importance in industrial R&D. As head of Vakutronik, he had often encouraged employees to express new ideas that occurred to them, saying that he preferred for employees to make 'ten suggestions, only one of which proves to be realistic and practical' rather than not to express any ideas out of fear of making a mistake.[39] He organised AME along functional lines rather than product lines. Thus, various departments had to work together on projects. His motto for AME was 'AME is one socialist laboratory'. He felt that his employees obtained a great deal of satisfaction from seeing that their own work had made a major contribution to an enterprise-wide project.[40]

Hartmann organised R&D in a way that was unusually risk-friendly by GDR standards. To meet the challenge of keeping up with technologies that were developed at an unprecedented pace, he had his staff develop microelectronics production methods and equipment at the same time rather than sequentially. This produced faster results, but there was a risk of failure all down the line. As research yielded new insights or worldwide trends shifted, multiple departments had to make adjustments or even break off a project. Hartmann worked to overcome resistance and frustration over what were, at times, wasted efforts. In addition, he organised specialised collaborative teams of staff from AME and HWF, the production facility associated with AME. This eased the transition from R&D to mass production, as well as adjustments to new technological realities. He also sent many recent hires, who often had no specific knowledge of electronics and microelectronics, to get practical training at HWF or Falter's institute, the IHT.[41]

State and SED leadership did not understand the technology or the innovative process well enough to support the kind of constant adjustment and adaptation that was necessary. A study conducted by Bernd Wenzel demonstrates this. An alternative to solid state electronics existed: thin film technique, a hybrid technology in which passive elements were sprayed onto ceramic wafers and active elements (such as transistors) were individually attached. The SED and Academy of Sciences mistakenly believed that this technology was the better choice for the GDR because it was cheaper. Hartmann kept an open mind towards various technological avenues. However, solid archival evidence shows that he thought that few resources should be devoted to thin film technique, which did not seem to be showing much progress in the West. Components that used this technology made Robotron computers very prone to break down. Valuable time and money were wasted.[42]

Holt's scale helps us to evaluate Hartmann's management style. He emphasised his authority vis-à-vis employees, which he saw as important in maintaining a high level of discipline, adherence to scientific and technical standards, and professionalism, while not allowing party officials to exercise undue influence. He also was the ultimate scientific and technical authority at AME, but he very much encouraged personnel to acquire expertise, for example through training or by attending conferences. Many of the characteristics described by Holt as part of the 'organic' managerial style apply to Hartmann: his encouragement of individual initiative and creativity; strong horizontal communication channels; dispersal of knowledge throughout the enterprise; and motivating of personnel by giving them a sense of 'involvement' in a larger mission and 'satisfaction of psychological needs'.

He also tried to fend off the autocratic, top-down tendencies of the planned economy and dictatorial system.

Running Afoul of the SED: Hartmann as external representative of AME

Hartmann was also the main representative of AME vis-à-vis the SED, the secret police, and other enterprises. Schulz and Welskopp have brought to the fore the question as to the extent to which East German managers could exercise some of the functions of their Western counterparts, seeking resources, negotiating with other enterprises, and getting the technology they needed. The rich documentation on AME provides a great deal of insight.

Soon after its founding, Hartmann became enmeshed in a never-ending struggle for funding, personnel, and work crews, despite repeated party resolutions aimed at rapid completion of AME. 'Back then', he writes, 'I came to realise for the first time that resolutions and directives were seen as goals unto themselves, and that the relevant issues were seen as having been taken care of, as having been seen through to the end'.[43] AME enjoyed a relationship of patronage with Apel, whose intentions were good, but who essentially had no power to allocate the resources needed by AME. In any case, Apel committed suicide in 1965.[44] Members of the Economic Council, which theoretically was in charge of the AME at that time, reacted to a presentation by Hartmann in December 1963 'like interested members of the audience rather than like the responsible representatives of the central state administration'.[45] This was an endemic problem in GDR industrial administration. No one wanted to take responsibility, facing as they did high odds of failure and a culture of recrimination and intimidation that made even upper-level administrators risk-averse.

Hartmann wrote hundreds of letters to officials throughout the 1960s, trying to convince them of the importance of microelectronics and the need to provide AME with greater resources. In meetings with officials great and small, he eloquently made AME's case, but was met at times with grandiose but empty promises, at other times with hostility. Official SED doctrine held that SED economic policies were based on Marxist-Leninism, which provided a scientific basis for the running of the socialist economy. Enterprise functionaries who showed initiative in ways that seemed to call into question the wisdom of the SED were thought to be motivated by self-interest and were often accused of 'subjectivism', that is, deviation from scientifically 'objective' SED policies.[46] Difficulties were blamed on individual, enterprise-level personnel. At a June 1964 meeting of the Research Council, top economics official Günther Mittag accused Hartmann of having neglected his 'responsibility for microelectronics'. Hartmann defended himself and AME. He returned to Dresden, dispirited, and recounted the entire episode to his department heads. They closed ranks, and the incident 'brought us closer together and forged us into a real community in which we could count on each other'.[47]

The solidarity shown by Hartmann's employees, if anything, discomfited SED officials, who hoped to weaken Hartmann's position at AME by making the enterprise's party secretary his deputy.[48] In 1967, Minister for Electrical Engineering and Electronics Otfried Steger told Hartmann that he was an 'objective obstacle to the development of microelectronics', apparently because Hartmann was not a member of the SED.[49] Hartmann tried to negotiate with various layers of party and state bureaucracy but was unable to get the kind of support that AME needed. As a result, it took AME until 1967 to produce its first integrated circuit, followed by a TTL (transistor-transistor logic) integrated circuit in 1968, though in the meantime it had, together with HWF, developed and transferred onto the production line a great deal of equipment for electronics and microelectronics production.

Innovation, the quest for technology transfer, and the secret police

By the mid-1960s, a major secret police crackdown was underway in high-tech industries. Hartmann and AME present an excellent case study of the impact of the Stasi on the innovation process in East German industry. Kristie Macrakis is very much on-target in her assertion regarding the Ministry for State Security that 'security concerns made them work against their own interests by restricting the needed international travel of scientists and by imposing other harmful security measures'.[50] AME was grappling with the problem of how to gain insight into rapidly proliferating technological advances. No one country, least of all a small country such as the GDR, could re-invent microelectronics or pursue original paths of development.

Hartmann and his employees sought to gain knowledge of international developments on trips to the West. They learned a good deal about clean rooms on a trip to West Germany in 1964, as well as from Soviet sources. Hartmann hoped to visit Fairchild, Texas Instruments and Motorola during a 1965 stay in the United States and learn more about how to conduct experimental production runs of integrated circuits. However, this, along with a trip to Japan, was called off at the last minute. For a few years, no delegations from the microelectronics or semi-conductor industries were allowed to go to the United States. Hartmann then turned to the Soviet Union for technical help, but to no avail. As in many other cases, the Soviet Union did not want to share its most advanced technologies with the GDR.[51]

It was in the 1960s that the SED—following the Soviet example, but also reacting to setbacks—decided that it was not worthwhile conducting independent R&D in many high-tech areas. Instead, GDR industry was ordered to start copying Western technologies. GDR industry had always tried to *imitate* Western technologies, but not to copy them exactly. One day in June 1967, the Minister for Electrical Engineering and Electronics showed up at Hartmann's enterprise with a briefcase filled with integrated circuits produced by Texas Instruments, which AME was ordered to produce copies of.[52] This strategy was, of course, to cause major problems later because the patent infringement was obvious to buyers of East German machinery and equipment in the West. Its immediate impact was worse, however.

In attempting to protect the guilty secrets of East German industry, the SED and the Stasi cracked down, not only on East–West contacts that might bring GDR patent violations to light, but also any and all contacts between enterprises and even within enterprises. The basic exchange of information, the passing along of know-how and practical applications of technology went from being the glue that held together the microelectronic industry's R&D infrastructure to being industrial secrets shared only on a need-to-know basis. Particularly problematic was the way these new security measures disrupted the close relationship between AME and HWF, which was crucial to the smooth transition from R&D to production. This greatly slowed down the microelectronics program.[53]

However, the SED failed to recognise that its own policies and the practices of the Ministry for State Security were to blame for delays. Once the SED realised the importance of microelectronics—around 1974—the hunt for scapegoats was on. The leadership's anxiety was increased by the Western CoCom embargo, which included microelectronics. Falsely accused of sabotage and espionage, Hartmann was ousted from his position and relentlessly pursued by the Stasi. He was accused of employing 'managerial methods of capitalist companies', favouring non-Communists in the hiring and promotion process, and being a tyrannical boss who 'suppressed all criticism'.[54] He allegedly spent too much time writing articles for scientific and technical journals.[55] His model of professionalism could no longer find a place in the East German system. He died, a broken man, in 1988.

There are parallels between Hartmann's case and those of upper-echelon chemical industry employees, discovered by Mark Schiefer. He explains these Stasi campaigns and the accompanying expansion of the ranks of the Ministry for State Security as a hostile reaction to greatly increasing contacts between East and West Germany since the détente era, along with growing pressure on GDR industry resulting from the debt crisis and an SED push to increase exports. The difference is that in the cases he analysed, the SED and the top chemical combine administrators put the brakes on Ministry for State Security attempts to put chemical industry personnel on trial or get them fired.[56] Perhaps because AME was a small, independent entity, the secret police were able to cause more trouble in the case of Hartmann, whose firing had serious consequences for AME and the microelectronics industry.

Carl Zeiss Jena: from traditionalism to a militarized model of management

Many of Carl Zeiss Jena's top R&D personnel had a similar background to Hartmann's—careers started in the Weimar era and built up in the Nazi era, deportation to the Soviet Union in 1945–46, and abstention from political commitments in the GDR. However, while AME was newly founded in 1961, Carl Zeiss Jena looked back on a storied tradition. Carl Zeiss Jena split off from the West German Zeiss Corporation and successfully revived a long tradition of excellence in optics and scientific and other precision instruments after the Second World War. A large number of its pre-war and wartime employees returned.[57] Thus, in terms of personnel and enterprise culture, Zeiss was characterised by significant continuities between the pre-Communist and Communist eras, unlike AME. Nonetheless, as a showcase enterprise, Zeiss was subject to a great deal of political pressure, which increased over time. This case study allows us to see the interplay between tradition and politically induced change, and the impact on management of innovation. An added advantage is that the material on Zeiss provides some insight into what happened to microelectronics after AME lost its leading role in this field, though more research is needed here.

One Zeiss researcher, Herbert Kortum, was able to apply work on automation that he had done for the Nazis and the Soviets to the building of the first East German computer, the Oprema, in 1954–55.[58] As director of development, Kortum oversaw the development of a large range of instruments and precision tools. In 1958, 24% of the running 366 projects were new instruments which were based on older technologies, while 38.8% were completely new. He was in charge of a successful program to build second-generation computers at Zeiss.[59] Kortum worked together with workers and professionals from other Zeiss divisions and sub-divisions, harnessing their enthusiasm to his projects. The factory head took exception with this, evidently because it cut across enterprise hierarchies and upset the chain of command.[60]

In a widely distributed report of 1958, Kortum complained bitterly about what he saw as very negative post-war changes in the R&D system at Zeiss, writing 'Unfortunately, it has not been possible to get back to the work style that we used to cultivate'. According to Kortum, bureaucrats with little technological understanding were unfairly critical of those working on technical projects. Morale suffered, particularly since technical personnel were blamed for failures but never encouraged, offered help, or praised for successes. Kortum asserted that this oppressive bureaucratic culture was driven by fear of being blamed for failures.[61] This critique was echoed by Kortum's superior and successor, Paul Görlich, Zeiss's director of research.[62] What they described was a creeping transformation into a mechanistic, innovation-unfriendly management culture, to use Holt's concepts.

However, the innovative capability of Zeiss's R&D division lived on, at least in some areas. Görlich's managerial style was rooted in personal relationships. His biggest contribution was in the area of lasers. A respected member of the international scientific community, he oversaw the incorporation of lasers into Zeiss devices and fended off a militarisation of Zeiss laser development. Görlich's aim was to preserve and protect Zeiss's traditional areas of strength—optics and precision instruments—while modernising its products. However, he erred on the side of traditionalism in resisting the integration of microelectronics into Zeiss devices. He appears to have been motivated by a desire to fend off professional challenges to long-year Zeiss personnel whose expertise lay in traditional areas.[63] Unfortunately, Görlich did not leave a detailed account of day-to-day management practices, but one can infer that he valued collegial relationships, autonomy, and a scientific orientation in research.

During the reform period of the NES (New Economic System, or *Neues ökonomisches System*, NÖS), 1963–1970, the state provided Zeiss with increased funds for R&D. Carl Zeiss Jena became the central enterprise in a socialist combine of the same name. It profited from state encouragement of cooperative relationships between industrial research divisions, universities, and Academy institutes. With greater state interest came greater state intervention. Leonid Brezhnev himself came to Jena in 1967 to force the Zeiss R&D establishment to begin to produce equipment for the microelectronics industry, such as photo repeaters.[64]

In 1966, a party stalwart, Ernst Gallerach, became the director of Zeiss. He tore apart the research division, ridding it of what he called its 'patriarchal management style'. He oversaw a Sovietisation and militarisation of Zeiss and a gradual withdrawal from traditional areas of specialisation. Zeiss began making use of technology procured from the U.S. military through espionage networks.[65]

This led to a ramping up of security at Zeiss. Görlich became the subject of Stasi and KGB investigations because of his professional friendships with Western technical and scientific experts, as well as because of his failure to join the SED. In 1967, he was prohibited from travelling to the West, thus cutting him off from the international contacts that underlay a transfer of technology from the West. In the end, he was allowed to retire.[66] Even greater changes of a technological, managerial, and political nature were afoot at Zeiss by 1970.

Erich Honecker's coming to power in 1971 brought, not a change of direction, but an intensification of trends already clear by the mid-to-late 1960s. The 'power trio' of state, SED, and Stasi worked to establish ever-greater control over the innovative process and management in microelectronics and at Zeiss. Wolfgang Biermann, general director of Zeiss 1975-1989 and a member of the Central Committee of the SED, sought to bring Zeiss under unquestioning SED control. He reinforced hierarchical structures and a style of management based on fear, subjecting Zeiss employees to 'daily tirades', something that they were not used to. This demotivated upper management. He allowed the Stasi to penetrate Zeiss, creating a dense web of informants. Draconian security regulations (for example, the total prohibition on contacts with West Germans) made it difficult to recruit highly qualified personnel. Promotion to managerial positions at Zeiss became dependent upon party membership and demonstrated political loyalty. Interestingly enough, he strenuously argued against the expansion of military research and production, convinced that Zeiss should instead concentrate on microelectronics. However, the SED was very receptive to Soviet insistence that Zeiss embark on an ambitious program of development of cutting-edge military technologies. Soviet defense minister Dmitri Ustinov visited Zeiss at the height of renewed East–West tensions (April 6, 1983) to deliver these marching orders. Military R&D was moved into a secretive division of its own.[67]

However, the head of the civilian research division, Klaus Mütze (born in 1933), a product of the post-war university system and a member of the party, promoted innovation and a collegial managerial style to the extent that he could. He very much wanted to preserve the Zeiss tradition of optics and precision instruments, but also promoted a modernisation of product lines through the incorporation of microelectronics into Zeiss products. Very reluctantly, he became a Stasi informant, but on several occasions defended Zeiss employees in reports to the Stasi. These reports make clear what he truly valued: publishing in international journals, ability to motivate one's work team and achieve good results, and tenacity in trying to solve difficult problems. However, Mütze could do next to nothing to solve underlying structural problems at Zeiss. When Zeiss was made the major GDR producer of microelectronics (in 1986), he became the head of the program. Copying Western technologies helped to bankrupt the GDR because it was so inefficient and expensive.[68] The destruction of traditional Zeiss strengths through militarisation, production of surveillance equipment for the Stasi, overexpansion, and oppression of middle management by Wolfgang Biermann fatally weakened sound managerial practices and undermined Zeiss's ability to continue to be an innovative powerhouse and major exporter. By the late 1980s, Zeiss's exports to the West were sharply declining.

The transition from an 'organic' to a 'mechanistic/authoritarian' culture of management went hand-in-hand with a shift from innovation to ever-greater reliance on industrial espionage, including in the microelectronics program, which Zeiss took over to a growing extent.

Conclusion

Both case studies demonstrate the usefulness of Holt's analytical categories in understanding the connection between managerial practices and innovation. In AME's most productive years, Hartmann's management style was 'organic', and thus conducive to innovation in important ways. He promoted communication and collaboration between functionally organised departments. His scientific and technical expertise towered over that of his employees, yet he encouraged them to become as knowledgeable, skilled, and independent as possible. His position of authority does not seem in any sense to have crushed their initiative. The relationship he forged between AME and HWF promoted the transfer from R&D to production—a very weak link in the East German system.

At Carl Zeiss Jena, highly innovative work was possible during Kortum's tenure as director of development in the 1950s. Kortum cultivated an 'organic' style of management, for example by organising collaboration on projects across departmental divides. By 1958, however, bureaucratisation and an ever-intensifying culture of blame and fear had undermined the ability to innovate, according to a widely distributed report by Kortum, who left Zeiss. R&D director Görlich promoted a collegial work style, fought off militarisation of R&D at Zeiss and defended staff scientists who were working in traditional areas of specialisation. He himself was an innovator, bringing laser technologies to Zeiss, though he resisted the use of microelectronics.

In answer to the question as to whether a socialist enterprise could function like a Western, capitalist one, the case studies examined in this article certainly point to such efforts. Hartmann tried to negotiate for the resources and funding AME needed, while marshalling the capabilities of his most valuable resource—his personnel—who, under conditions of scarcity, managed to achieve a fair amount. The reasons that AME was not given the resources needed to build up an independent microelectronics industry in the GDR are many: endemic shortages in the GDR economy; an emphasis on production over innovation; a lack of understanding of the importance of microelectronics on the part of top economic and scientific officials; and Soviet reluctance to share cutting-edge technologies with Eastern bloc nations. But the problems were also political in nature. The kind of initiative that Hartmann displayed was unsettling in a system that looked to the SED to show the path forward, particularly since he refused to join the party.

At Zeiss, a break with older managerial practices in R&D took place in the Honecker era, and the relationship between the party and the enterprise underwent radical transformation. Increased production for the Soviet military and for the Ministry of State Security created an island within Zeiss that was cloaked in secrecy and under strict SED and Stasi control. Areas of research and production that played to Zeiss's traditional strengths were starved of resources as microelectronics came to dominate Zeiss civilian R&D and production.

A major question in the literature regards the role played by the Stasi in innovation. My findings indicate that Stasi interventions increased *before* the détente era. This raises the possibility that it was not fear of Western disruptions that prompted this ramping up of secret police attention to industry. In high tech, Soviet interest in mobilising East German expertise for military purposes may have been a major factor, but further research is needed. The timeline of the tightening of CoCom restrictions may also be relevant.

Hartmann was one of many leading managers of innovation who were investigated and harassed by the Stasi. Hartmann suffered a worse fate than those whose cases were uncovered by Schiefer. A forthcoming book by Reinhard Buthmann can be expected to add to this picture.[69] Hartmann may have fallen victim to a personal vendetta. Or perhaps the decisive factor was that AME did not enjoy the protection of a powerful socialist combine.

Secret police intervention contributed to fundamental changes in the innovation process. A model of technology acquisition through espionage condemned the GDR to lag years behind worldwide technological developments and caused problems due to patent law violations. As Meyersson and Glitz have pointed out, dependence on stolen proprietary knowledge set up some East German industries for failure after 1989.

An important finding of this article is that the SED-imposed model of innovation-through-espionage undermined and, in some cases, destroyed what had been a constructive and relatively successful culture of management of innovation in some fields. In the case of AME, communication and collaboration across units and enterprises was virtually shut down, undermining a highly functional system of innovation. However, the older patterns in the management of the innovative process never disappeared entirely. At Zeiss, Klaus Mütze tried to preserve traditional product lines while ushering them into the microelectronics age. He also defended innovative researchers who did not adhere entirely to the new model of the political conformist. This hints at deep continuities in professional ethos and the conception of what managerial practices were conducive to innovation. However,

R&D managers no longer had enough influence to positively affect the overall direction of the GDR economy.

Notes

1. This question is asked in: Schulz and Welskopp (2017).
2. Two of the most important scholars to have brought about a historicised understanding of the GDR economy are André Steiner and Raymond Stokes: Steiner (2010) and Stokes (2000).
3. This conception of management as anathema to socialism was part of official doctrine. See Jahn and Schulz (1959). "Real socialism" was a term first used by Erich Honecker in 1973 to describe the system of the GDR.
4. Augustine (2007).
5. Ahrens and Boldorf (2012)
6. Ahrens (2014). For further details, see Ahrens (2016).
7. Schulz and Welskopp (2017, Wieviel, esp. pp. 336–337). Simson motorcycles and mopeds enjoyed brand-name recognition in the GDR and in some foreign markets.
8. Fengler (2013).
9. Macrakis (2008).
10. Glitz and Meyersson (2020).
11. Example in Carl Zeiss Archive (Jena), NG 148, letter from the general director of Zeiss, Schrade, to the general director of the socialist combine (VVB), dated September 30, 1965.
12. The New Economic System of 1963–67 loosened the planning system, allowing enterprises to orient their decision-making according to criteria that mimicked market mechanisms. The Economic System of Socialism brought about a concentration of investments in what were deemed key technologies. See Steiner (2010, Chapter 4).
13. Schiefer (2018, pp. 196–216, 220–230, 260–263, 277–287, 309–312, 324–332, 338–348 and 452–453). On the debates regarding the role of the Ministry for State Security, see pp. 333–347 and literature cited therein.
14. See Macrakis (1999, p. 120).
15. Holt (1970). He derived this conceptual framework from: Burns and Stalker (1959).
16. See Brown and Eisenhardt (1995, esp. pp. 356–358) and Meissner and Sprenger (2011).
17. See Mick (2000).
18. Connelly (2000).
19. The CoCom (Coordinating Committee for Multilateral Export Controls) embargo applied to technologies with military applications. See Mastanduno (1992, esp. p. 110).
20. Roesler (1998).
21. The entire memoir is housed in the Technische Sammlungen Dresden (TSD). First publication on this memoir: Dörfel (2003).
22. Originally under the Economic Council, it came under the authority of the Ministry for Electrical Engineering and Electronics in 1965.
23. See Ash (2010) and Macrakis (1993).
24. Maier (2007, vol. 1, p. 150; also see p. 180).
25. TSD, Nachlaß Hartmann, vol. D, p. 1.
26. Wagner-Kyora (2009).
27. TSD Dresden, Nachlaß Hartmann, vol. F, pp. 55–56; quotation on pp. 45–46. See also Mick (2000).
28. Riordan and Hoddeson (1997).
29. BArch (German Federal Archives, Lichterfelde) DF4 40751, State Planning Commission report of October 16, 1959; "Bemerkungen der sowjetischen Delegation," dated December 22, 1959.
30. BArch DF4 40751, memorandum dated August 14, 1958. Also confirmed in SAPMO/BArch (Party Archives in the Federal German Archives) DY 30/IV 2/6.07, Nr. 71, pp. 88–90.
31. TSD, Nachlaß Hartmann, vol. G, p. 95.

32. TSD, Nachlaß Hartmann, vol. H, pp. 18–20; BstU (Ministry for State Security Archives) MfS Archive Number 1902/67, vol. 1 [part 1] (file Matthias Falter), pp. 26–27. (Abt. XVIII/1 der BV Dresden, report of September 14, 1964.)
33. TSD, Nachlaß Hartmann, vol. D (on his educational background), vol. F (on his years in the Soviet Union), vol. G (on his time as head of Vakutronik), and vol. H, pp. 6–18 (on the founding of AME).
34. Author's interview with Hans Becker, July 2000.
35. TSD, Nachlaß Hartmann, vol. H, passim.
36. Author's interviews with Hans Becker and Günter Dörfel, July 2000 and with Günter Dörfel (by telephone), June 2020.
37. TSD, Nachlaß Hartmann, vol. H, pp. 31, 40, 50, 54–56, 70, 90, 94, 126–129, 171–172. Interviews with Renée Gertrud Hartmann, Günter Dörfel and Hans Becker, July 2000. BStU Dresden AOP 2554/76, vol. 3, p. 150.
38. TSD, Nachlaß Hartmann, vol. G, pp. 36–37.
39. TSD, Nachlaß Hartmann, vol. G, p. 99.
40. TSD, Nachlaß Hartmann, vol. H, pp. 28–30, 54–56.
41. TSD, Nachlaß Hartmann, vol. H, pp. 52–54.
42. See Wenzel (1989). SAPMO DY 30/IV A2/6.07 171, Protokoll der Beratung über Grundfragen der Mikroelektronik am 1.2.1965, p. 9. Landesarchiv Berlin [Provincial Archives of Berlin], Rep. 404, Nr. 525, Darlegung zur Perspektivplankonzeption der VVB RFT Bauelemente und Vakuumtechnik, dated April 4, 1966; Stellungnahme zur Darlegung, dated May 18, 1966, pp. 5–8. TSD, Nachlaß Hartmann, vol. H, pp. 251, 253.
43. TSD, Nachlaß Hartmann, vol. H, p. 40. Hartmann's account confirmed in: SächsHStA (Saxon Main State Archive) Bestand Zentrum für Mikroelektronik, 1903/1, report dated September 23, 1964.
44. TSD, Nachlaß Hartmann, vol. H, p. 36. Also SächsHStA, collection Zentrum für Mikroelektronik 2158, memorandum L-Nr. 108/62, dated September 14, 1962. Example of Apel's attempts to resolve problems faced by the semiconductor industry: SAPMO/BArch DY 30/IV 2/6.07/63. On Apel's suicide, see Karlsch and Tandler (2001).
45. SAPMO/Barch DY 30/IVA 2/6.07 171, "Konzeption," dated December 28, 1963, sec. 3, p. 8.
46. Schiefer (2018, p. 324).
47. TSD, Nachlaß Hartmann, vol. H, pp. 61–63.
48. SAPMO/Barch DY 30/IV A 2/607 171, Protokoll der Beratung über Grundfragen der Mikroelektronik am 1.2.1965 im Staatssekretariat für Forschung und Technik, p. 8.
49. TSD, Nachlaß Hartmann, vol. H, p. 136.
50. Macrakis (2008, p. 118).
51. TSD, Nachlaß Hartmann, vol. H, pp. 71–75, 81–86, 89–91, 109–110.
52. TSD, Nachlaß Hartmann, vol. H, p. 121, quotation on p. 86. The minister's orders to begin copying of Texas Instruments devices are mentioned in BStU AP 444/87 (file Werner Hartmann), p. 165.
53. TSD, Nachlaß Hartmann, vol. H, pp. 130, 131, 140, 147.
54. BStU Zentralarchiv HA XVIII, Nr. 9910, p. 12.
55. BStU AP 444/87, p. 7.
56. Schiefer, (2018, pp.192–193, 196, 220–229, 230, 324–332, 338–340, 449–452, 460).
57. For a history of Carl Zeiss Jena, see Mühlfriedel and Hellmuth (2004).
58. Carl Zeiss Archive (Jena) BACZ 27995; Carl Zeiss Archive (Jena), BACZ 24500, report from May 1958, pp. 95–104. See also Mühlfriedel and Hellmuth (2004, pp. 175–177).
59. Carl Zeiss Archive (Jena), BACZ 24500, report from May 1958, pp. 87–88.
60. Carl Zeiss Archive (Jena), BACZ 24500, pp. 4, 95–104.
61. Carl Zeiss Archive (Jena), BACZ 24500, report from May 1958.
62. Carl Zeiss Archive (Jena) NG 91, "1. Entwurf," 1959.
63. See Pröger (2003, pp. 143–147), Albrecht (1996), and Neunhöffer (2001).
64. See Kaschlik (2004, p. 22).
65. BStU Zentralarchiv MfS-HA-XVIII, Nr. 13337, p. 55 ("Erfüllung eines Beschaffungsauftrages für das V-System im VEB Carl Zeiss Jena," dated January 2, 1970). On Gallerach, see Mühlfriedel and Hellmuth (2004, pp. 184–200).

66. BStU, Archive number 14254/69, vol. 1, pp. 10, 42, 43, 62; vol. 2, pp. 166–170; vol. 6, p. 108; vol. 7, pp. 98–99, 100–102, 166–167, 168–169, 216; vol. 11, p. 259.
67. I found very few documents on this division. On Biermann and the changes at Zeiss in this period: BStU Zentralarchiv HA XVIII, Nr. 6900, pp. 13, 14; BStU Zentralarchiv HA XVIII, Nr. 5519, p. 5; BStU Zentralarchiv HA XVIII, Nr. 8649, p. 32; BStU Zentralarchiv HA XVIII, Nr. 9110, p. 8; BStU ASt. Gera XV/1890/77 "Michael," Part I, vol. 2, p. 111; BStU ASt. Gera XV/1890/77 "Michael," Part I, vol. 2, p. 121; BStU ASt. Gera JHS 22052, pp. 80–85. Also see Reinhard Buthmann (1997, pp. 48–68, 80, 87, 94–95, 104–110); Mühlfriedel and Hellmuth, (2004, pp. 295–296, 298, 342, 371); Hellmuth, (2004, p. 119); Barkleit (2001); Schreiner (1999, pp. 20–26).
68. See Mühlfriedel and Hellmuth (2004, p. 315. My sources: BStU ASt. Gera XV/1890/77 "Michael," Part I, vol. 2, p. 88 and p. 94. BStU ASt. Gera XV/1890/77 "Michael," Part II, vol. 1, pp. 131 and 151–158. Examples of protecting Zeiss employees: BStU ASt. Gera XV/1890/77 "Michael," Part I, vol. 2, pp. 97, 174–176, 193. Further examples in BStU ASt. Gera XV/1890/77 "Michael," Part II, vol. 1, pp. 12–14, 204, 233, and 237–240.
69. Buthmann (2020). I was not able to obtain a copy of this book before the submission of this article.

Disclosure statement

No potential conflict of interest was reported by the authors.

References

Ahrens, R. (2014). Planning priorities, managing shortages: Industrial policy in the German Democratic Republic, from Stalinism to Welfare Dictatorship. In C. Grabas & A. Nützadel (Eds.), *Industrial policy in Europe after 1945. Wealth, power and economic development in the Cold War* (pp. 300–320). Palgrave Macmillan.

Ahrens, R. (2016). Eine alte Industrie vor neuen Herausforderungen. Aufbrüche und Niedergänge im ost- und westdeutschen Maschinenbau seit den 1960er Jahren. In W. Plumpe & A. Steiner (Eds.), *Der Mythos von der postindustriellen Welt. Wirtschaftlicher Strukturwandel in Deutschland 1960 bis 1990* (pp. 55–119). Wallstein Verlag.

Ahrens, R., & Boldorf, M. (2012). Einleitung: Systembedingte Innovationsschwäche und betriebliches Innovationsverhalten in der DDR. *Technikgeschichte, 79*, 3–9.

Albrecht, H. (1996). Laserforschung in Deutschland 1960–1970 [Habilitation thesis]. University of Stuttgart.

Ash, M. (2010). Die Kaiser-Wilhelm-Gesellschaft im Nationalsozialismus. *NTM Zeitschrift für Geschichte der Wissenschaften, Technik und Medizin, 18*, 79–118. https://doi.org/10.1007/s00048-009-0011-8

Augustine, D. (2007). *Red Prometheus: Engineering and dictatorship in East Germany, 1945–1990.* MIT Press.

Barkleit, G. (2001). Moderne Waffensysteme für die Sowjetunion. In H. Timmermann (Ed.), *Deutsche Fragen. Von derTeilung zur Einheit* (pp. 39–52). Duncker & Humblot.

Brown, S., & Eisenhardt, K. (1995). Product development: Past research, present findings, and future directions. *Academy of Management. The Academy of Management Review, 20*(2), 343–378.

Burns, T., & Stalker, G. M. (1959). *The management of innovation*. Travistock.

Buthmann, R. (1997). *Kadersicherung im Kombinat VEB Carl Zeiss Jena*. Ch. Links Verlag.

Buthmann, R. (2020). *Versagtes Vertrauen: Wissenschaftler der DDR im Visier der Staatssicherheit.* Vandenhoeck & Ruprecht.

Connelly, J. (2000). *Captive University: The Sovietization of East German, Czech and Polish Higher Education, 1945–1956.* University of North Carolina Press.

Dörfel, G. (2003). Werner Hartmann—Industriephysiker, Hochschullehrer, Manager, Opfer. In D. Hoffmann (Ed.), *Physik im Nachkriegsdeutschland* (pp. 221–230). Verlag Harri Deutsch.

Fengler, S. (2013). Innovation in a centrally planned economy: The case of Filmfabrik Wolfen. In H. Berghoff & U. Balbier (Eds.), *The East German Economy, 1945–2010: Falling behind or catching up?* (pp. 145–160). The German Historical Institute.

Glitz, A., & Meyersson, E. (2020). Industrial espionage and productivity. In *IZA Institute of Labor Economics, Discussion Paper Series*, IZA DP No. 10816. http://ftp.iza.org/dp10816.pdf, accessed on July 1, 2020.

Hellmuth, E. (2004). Investitionen als Indikator von Entwicklungsschwerpunkten im VEB Carl Zeiss Jena von 1978 bis 1987. In K. Schreiner (Ed.), *Schaltkreise: Die Anfänge der Mikroelektronik im VEB Carl Zeiss Jena und ihre Folgen* (pp. 102–141). Thüringer Forum.

Holt, K. (1970). Management of technological innovation. *Management International Review, 10*(4/5), 21–29.

Jahn, G., & Schulz, G. (1959). *Sozialistische Arbeitsweise contra Managertum*. Verlag Die Wirtschaft.

Karlsch, R., & Tandler, A. (2001). Ein verzweifelter Wirtschaftsfunktionär? Neue Erkenntnisse über den Tod Erich Apels 1965. *Deutschland Archiv, 34*, 50-64.

Kaschlik, K. (2004). Zwanzig Jahre Mikrolithografie-Entwicklung bei Carl Zeiss Jena. In K. Schreiner (Ed.), *Schaltkreise: Die Anfänge der Mikroelektronik im VEB Carl Zeiss Jena und ihre Folgen*. Thüringer Forum für Bildung und Wissenschaft.

Macrakis, K. (1993). *Surviving the swastika: Scientific research in Nazi Germany*. Oxford University Press.

Macrakis, K. (1999). Espionage and technology transfer in the quest for scientific-technical prowess. In K. Macrakis & D. Hoffmann (Eds.), *Science under socialism* (pp. 82–121). Harvard University Press.

Macrakis, K. (2008). *Seduced by secrets: Inside the Stasi's spy-tech world*. Cambridge University Press.

Maier, H. (2007). *Forschung als Waffe. Rüstungsforschung in der Kaiser-Wilhelm-Gesellschaft und das Kaiser-Wilhelm-Institut für Metallforschung. 1900–1945/48* (2 vols.). Wallstein Verlag.

Mastanduno, M. (1992). *Economic containment. CoCom and the politics of East-West trade*. Cornell University Press.

Meissner, J., & Sprenger, M. (2011). Mixing methods in innovation research: Studying the process-culture-link in innovation management. *Historical Social Research/Historische Sozialforschung, 36*(1), 180–198.

Mick, C. (2000). *Forschen für Stalin. Deutsche Fachleute in der sowjetischen Rüstungsindustrie 1945–1958*. R. Oldenbourg Verlag.

Mühlfriedel, W., & Hellmuth, E. (2004). *Carl Zeiss in Jena 1945–1990*. Böhlau Verlag.

Neunhöffer, R. (2001). Jenaer Lasertechnik zwischen Wissenschaft, Wirtschaft und Staatssicherheit [Dr. phil. diss.]. University of Stuttgart.

Pröger, H. (2003). *Mikrostrukturen. Erinnerungen an ein Arbeitsleben bei Carl Zeiss Jena*. Thüringer Forum für Bildung und Wissenschaft.

Riordan, M., & Hoddeson, L. (1997). *Crystal fire. The birth of the information age*. Norton.

Roesler, J. (1998). Wirtschaftspolitik der DDR—Autarkie versus internationale Arbeitsteilung. *Dresdner Beiträge zur Geschichte der Technikwissenschaften, 25*, 2–14.

Schiefer, M. (2018). *Profiteur der Krise: Staatssicherheit und Planwirtschaft im Chemierevier der DDR 1971-1989*. Vandenhoeck & Ruprecht.

Schreiner, K. (1999). *Das Zeiss-Kombinat: Fragmentarisches Zeitzeugnis 1975/1989*. Jenaer Forum für Bildung und Wissenschaft.

Schulz, U., & Welskopp, T. (2017). Wieviel kapitalistisches Unternehmen steckte in den Betrieben des real existierenden Sozialismus?: Konzeptionelle Überlegungen und ein Fallbeispiel. *Jahrbuch für Wirtschaftsgeschichte/Economic History Yearbook, 58*(2), 331–366.

Steiner, A. (2010). *The plans that failed: An economic history of the GDR* (E. Osers, Trans.). Berghahn Publishers.

Stokes, R. (2000). *Constructing socialism: Technology and change in East Germany, 1945–1990*. Johns Hopkins University Press.

Wagner-Kyora, G. (2009). *Vom "nationalen" zum "sozialistischen" Selbst. Zur Erfahrungsgeschichte deutscher Chemiker und Ingenieure im 20. Jahrhundert*. Franz Steiner Verlag.

Wenzel, B. (1989). *Ein Beitrag zur Geschichte der Mikroelektronik unter besonderer Berücksichtigung der Entwicklung der Halbleiter- und Mikroelektronik in der DDR* [Dissertation B]. Technical University of Dresden.

Workers against technocrats: The failed economic reform and the rise of consumer socialism in the German Democratic Republic

Eszter Bartha

ABSTRACT
The article seeks to investigate the working-class background of the failure of the economic reform of the 1960s in the German Democratic Republic (GDR). The reform attempted to bring more incentives and market-like elements into labour organisation and management practices. However, there was an essential discrepancy between loyal party work and strong ideological commitment, and the 'capitalist' managerial practices. Despite the fact that the SED (the Communist Party of the GDR) invested a lot in the training of socialist technocrats, the regime's rigid ideology and its political constraints severely curtailed the extent to which technocrats could deploy their expertise. Egalitarianism and the 'workerist' ideology of the Party were effective obstacles in the implementation of the 'scientific-technical revolution', thus making a case for an aborted Fordism or a failed socialist modernity.

Introduction: revisiting the 'workers' state'

A Worker in a Worker's State was originally the title of a manuscript written by the Hungarian dissident intellectual, Miklós Haraszti in 1972 and published in English in 1977 with a foreword by Heinrich Böll (Haraszti 1977).[1] The book soon became a classic in the study of socialist societies, and it is still referred to in the international literature[2] while it remained barely noted in Hungary, even after the collapse of state socialism.[3]

In line with the interpretation of many contemporary Western leftists, who at best saw the Soviet Union as an aborted workers' state,[4] Haraszti described his work experience in a socialist factory as a form of commodification and alienation. He claimed no less than that workers are exploited to the same effect under 'actually existing' socialism as under capitalism; moreover, workers are very much conscious of their exploitation. Since they do not consider the factory as theirs, they would use all small tricks to cheat the proprietor State and its local representatives (factory management, trade union leaders, foremen). They refuse to follow labour protection regulations, they falsify work-sheets, they cheat at the calculation of norms (they are 'looting') they feel alienated and lonely in the brigades, they misappropriate materials and use state-owned machinery and equipment for private purposes, e.g. fabricating grill ovens, renovating cars or building their own homes (such workers are called 'homers', who are portrayed as thieves in the satirical journals) and they do not consider the misappropriation of state property as stealing. Given their exploited situation, they hold the party and trade union functionaries to be parasites on the back of the working class.[5]

These statements were seen as a direct attack against the regime, which based its legitimacy on the thesis that the ruling Communist Parties of Eastern Europe represented the working class, which was conceived as unified, homogenous and possessing a revolutionary consciousness.[6] Haraszti's manuscript, which he finished in 1972, provoked a show trial against the author, which also served as a warning to all dissidents in Hungary, many of whom were selected to appear before the court.[7] In the capitalist West, the book became an academic 'bestseller' precisely for giving fieldwork evidence for the real-life alienation of workers from the 'workers' state'.[8]

A Worker in a Worker's State can, nevertheless, provide novel insights into labour history beyond Cold War stereotypes of East and West. In 1991 Michael Seidman wrote a controversial book, *Workers against Work*, in which he also referred to Haraszti's experience, arguing that typical 'technocratic' catchwords such as labour efficiency, competitiveness, performance stand in direct opposition to the rational interests of the workers *independently of who is the proprietor*. Rational calculations, then, would necessarily turn workers against technocrats, no matter how a socialist economy is organised.

After examining the responses of the East German workers to the labour policies introduced by the SED as an attempt to increase labour efficiency, Jeffrey Kopstein (1996), however, concluded that the rational choice/individualistic models were not sufficient to account for the two most important moments when the East German working class – alongside other segments of the population – rebelled against the regime: the great strikes and demonstrations of 17 June 1953 and the actual collapse of the SED-dictatorship. True, the revolt of 17 June was preceded by the increase of the norms by 10% and price increases, but in Kopstein's analysis, 17 June should be understood in the context of a moral economy rather than the rational choice theory.[9] It was a moment when the workers collectively turned against the regime, which denied their right to what was considered an acceptable standard of living that the workers' state should guarantee to them. Kopstein speaks of a solidarity, which united different groups of workers, thus supporting the case for a working-class revolt.

The memory of the revolt of 17 June 1953 remained deeply embedded in the consciousness of the SED-leaders. The lesson that they learnt was that in order to make a tacit agreement with the working class, they have to respect and satisfy the workers' moral economy claims. This expectation severely limited the room for manoeuvre of the SED to reform the planned economy, which in the long run was unable to meet the moral economy demands of the workers. While it has been itself a question in the literature to what extent working-class resistance contributed to the demise of the regime, for Kopstein, the answer lies in a repeated cross-national case of a moral economy. Working-class expectations of consumption levels, which were at equal footing with their West German counterparts, played a crucial role in immobilising the regime, rendering it impossible for the state to 'renew' socialism.

While accepting Kopstein's argument of the moral economy of the workers that curtailed the introduction of pro-market (or pseudo-market) policies, which could have resulted in higher competitiveness with the West (in our case, West Germany), the moral economy explanation also has its limits. At the demise of the SED-dictatorship, most workers opted for more rather than less consumerism: when expecting the West German standard-of-living, they said yes to a capitalist society, where inequalities were considerably greater than what they had been accustomed to under socialism. Taking the moral economy argument seriously, 17 June 1953 was indeed a moment of collective resistance, while labour interests played a directly *opposite* role in the demise of the regime. Instead of strengthening the 'really' socialist institutions, notwithstanding marginal attempts at renewing socialism, the majority of the people voted for a different, capitalist regime.

This paper sets out to combine some insights of Haraszti and Kopstein with a case study of the relationship between workers and socialist managers in another turbulent period in the labour history of the GDR: the era of the failed economic reform of the 1960s on the example of the giant enterprise of Carl Zeiss Jena. Regarding the moral economy argument, Haraszti and Kopstein do not stand so far from each other: the homers offer an example for a similar form of everyday resistance that Kopstein examines in the light of archival sources. The common element is the shared working-class solidarity: the homers (mis)used state property because they felt to be entitled to this 'theft' in the light of the low wages, and workers provided mutual aid to each other in order to achieve private goals (building a home is the most well-known example in the Hungarian case).

This paper seeks to bring in three novel aspects. Firstly, the case study reverses Haraszti's conclusion and extends the theory that Kopstein develops. For Haraszti, as a dissident intellectual, the conclusion was natural: the 'workers' state' betrayed the workers, and – contrary to Marx's vision of socialism – sustained a regime, which was characterised by social inequalities, an unequal wealth redistribution, and the exploitation and alienation of the working class. For Kopstein, the workers' state had to give significant concessions to the workers, and therefore, the SED-leaders had only a limited room for introducing labour policies, which violated the moral economy of the socialist working class. This paper adopts a similar view by arguing that the SED had a greater need for the workers than the workers had for the SED. The moral economy of the workers therefore had to be taken seriously as it was central not only to the legitimating ideology but also the *legitimacy* of the regime (see e.g. Hübner 1993).

As for the second aspect, the paper intends to contribute to a mushrooming literature, which utilises core notions of labour history such as labour control, factory hierarchy, labour interest representation, shopfloor relations, etc.[10] Such approaches question the assumption inherited from the totalitarian school that factories in the 'East' were only characterised by a one-sided dependence on politics, coercion and repressive apparatuses. The English historian Mark Pittaway (2012) showed that the ideology had to be adjusted to shopfloor realities even in the era of high Stalinism in Hungary. Instead of a one-sided dependence, there was a mutual interplay between the political, the economical and the social interests of both the party and the workers; and the outcome was the result of a continuous struggle rather than a set of political directives (many of which remained on paper).

Thirdly, an attempt is made to complement Kopstein's insights with the argument that the failed reform of the 1960s also offers a case of workers' protest based on a widely shared moral economy. Albeit the technocrats were not 'capitalists', serious efforts have been made to render the wages more competitive, and break with the wage policy of levelling. Indeed, the immediate context of Haraszti's ethnographic study was the introduction of piece-rates in the factory where he worked (Haraszti 1980); and, according to the testimony of contemporary Hungarian sociologists, working-class outrage and grievance were expressed in the same way in other factories, where piece-rates were introduced.[11]

The findings of the post-1989 labour history on Eastern Europe also suggest that factory work under socialism had more in common with wage-work in a capitalist factory than what had been previously assumed. Kopstein (1996, p. 403) already spoke of *corrupted Taylorism* in relation to the attempts of the SED to 'discipline' the workers in the factory, while Thomas Lindenberger (2018) referred to the work-based societies of the state socialist countries as a case of *failed or obsolete Fordism*. Phil Scranton (2018) argued that concerning market economy and management practices, the 1960s triggered an important change in the mentality of making business in East-Central Europe: as the significance of (Western) exports and hard currency replaced the previous war economy, where only tons mattered, a new style of a managerial way of thinking started to develop in these countries – including even the establishment of managerial schools e.g. in Hungary.[12]

Following the aborted reform of the 1960s in the GDR, Honecker created a workers' state, which perfectly fitted in with the demands of a levelling moral economy. The giant enterprises (*Kombinats*), whose organisation was finished under Honecker, became 'centres of socialization' *(Vergesellschaftungskerne)*,[13] while the social policy of the state and public welfare also centred on the large plants (Hübner 1995), providing for various services, such as clinics, day-care centres, kindergartens, vacation houses, cultural centres, shopping areas, repair services, and even soccer teams. Working-class identities were, thus, forged in the *Betriebe* (plants); it is with reference to this that Dorothee Wierling called the GDR a 'society of the workplace'.[14] We can also mention here Christoph Klessmann's magisterial portrait of the workers in the workers' state' (2007). Lindenberger (2018) also raised the 'unorthodox' point that there could be more continuity in the labour history of the GDR with the German past than what has been previously assumed: since the welfare scheme of the Kombinats to a large extent resembled the welfare policies the philanthropist capitalist enterprises (e.g. Zeiss) adopted in the late nineteenth and the early twentieth centuries.

Konrad Jarausch (1999) was the first to use the term 'welfare dictatorship' (*Fürsorgediktatur*) to highlight the centrality of social policy (*Sozialpolitik*) for the legitimacy claims of the GDR. Martha Lampland (1996) demonstrated that the state socialist regimes and planned economies also produced commodified labour. My argument is that the *Fürsorgediktatur*, which grew out a levelling moral economy, eventually forged a commodified consciousness also within the ranks of industrial labour which, in 1989 proved to be one of the gravestones of the workers' state.

Socialist fordism – squaring the circle?

While both the turbulent era of the 1960s[15] and Honecker's welfare dictatorship[16] belong to the well-researched areas, the novelty of this paper is to link the two by simultaneously using and reversing the moral economy argument Kopstein (1996) has applied to the GDR. The economic reform Ulbrich initiated aimed at the reorganisation of labour production, factory hierarchies and workers' consumption levels in order to increase the efficiency of the economy of the GDR, and prepare it for an export-driven growth, which inevitably meant a direct business competition with the capitalists of the Western world. As Kopstein (1994) observed, the reform, which aimed at decentralisation and deregulation, had two central components:

(1) improving enterprise performance without introducing a labour or a capital market and (2) upgrading the quality and qualifications of leading economic personnel without sacrificing a commitment to socialist values.

Kopstein further argues that an *internal* political struggle lay at the centre of the reforms from the very onset and that East German leaders were given far more autonomy than in the conventional histories of the period. On the one hand, the new technocrats pushed for more reforms, on the other hand the 'old Communists' opposed even Ulbricht's moderate economic reforms. While Kopstein analyses in detail the internal struggle at the top, this paper turns attention to labour struggles at the bottom. I seek to show with the example of the emblematic socialist enterprise Carl Zeiss Jena (which from the onset competed with the capitalist Zeiss in Oberkochen) how the struggle over labour reorganisation took place among the new and old managers, and how workers on the shopfloor reacted to this conflict.

Ironically, the turbulence of the 1960s is best shown by what has *not* been written in the Honecker era. While the factory documents report on many labour conflicts from these times, later on, criticism disappeared from the documents. This supports Kopstein's analysis of the internal struggle within the party: the local party leaders transmitted – or even amplified – workers' criticism in order to argue *against* the reform. The shadow of 17 June proved to be long, and the opponents of the reform could always use labour unrest as a *threat* to the socialist order that obviously none of the leaders wanted to overthrow. Thus, the workers' moral economy was (also) exploited to *reverse* the course of the economic reform.

This reversal put an end to Ulbricht's dreams of paving the way of an export-driven growth of the GDR, and it also meant an end to his political career. However, with Honecker's rise to power, the welfare dictatorship proved to be unable to compete efficiently with the advanced capitalist economies. As Raymond Stokes (1997) observes, the East German economic problems did not result from the 'incompetence' of the 'bourgeois' technocrats; it was essentially the politics that decided the production of artefacts, which could not compete with the Western world. Stokes mentions among the factors, which impeded the 'scientific-technical revolution', 'an exaggerated interest in mass production owing both to egalitarian ideological precepts and resource scarcities' (Stokes, 1997, p. 237). Egalitarianism was, however, not only an ideological precept; it was widely shared by the working-class 'masses', who eventually decided the fate of the reform.

Methodologically, the paper draws examples from the *Betriebsgeschichte* (factory history), which Lindenberger (2018) called a promising area of GDR labour history, whose potential was, unfortunately, severely limited by ideological constraints. Factory history has also been recently promoted as a useful tool for labour history by Görkem Akgöz et al. (2020).

The paper presents archival materials from the enterprise Carl Zeiss Jena in order to reconstruct industrial *Alltagsgeschichte* in the late 1960s and early 1970s. The main aim of the following sections is to introduce examples from 'above' and from 'below', which show the conflictual relationship between workers and technocrats. I also seek to demonstrate that the political powers used this working-class discontent to blackmail or outright discipline technocrats, which in turn had a disastrous effect on the managerial performance and the eventual outcome of the 'scientific-technical revolution', which was placed at the centre of Ulbricht's hopes to create a triumphant socialist state.

Planning the impossible? The lessons from Carl Zeiss Jena

The enterprise Carl Zeiss Jena was selected because (1) its workers already enjoyed a privileged position before World War II, thanks to the generous social policy of the enterprise (2) after the war, refugees to the West established a 'Western' Carl Zeiss; thus, the competition of the two enterprises mapped the rivalry between the two Germanies (3) the enterprise had a special role in the New Economic System (NES) and the building of an export-driven industry: the importance of microelectronics and lasers—produced by Zeiss—grew exponentially during the 1960s (Augustine 2000, p. 4).While Dolores L. Augustine (2020) makes a strong case for how Ernst Gallerach, the general director of Carl Zeiss from 1966, a loyal supporter of Ulbricht oversaw a Sovietisation and militarisation of Zeiss (Augustine 2020, p. 11), I argue that (1) he was under increasing attack both in the factory and the party committee of the district Gera, under which Jena belonged (2) the reforms that he supported also served the purpose of an export-driven growth of the factory, which could do (more) business in the West.

Carl Zeiss was, indeed, envisaged as a laboratory for the NES, because of its export output and its scientific-technical potential. That said, already in 1964, a socialist working group was formed with the task of developing the principles of the application of the new system in the enterprise. Even more important was the task of elaborating a prognosis for the long-term (15–20 year) development of the Zeiss factory, which Gallerach presented at the Seventh Party Congress in 1967. The members of the working group received state awards for their work – according to later memoirs they spent many nights at their workplace in order to accomplish the task.[17] In April 1968 the Political Committee of the SED decided that the enterprise would be the centre of the research of the rationalisation and automation technology in the GDR, and relevant production would be also concentrated in the town.[18] When Ulbricht visited Jena, he also promised to invest in the development of the town; he criticised the crumbling houses and declared that such conditions were unworthy of a town which hosted the internationally recognised Zeiss factory.[19]

In spite of the promising beginnings and the increased attention of the central party leadership, the reform of the economic management in the enterprise was not at all a success story – on the contrary, in the light of the local sources, the chaos of the last years of the NES was strongly felt in the factory. The price reform had a very negative effect on the management of Zeiss because the cost of raw materials significantly increased while the price of industrial products could not be increased accordingly because of political considerations. The increase of energy prices, on which they likewise could not spare much, added to the financial difficulties of the enterprise: in 1964, the cost of energy increased by 1.6 million M, while the enterprise could only spare 125,000 M with rationalisation.[20] In addition, there were huge arrears in export performance. The ambitious and taut plans of 1969 and 1970 worsened the situation of the factory to the extent that it could only avoid bankruptcy with significant state support.[21]

Augustine (2020) argues that there was a sharp conflict between the old 'Zeissianers' (Zeiss-employees) and Gallerach, who, e.g. tore apart the research division, ridding it of what he called its 'patriarchal management style'. However, an in-depth study of the local party materials can modify this picture, which suggests that Gallerach adopted – or could adopt! – a one-man rule in the enterprise. As I demonstrate below, the party documents inform of frequent conflicts between the new and old managers, who even openly question the competence of the new director. The conflicts also testify to an internal struggle between the 'old' and 'reformer' Communists, where the former were interested in *transmitting*, or even amplifying the local struggles to the central leadership.

Gallerach's will to change the managerial style and way of thinking of the economic personnel is reflected in several documents. On the 'Day of the Socialist Leader' (*Tag des sozialistischen Leiters*) the director argued that the managers of VEB Carl Zeiss Jena had no reason to be complacent, let alone conceited:

> There are managers even among our colleagues, who accustomed themselves to passivity, and they examine every question of our development from the perspective of an observer. We don't need observers and yes-men here, but we need active combatants.[22]

One month later Gallerach again laid into the old-fashioned methods and the lack of initiative of much of management in front of the factory party committee:

> Today's most important problem is the elimination of deficiencies in the organization of production in our enterprise. I think that the greatest obstacle to this is complacency and managers' attachment to traditional, outdated methods. We need to pay more attention to the *education of managers*.[23] In the factory I experience signs of resignation among part of the management. We need to treat this question as a political one. A manager needs socialist education, if he wants to educate others.[24]

The East German party jargon hid the most important element of the speech: the chief director sought to transform the mentality of the managers in order to be adjusted to the requirements of the NES. Failure to do so resulted in repeated problems with the fulfilment of the plan – apart from the objective difficulties, which resulted from the internal contradictions of the NES: to introduce market incentives without bringing back the market. In 1968 Gallearch listed the following problems at a factory party leadership meeting:

> There is no discipline in the instrument plant, the managers do what they want, they permanently disregard the plan, the direct production managers and shop managers are making their own plans (I can prove it with a number of concrete examples), of which the majority of the workers are not informed. In addition, shift work is unsolved, and the management of the plant has not dealt with the E-system[25] for a year.[26]

While Gallerach had to speak of the 'incomplete' political education of the managers, the listed problems inform of deficiencies in labour organisation and management rather than a missing party loyalty. Peter Hübner (1998) demonstrated that there was a change in the economic personnel in the GDR: the old working-class leaders, who often lacked the necessary education, were gradually replaced by the new technocrats. While both the old and the new guard asserted their loyalty to the party, what was at stake was the political influence rather than the actual political sympathies.

The difference in the mentality between the old Zeiss-employees and the new managers was voiced in a report of the supervisory committee of 1969:

> The ideological reasons lie primarily in the missing political and *professional qualifications*[27] and the weak fighting spirit of middle management, who fail to recognize their responsibility for the political education of the collective and they content themselves with the management of the technological-economic processes only. This is manifest in the deficiencies of socialist democracy, the lack of commitment in problem-solving, the adoption of a passive attitude and the toleration of mediocrity, complacency and conceit. Many employees think that they only have

to wait and see. This attitude results from the failure of the management to put the resolutions of the party into practice creatively, because *they have not yet fully understood our structural policy*[28] and they don't trust enough in the working ability of the Zeiss-collective.[29]

The italicized parts in the above citation support the argument that my paper shares with Hübner's findings: that the described conflict was not only between the 'old' and the 'new' managerial mentality but also *within* the economic personnel.

My second argument concerning the internal struggle within the party is supported by the fact that the weaking of Ulbricht's position also undermined Gallerach's authority. In 1970 he had to exercise self-criticism in front of the district party leadership (which, in the Communist jargon, was one step before the 'fall'):

> We have done significant damage to the Soviet Union because we could not find a satisfactory solution to the problem of the E-system. The GDR has always distinguished itself as a reliable partner of the Soviet Union. Our behaviour undermined this confidence, seriously threatening the reputation of the VEB Carl Zeiss Jena in the Soviet Union. We have to admit that we underestimated the difficulty of the task, we badly managed the project, and we failed to mobilize the resources of the VEB Carl Zeiss Jena in order to solve this problem.[30]

A report at the end of the year of 1970 expressed even stronger criticism than before, again blaming the management of the enterprise for the repeated failures.

> The export plan was not fulfilled mainly because of the mistakes of management. These mistakes are the following: deficiencies in the professional qualifications of management, and their Marxist–Leninist organizational work; failure to realize democratic centralism; chaos in management, lax discipline, a lenient, and sometimes careless working style; formalism in the management of the socialist labour competition. Efforts to improve labour organization have not yet ensured continuous production. It takes too much time to solve problems, even with the help of electronic data processing. The result is that production stoppages alone caused losses of 50 million Marks in the instrument plant. Why? The reasons are that they could not set the technical parameters that were negotiated with the Soviet partner; the central plants did not allow for sufficient capacity; there was not enough cooperation between the producers of the various optical components; we could not solve the material supply problems; the prefabricating and mounting plants performed very poorly (they under-fulfilled the plan by 550,000 hours). The labour plan was likewise not realized.[31]

High party functionaries also started to blame the whole management, which reflected Gallerach's weakening position at the enterprise. At the beginning of 1971 the first secretary of the factory party organisation sent a personal letter to the district party secretary, in which he criticised the political (meaning: economic) work of the entire management:

> In my judgement, the managers and colleagues of the departments of research, development and foreign trade even today do not understand that what we need here primarily is *achievement and efficiency*. The elections especially showed us that the employees do not have the fundamental information to engage with economic plans....[32]

Gallerach's eventual removal was decided at a higher political level than the local party committee; but precisely the attack against the director, who was appointed by the central leadership reflects a deeper conflict within the party than what any economic considerations could justify. In addition, the local organs 'normally' were not in the position to criticise a cadre, in whom the higher party organs placed their trust.

The above citations amply support the argument of Kopstein (1994) that the management under the SED enjoyed more autonomy than what has been previously assumed. The clash between the old and new guard has been somewhat hidden by the monotonous East German jargon, in which both sides used the party language in order to gain political support. However, the highlighted citations are in line with Hübner's argument (1998), who showed that the conflict between the old and new technocracy also arose from a different education and mentality how to do business – referring back to Scranton (2018). It is a question to what extent the economic reform could have solved the problem of making business in the West *without* integrating into the capitalist world economy. In any case, the internal struggle within the party alongside the hardening of the Soviet line and the suppression of the Prague Spring determined the fate of economic reform in the GDR. The new technocrats had to come to terms with Honecker's workers state, where the workers' interests took precedence over the demands of efficiency and rationalisation – and indeed, over the dream of making business in the West.

Where were the workers? A view from the shopfloor

It is hard to reconstruct workers' voices – which have not been transmitted by the party cadres – in the lack of the relevant sources. The surviving minute-books of an investigation conducted in the instrument plant in 1969 therefore constitute a unique source, not only because they address the conflict between workers and managers but also because they bring up an issue, which is totally missing from the local party materials produced in the Honecker era: the controversial relationship between the party and the ordinary workers.

The investigation was conducted by a commission that the SED appointed to examine the situation in the instrument plant, which produced strikingly bad results. The managing director also criticised the poor performance of this plant in a speech in front of the factory party leadership.[33] The members of the commission visited several departments and they talked with many people in different positions, from managers to workers. The minute books obviously give no information about the conditions in which the conversations were held; it is, however, remarkable that workers and grass-roots party members vehemently criticised their managers, whom they charged with incompetence and even with the deception of their superiors.

The inquiry in the turners' shop, for instance, concluded: 'The workers think that it is impossible working properly in these conditions. The instructions are being changed from one day to the next, and they often completely contradict each other. The plan tasks do not at all correspond to the regular norms, which are always changed.'[34] Workers in the turners' shop also had a low opinion of their party leaders and the formality of the party meetings:

> The APO-leaders[35] and the party groups summon people to regular meetings where they say nice things to us, but nothing happens afterwards... Neither are the meetings of the party groups of a particularly high standard. At these meetings officials and the state leaders speak only, workers never make any comments.[36]

The investigation detected several other 'ideological deficiencies', which reveal much of the tense relationship between the party cadres and the workers, including the practice of simply thrusting party membership involuntarily on workers[37] as the party had to demonstrate its working-class origins.

Apart from expressing strong criticism of their superiors and the party, which – in the light of their testimonies – they did not feel to be theirs, we are informed of forms of everyday resistance, which are also mentioned by Hübner (1995) and Kopstein (1996); e.g. cheating with the norms,[38] refusing to pay party duties,[39] terminating their party membership,[40] giving false calculations on the wage sheets,[41] falsifying technological documents,[42] failing to fulfil the plan for eight years, doubting whether the plan can be fulfilled at all, etc.[43] The management not only tolerated these practices, but they in fact gave significant pay increases to the workers,[44] who could also make extra money from shift work and overtime.[45]

As to concrete examples: a brigadier reported that the 'Sixth Congress' brigade undertook eight hundred extra hours alongside the twelve hundred that they had already accomplished. He also spoke of his problems concerning party-work in the brigade: out of the eleven members of the brigade only two were members of the party, and when they asked three workers to be candidates, they refused, saying that party membership would mean too much extra work for them.[46] At the same time, workers in the mill shop denounced the 'Sixth Congress' brigade as well: it turned out that they undertook weekend work instead of the second shift only because it was better paid by the enterprise. With respect to party life, the mill shop could not boast of better results than the 'Sixth Congress' brigade: their workers likewise did not hold regular party meetings. There were evidently more 'ideological problems': the meetings of the party leadership of the base organisation were often not recorded and the campaign plan for the elections of 1969 was 'nowhere to be found'. According to the information of many grass-roots members the secretary of the base organisation was hardly ever seen in the workshops: in the previous year he attended the mill shop only once even though he was invited many times to come.[47]

With respect to the relationship between the SED and the factory it is worth quoting the summary of comrade W, who singled out the following problems in the plant:

> Part of the workforce believes that socialism has been already realized and now people can have a rest, but *they should get their rightful reward*;[48] many colleagues work conscientiously because of their old loyalty to Zeiss, but not because of political consciousness or in the defence of a political standpoint on the basis of their class category.[49]

In addition, comrade W. also complained about the bad norms and rocketing wages of the workers. However, if these practices were tolerated by the management, it clearly shows that workers could exert considerable *informal* pressure on the shopfloor.

Socialist workers, then, defiantly – we can even say, militantly – refused to accept Taylorist practices, which would have upset the moral economy that they have built of a socialist state. The conversations with people in different positions confirm the central argument of the paper: that next to the internal division within the management, workers also refused to side with the 'Taylorist' technocrats, and this double pressure – at least domestically – severely curtailed the effect to which the reform could have been carried out. The regime had a pronounced policy towards the workers, which manifested itself not only in ideology – there was, for instance, no attempt to shift the responsibility for failure onto workers – but the managers had to offer several material concessions to the workers either in form of direct pay increases or by overlooking the above described forms of everyday resistance. For the fulfilment of the plan, managers needed experienced and skilled workers, who were keen on securing what they perceived as their 'rightful' reward.

Workers' protests also impeded the reform of the price system (Hübner 1995), which reversed the objective of the economic reform to break with egalitarianism.

Honecker came to power as a direct consequence of the failure of Ulbricht's reform. He set out to realise the 'true' workers' state by further limits on the (remaining) private sector, nationalisation, and a generous social welfare program, which promised ever increasing consumption levels that could beat West Germany to *every* GDR citizen. The attempt of this paper was to link the wide coverage of social consumption under Honecker with some findings of labour history by exploring the political roots of the *Fürsorgediktatur* through a case study which intended to analyse the NES *both* from the perspectives of the managers and the workers. The memory of 17 June and the failure of the economic reform both showed the *strength* of the working class and the pressure that they could exert on the party and the technocracy in order to reverse repeated attempts of introducing Taylorism into the planned economy. The moral economy of the workers and the egalitarian ideology of the party were effective obstacles in the implementation of the 'scientific-technical revolution', thus making a case for an aborted Fordism or a failed socialist modernity.

Conclusions

This paper investigated the local factory and party documents of Carl Zeiss Jena in order to make the argument that during the turbulent times of the 1960s, there was an endeavour on behalf of the political power to train a new, professional, efficiency-oriented management instead of the former working-class leaders, who were selected on the basis of their political loyalty to the regime (see also Hübner 1998). In spite of Ulbricht's efforts to set the GDR on a new course of export-driven growth, the old party stalwarts – both at local and central levels – did their best to exaggerate workers' discontent and sharpen the conflict between the 'new' management and the 'old' working class. The 'Taylorist' practices alongside the planned price reform posed a threat to the egalitarianism, which was not only an ideological requirement, but it was also central to the moral economy of the workers. Albeit the NES did not lead to an open working-class revolt, the failure of the reform can be still seen as yet another example of the triumphant everyday resistance of the workers.

This informal way of exerting pressure on the nomenklatura could not, however, translate into granting the workers real political rights. Honecker reversed the course of the NES in order to appease the workers; in addition, he created a *Fürsorgediktatur*, which realised many objectives of the social democratic labour movement, so influential in Germany in the twentieth century. However, socialist consumerism was a double-edged solution: while the planned economy could not make a lucrative business in the West, the desire for the Western products spoilt the moral economy of the workers, creating differences between those who had access to the Western money (and goods) and those, who lacked this resource. As Stokes (1997) observed, politics made artefacts as much as artefacts made politics. In the late 1960s, workers said no to the labour organisation and management practices, which were designed to compete with the West at an equal footing. Socialist consumerism under Honecker, however, developed a consciousness, which grew increasingly distant from the workers' moral economy. In the late 1980s, the working class *en masse* refused to stand up for a different socialism based on grassroots democracy rather than 'democratic centralism'. Albeit there were attempts to organise labour (Denis 2007), the 'masses' demanded national unity and the long-desired Western currency and market stores full with consumer goods. The *cul-de-sac* of socialist modernity effectively undermined the faith in a socialist revival, and triggered illusions that egalitarianism *and* capitalism can be reconciled.

The awakening was bitter, not only in Eastern Germany. High unemployment rates (the average of the Eastern part of the country is still double of the Western average), the closing or selling of the factories, the de-industrialization of many regions, where traditional industries were located, the migration of skilled and educated groups – and in particular, the youth – to the West – to name just some of the crisis symptoms – even today set apart Eastern and Western Germany. Kopstein and Ziblatt (2006) showed that this division continued to be present also in the political sphere, which triggered 'unlikely' coalitions instead of the traditional West German party alliances. The German far left – and nowadays the far right – 'performed' much better in Eastern Germany than in the Western provinces. This, however, cannot be attributed (only) to the Communist political legacy. Workers' disappointment in a capitalism, which was very far from being egalitarian and rendered many of them second-class citizens again restored the moral economy, which, in 1953, led to the memorable working-class revolt. It (still) poses a challenge not only for Germany what kind of political responses and alliances this moral economy will generate.

Notes

1. The book was first published in Hungarian in Paris in 1980, under the title: Piecework (*Darabbér*).
2. Seidman (2012). See also the pioneering study of Michael Burawoy (1985) of the similarities between the socialist and capitalist factory regimes. His fieldwork for the book was admittedly inspired by Haraszti's work.
3. This is in the context that labour history was effectively marginalized in Hungary after 1989 See: Zimmermann (2018).
4. See Linden (2007a).
5. Haraszti (1977).
6. On the "old" labour history see Welskopp (1993); Linden (2007b); Lindenberger (2018).
7. Information by Michael Wright, the translator of the book in Haraszti (1977), 17.
8. On the internal fights of the Western left concerning labour history in the 1970s see Seidman (2012). See also Konrád & Szelényi (1979), who argued that under "mature" socialism the intelligentsia developed into a new ruling class.
9. Kopstein bases this argument on E. P. Thompson's classic study of the nascent English working class. Thompson showed that the moral economy of the crowd in 18th century England severely limited the introduction of pro-market policies.
10. See Grama and Zimmermann (2018) and Brenner & Heumos (eds. 2005).
11. Information by Michael Wright, the translator of the book in Haraszti (1977), 17.
12. Scranton, 2018.
13. Kohli, 1995.
14. Wierling, 1996, 54.
15. See, especially Keren (1973); Leptin-Melzer (1978); Kopstein (1994); Steiner (1999); Haupt (ed., 2004); Szobi (2014); Evans (2010).
16. On socialist consumerism see Fulbrook (2005), who spoke of participatory dictatorship; Kaminsky (2001); Merkel (1999a, 1999b); Madarász (2003); Harsch (2006); Zatlin (2007); Bartha (2013).
17. Ulbricht held economic prognoses so important that he himself undertook the leadership of the working group created within the Political Committee, which dealt with long-term (15–20 year) strategic planning. For a discussion of the development of prognosis in Carl Zeiss see: Neumann (2000).
18. The Political Committee's resolution of 26 April 1968 is quoted in: Mühlfriedel & Hellmuth (2004), p. 206.
19. The first secretary visited the factory with his wife on 25 April 1968, on the occasion of the laying of the foundation stone of the building of 6/70. Mühlfriedel & Hellmuth (2004), p. 205.

20. Ibid., 186.
21. Ibid., 214–15.
22. Thüringisches Staatsarchiv, thereafter: ThStA, Rudolstadt, Bezirksparteiarchiv der SED Gera. Nr. IV B-2/3/255, Informationsbericht des 1. Sekretärs der IKL (Industriekreisleitung) Zeiss, Tag des sozialistischen Leiters, 16 Oktober 1968.
23. Stress is mine.
24. ThStA, Rudolstadt, Bezirksparteiarchiv der SED Gera. Nr. IV B-2/3/255, Informationsbericht des 1. Sekretärs der IKL Zeiss, 12 November 1968.
25. Electric data system.
26. ThStA Rudolstadt, Bezirksparteiarchiv der SED Gera, IV B-4/13/79, IKL-Sitzung, 15 and 18 August 1969.
27. Stress is mine.
28. Stress is mine.
29. ThStA, Rudolstadt, Bezirksparteiarchiv der SED Gera. Nr. IV B-2/3/79, Protokoll der Sekretariatssitzung, Bericht der IKL VEB Carl Zeiss JENA über Probleme der politisch-ideologischen Arbeit und der Erziehung der Leiter bei der Gestaltung des ökonomischen Systems des Sozialismus als Ganzes, 30 Januar 1969.
30. ThStA, Rudolstadt, Bezirksparteiarchiv der SED Gera. Nr. IV B-2/3/269, Kreisleitungssitzung, 22 Mai 1970.
31. ThStA, Rudolstadt, Bezirksparteiarchiv der SED Gera. Nr. IV B-2/3/269, Informationsbericht des 1. Sekretärs der IKL Zeiss, 12 November 1970.
32. ThStA, Rudolstadt, Bezirksparteiarchiv der SED Gera. Nr. IV B-2/3/283, Persönlicher Brief des 1. Sekretärs der IKL/SED des VEB Carl Zeiss JENA an den 1. Sekretär der BL (Bezirksleitung), 17 Februar 1971.
33. Protokoll der IKL-Sitzung, 15 und 18 August 1969, op. cit.
34. ThStA Rudolstadt, Bezirksparteiarchiv der SED Gera, IV B-4/13/79, Bericht, 19 September 1969.
35. Abteilungsparteiorganisation (departmental party organization).
36. Bericht, APO-Leitung, 19 September 1969.
37. ThStA, Rudolstadt, Bezirksparteiarchiv der SED Gera. Nr. IV B-4/13/79, Bericht der IKPKK (Industriekreis-Parteikontrollkommission), GDREH 1, 19 September 1969.
38. Bericht der IKPKK (Gen. Z, Ökonom), op. cit.
39. Bericht der IKPKK, GDREH 1, op. cit.
40. Ibid.
41. Bericht der IKPKK (Gen. Z, Ökonom), op. cit.
42. Ibid., Bericht (Gen. N, GO-Leitung).op. cit.
43. Bericht der IKPKK (Gen. Z, Ökonom), op. cit.
44. ThStA Rudolstadt, Bezirksparteiarchiv der SED Gera, IV B-2/3/269, Referat des ökonomischen Direktors des VEB Carl Zeiss Jena, 17 Januar 1969
45. Bericht der IKPKK (Gen. Z, Ökonom), op. cit.
46. Ibid.
47. Ibid., Bericht (GFRÄS1).
48. Stress is mine.
49. Bericht der IKPKK (Gen. W), op. cit. Welche Probleme sieht der Betriebsleiter?

Disclosure statement

No potential conflict of interest was reported by the author.

Funding

Hungarian Scientific Research Fund, project NKFIH-OTKA K_120010.

References

Akgöz, G., Croucher, R., & Pizzolato, N. (2020). Back to the factory: The continuing salience of industrial workplace history. *Labor History, 61*(1), 1–11. https://doi.org/10.1080/0023656X.2019.1681632

Augustine, D. (2020). Management of technological innovation: high tech R&D in the GDR. *Business History*, 1–17. https://doi.org/10.1080/00076791.2020.1848489 Accessed: 10 January 2021.

Bartha, E. (2009). Would you call the capitalists back? Workers and the beginning of market socialism in Hungary. *Social History*, (*34*) (2), 123–144. https://doi.org/10.1080/03071020902879515

Bartha, E. (2013). *Alienating labour: Workers on the road from socialism to capitalism in East Germany and Hungary*. Berghahn Books, Series: International Studies in Social History.

Brenner, C. & Heumos, P. (eds). (2005). *Sozialgeschichtliche Kommunismusforschung. Tschechoslowakei, Polen, Ungarn und DDR 1945–1968*. Bad Wiesseer Tagungen des Collegium Carolinum, 27.

Burawoy, M. (1985). *The politics of production: Factory regimes under capitalism and socialism*. Verso.

Denis, M. (2007). *Labor in the Collapse of the GDR and Reunification: A Crucial, Yet Overlooked Actor. Dissertation*, Humboldt Universität zu Berlin.

Evans, A. (2010). The last Gasp of socialism: Economics and culture in 1960s East Germany. *German Life and Letters, 63*(3), 331–344. https://doi.org/10.1111/j.1468-0483.2010.01502.x

Fitzpatrick, S. (2007). Revisionism in soviet history. *Slavic Review, 46*(4), 77–91.

Fulbrook, M. (2005). *The people's state. East German society from Hitler to Honecker*. Yale University Press.

Gleason, A. (1995). *Totalitarianism: The inner history of the cold war*. Oxford University Press.

Grama, A., & Zimmermann, S. (2018). The art of link-making in global labour history: subaltern, feminist and Eastern European contributions. *The Art of Link-Making in Global Labour History: subaltern, Feminist and Eastern European Contributions' European Review of History: Revue Européenne D'histoire, 25*(1), 1–20. https://doi.org/10.1080/13507486.2017.1374927

Haraszti, M. (1977). *A worker in a worker's state: Piece-rates in Hungary*. Penguin Books.

Haraszti, M. (1980). *Darabbér*. Magyar Füzetek, 1.

Harsch, D. (2006). Dictatorship and demand. The politics of consumerism in East Germany. *Central European History, 39*(3), 528–531. https://doi.org/10.1017/S0008938906360177

Haupt, H. G., et al. (2004). (eds) *Aufbruch in die Zukunft. Die 1960er Jahre zwischen Planungseuphorie und kulturellem Wandel. DDR, ČSSR und Bundesrepublik Deutschland im Vergleich*. Wissenschaft Verlag.

Hübner, P. (1993). Balance des Ungleichgewichtes. Zum Verhältnis von Arbeiterinteressen und SED-Herrschaft. *Geschichte Und Gesellschaft, 19*(1), 15–28.

Hübner, P. (1995). *Konsens, Konflikt und Kompromiß: Soziale Arbeiterinteressesn und Sozialpolitik in der SBZ/DDR 1945-1970*. Akademie Verlag.

Hübner, P. (1998). Industrielle Manager in der SBZ/DDR. Sozial- und mentalitätengeschichtliche Aspekte. *Geschichte Und Gesellschaft, 24*(1), 55–80.

Jarausch, K. & Duffy E. (eds). (1999). *Dictatorship as experience: Towards a socio-cultural history of the GDR*. Berghahn.

Kaminsky, A. (2001). *Wohlstand, Schönheit, Glück: Kleine Konsumgeschichte der DDR*. C. H. Beck.

Keren, M. (1973). The new economic system in the GDR: An obituary. *Soviet Studies, 24*(4), 554–587. https://doi.org/10.1080/09668137308410891

Kleßmann, C. (2007). *Arbeiter im "Arbeiterstaat" DDR: Deutsche Traditionen, sowjetisches Modell, westdeutsches Magnetfeld 1945 bis 1971*. Dietz.

Kohli, M., et al. (1995). Die DDR als Arbeitsgesellschaft? Arbeit, Lebenslauf und soziale Differenzierung. In Kaelble H. (Eds.), *Sozialgeschichte der DDR* (pp. 31–61). Klett-Cotta.

Gy, K., & Szelényi, I. (1979). *The intellectuals on the road to class power*. Harcourt Brace Jovanovich.

Kopstein, J. (1994). Ulbricht embattled: The quest for socialist modernity in the light of new sources. *Europe-Asia Studies*, *46*(4), 597–615. https://doi.org/10.1080/09668139408412185

Kopstein, J. (1996). Chipping away at the state: Workers' resistance and the demise of East Germany. *World Politics*, *48*(3), 391–423. https://doi.org/10.1353/wp.1996.0011

Kopstein, J., & Ziblatt, D. (2006). Honecker's revenge: The enduring legacy of German Unification in the 2005Election.*GermanPoliticsandSociety*,*24*(1),134–147.https://doi.org/10.3167/104503006780935261

Lampland, M. (1996). *The object of labor. Commodification in socialist Hungary*. The University of Chicago Press.

Leptin, M., & Melzer, M. (1978). *Economic reforms in East German industry*. Oxford University Press.

Linden, M. (2007a). *Western Marxism and the Soviet Union: A survey of critical theory and debates since 1917*. Brill.

Linden, M. (2007b). Labour history: The old, the new and the global. *African Studies*, *2–3*(66), 169–180.

Lindenberger, T. (2018). From cold war battleground to a footnote to history? Labour history in divided and unified Germany. *European Review of History: Revue Européenne D'histoire*, *1*(25), 61–78.

Madarász, J. (2003). *Conflict and compromise in East Germany, 1971-1989. A precarious stability*. Palgrave MacMillan.

Merkel, I. (1999a). *Utopie und Bedürfnis: Die Geschichte der Konsumkultur der DDR*.

Merkel, I. (1999b). Working people and consumption under really-existing socialism: Perspectives from the German Democratic Republic. *International Labor and Working-Class History*, *55*, 92–111. https://doi.org/10.1017/S0147547999003208

Mühlfriedel, W., & Hellmuth, E. (2004). *Carl Zeiss in Jena 1945-1990*. Böhlau.

Neumann, P. (2000). "… bisher nicht Gedachtes denken …": Zur Bedeutung der Prognostik im Neuen Ökonomischen System. Das Beispiel des VEB Carl Zeiss Jena. *manuscript.*, Friedrich-Schiller-Universität.

Pittaway, M. (2012). *The worker' state: Industrial labor and the making of socialist Hungary* (pp. 1944–1958). Pittsburgh University Press.

Scranton, P. (2018). Managing communist enterprises: Poland, Hungary and Czechoslovakia, 1945-1970. *Enterprise & Society*, *19*(3), 492–537. https://doi.org/10.1017/eso.2018.13

Seidman, M. (1991). *Workers against work: Labor in Paris and Barcelona during the popular fronts*. University of California Press.

Seidman, M. (2012). *The Strange History of "Workers against Work". The Vicissitudes of a Book*. Manuscript.

Steiner, A. (1999). *Die DDR-Wirtschaftsreform der sechziger Jahre: Konflikt zwischen Effizienz- und Machtkalkül*. Akademie-Verlag.

Stokes, R. (1997). In search of the socialist artifact. Technology and ideology in East Germany, 1945-1962. *German History*, *15*(2), 221–239. https://doi.org/10.1093/gh/15.2.221

Szobi, P. (2014). Between ideology and pragmatism: The ČSSR, the GDR and West European companies in the 1970s and 1980s. *European Review of History: Revue Européenne D'histoire*, *21*(2), 255–269. https://doi.org/10.1080/13507486.2014.888705

Viola, L. (2002). The Cold War in American Soviet historiography and the end of the Soviet Union. *The Russian Review*, *61*(1), 25–34. https://doi.org/10.1111/1467-9434.00203

Welskopp, T. (1993). Von der verhinderten Heldengeschichte des Proletariats zur vergleichender Sozialgeschichte der Arbeiterschaft – Perspektiven der Arbeitergeschichtsschreibung in den 1990er Jahren. *1999 Zeitschrift Für Sozialgeschichte Des 20. und 21. Jahrhunderte*, *3*(8), 34–53.

Wierling, D. (1996). Work, workers and politics in the German Democratic Republic. *International Labor and Working-Class History*, *50*, 44–63. https://doi.org/10.1017/S014754790001320X

Zatlin, J. (2007). *The currency of socialism. Money and political culture in East Germany*. Cambridge University Press.

Zimmermann, S. (2018). Eastern Europe. In Hofmeester, Karin & Linden, Marcel van der (Eds.), *Handbook global history of work* (pp. 131–156). De Gruyter Oldenbourg.

Entrepreneurs as saviours of socialism? The complicated relationship between East German state socialism and entrepreneurship

Max Trecker

ABSTRACT

The economic policy agenda of the SED has often been described as extremely orthodox in nature and—with the exception of a short period in the 1960s—hostile to reform. It is often overlooked that the GDR entertained the largest private sector of any of the CMEA economies up till the early 1980s. Besides the official propaganda, the SED leadership at no point abolished private entrepreneurship completely in the GDR. In this article, I analyze the ambiguous relationship between the state party and private entrepreneurship. I focus particularly on the late 1980s and the role private entrepreneurs were supposed to play in reforming and saving socialism in East Germany.

Introduction

When Christa Luft took the stage of the International Congress Center in West Berlin on February 13 1990, she delivered an unusual speech for an East German government official and member of the Socialist Unity Party (SED). Having served as Chancellor of the East German School of Economics,[1] she became minister of economic affairs in the Modrow government in November 1989.[2] The West Berlin congress that focused on the prospects of small and medium-sized companies she attended a few months later in her official position as government representative was organized by the Association of German Chambers of Industry and Commerce.[3] She was an outsider at that conference not only because she came from a communist country but because she was one of the very few women who were allowed to say something in this otherwise almost exclusively male world of businessmen. In her speech which she titled 'Small and Medium-sized Enterprises Are Given a Key Role',[4] Christa Luft praised the virtues of innovative small businesses and entrepreneurs and spoke to her West German audience about an emerging social and ecological market economy in East Germany.[5] She thereby repeatedly evoked the multi-faceted meanings of the German term 'Mittelstand' which in a popular West German belief was key to the economic success of the country in the post-war era.[6]

I therefore want to ask in this article what actually were the goals for economic reform of the last socialist government of East Germany in respect to the future role of private companies and entrepreneurs? How did these reform ideas relate to previous policies of the SED and what was so special about the East German 'Mittelstand' in comparison to the economic landscape to be found in other state socialist countries after the war? I argue that the economic reform attempts of the Modrow government were of a particularly 'reactionary' character in the sense that they wanted to go back to an imagined harmonious past to be identified in the 1960s when small private enterprises and large public combines had allegedly established an effective division of labor. A reemergent private sector should eventually stabilize the state economy of the GDR, by no means should the private sector render the large state combines obsolete and open the path to some kind of 'shock therapy'.

Although the reform ideas of the Modrow government had hardly any general long-term effect, it was far from clear in the winter of 1989/90 how the future would look like for East Germans and if the GDR would continue to be a sovereign state. However, when it comes down to the East German Mittelstand, the reforms discussed, and laws passed by the last socialist government of the GDR left a lasting mark and set the frame for future actions by the privatization agency, the Treuhandanstalt, which was founded in early 1990 and became the main vehicle of economic and social transformation in East Germany only after reunification.

The German term Mittelstand conveys a multitude of meanings: In essence it encompasses companies run by owner-managers. These can be artisanal shops, as well as trading companies and industrial enterprises with several hundred employees. The latter are often called 'hidden champions', because many German mid-sized manufacturing companies operate successfully on the world market. This is a phenomenon that dates back till the early 1900s for many companies. Enterprises run by owner-managers form the backbone of the German economy in a practical and theoretical sense. They are at the core of the social market economy designed in the 1930s and 1940s after the shock of the Great Depression and the war economy. They perform an economic as well as a societal role in the social market economy. A capable Mittelstand is seen as guardian of economic fairness and democracy.[7] These assumed societal benefits apply to plumbing shops and mid-sized high-tech companies alike. The 1980s witnessed a debate in the West—particularly the Anglo-Saxon world—on the future of mass production and the need for flexible specialization regimes in the economy to enter a new era of prosperity.[8] These debates had already occurred with similar arguments in the German-speaking world in the 1930s and 1940s.

Ideological flexibility

The economic policies of the SED are often chracterized as 'orthodox' and except for a short period in the mid-1960s as hostile to the experiments with economic reform undertaken by their Hungarian or Polish counterparts.[9] While some kind of entrepreneurial class emerged in Hungary and Poland from the 1960s onwards—so the narrative goes—East German party heads and economic functionaries basically sided with the Soviet representatives in the Council for Mutual Economic Assistance and stuck to old-school central planning.[10] This popular view of an ossified East German leadership was fostered by the hostility of Honecker and the Politburo to Gorbachev's reforms in the late 1980s. However, this outside view conceals important differences between the GDR and its socialist peers. At a second glance, the legacy of the Ulbricht and Honecker regimes could ignite sparks of hope in advocates of capitalism and of reformed socialism—like Christa Luft—alike.

In contrast to Poland and Czechoslovakia, where even the shops of small artisans and craftsmen were nationalized in the early 1950s, the newly established Stalinist regime in East Berlin never tried to nationalize the whole economy but established a fragile compromise with private entrepreneurs in its territory.[11] The southern parts of the GDR—Saxony and Thuringia—had traditionally been highly industrialized and dominated by small and medium-sized industrial companies. A sizable chunk of the owners of these companies fled to West Germany prior to 1961 taking their know-how and often their most skilled engineers with them. But a large part remained. They were given a choice: accept the supremacy of party rule and you can remain majority owner of your company. The party agitators were using the paroles that had worked well for the National Socialist Party in the 1930s by promising to shield the East German Mittelstand from global competition and offer guaranteed access to domestic markets.[12]

While the East German regime had nationalized all big industrial and trade companies, by the early 1950s small and medium-sized private companies still contributed 40 percent to domestic economic output.[13] This fact rendered any quick nationalization scheme dangerous and made compromise appear prudent. In the 1950s and early 1960s, when the SED introduced laws that privileged private companies which accepted a minority government interest and punished those companies which did not. Whatever its intentions, this move was no economic death sentence for private entrepreneurs in the GDR. While the number of private companies decreased in the GDR throughout the 1950s and 1960s, those who survived often prospered, became larger and were able to modernize their workshops and factory floors. This resilience and adaptability of the private sector led to repeated outbursts of anger in the Politburo, as on the occasion of one of its meetings in 1958 when the Politburo members were briefed that the remaining private sector in the GDR was accumulating capital at a faster rate than the state sector.[14] This made it clear to the SED leadership that without drastic political measures in the future private entrepreneurship would not simply fade away.

The end result was the emergence of a numerically diminished but decently capable East German Mittelstand that found its raison d'être as supplier of the large state combines.[15] This had basically happened in West Germany, as well, inspite of most large companies being privately owned.[16] This was also the state of cohabitation the last Communist government of the GDR wanted to get back to in 1989/90 that proved so unique in the Eastern Bloc. However, the situation of the 1960s was precarious and only appeared to have been harmonious in nature with hindsight and a great deal of selective perception.[17] (Semi-)Private entrepreneurs in the GDR operated under different levels of constant political pressure and were always in danger of being expropriated. In their day-to-day affairs they often had to live with the presence of a party cell and a party secretary in their companies who watched every move of the owner and were looking for remarks in opposition to the official party line.[18]

Paradise lost?

Although Walter Ulbricht had publicly guaranteed the existence of the East German Mittelstand in a socialist society up to the year 1990,[19] the events of 1972 proved a heavy but not fatal blow to East German entrepreneurs. In January 1972 the Politburo passed a set of laws that led to the nationalization of any private company with more than 10 employees. The reasons for this drastic measure are still disputed and not entirely clear. Although the GDR had enacted tax laws in December 1970 that made life for private companies harder in the GDR, it is possible that Honecker pushed for complete nationaliaztion to distance himself from the policies of his former mentor Walter Ulbricht.[20]

It is interesting to note that the GDR was nationalizing large parts of the remaining Mittelstand, while the rest of the world, in East and West alike, was slowly rediscovering the alleged benefits of having a vibrant sector of small and medium-sized companies. In the 1970s this applied particularly to the West. The crisis of large manufacturing companies that was fueled by the oil shock sparked a debate in economics and in society in general about the benefits of a social-economic model based on the wellbeing of 'big business'.[21] As the socialist development model hit more and more road blocks in the late 1960s and 1970s, interest in the development of small and medium-sized companies started to rise, as well.[22]

However, in the eyes of the SED leadership, the social and ideological costs of the relative economic success of the Mittelstand were at the root of the perceived problem. As parts of the Mittelstand were thriving in the 1960s, thus increasing the social differences between the companies' owners and the living conditions of the average East German citizen.[23] This could only increase the tensions between ideology and reality in East Germany. On the eve of the last big nationalization campaign in 1972, the share of (semi-)private companies in economic output amounted to ca. 15 percent and had remained stable since the building of the Berlin Wall.[24] This number was much lower than in the early 1950s but still much higher than in any other socialist country in East Central Europe. The events of 1972 affected ca. 12,000 companies with 500,000 employees which were hastily integrated into the large state combines.[25]

Nevertheless, the events of 1972 did not prove to be the end for the Mittelstand. On the one hand, most small companies could still operate under private ownership. On the other hand, a majority of the owners of the companies that were nationalized were later appointed managing directors transforming them from manager-owners to manager-employees.[26] The government of the GDR slightly reversed course four years later when new laws were enacted that encouraged private companies working in scarcely available crafts.[27] In 1980, the private sector in the GDR still employed 5.2 percent of the non-agricultural workforce. In Poland and Hungary the numbers stood at 4.9 and 3 percent respectively the same year.[28] In the mid-to-late 1980s there were more than one hundred thousand active private entrepreneurs left in the GDR. Although they only contributed 4 percent to economic output[29]—now less than their Polish counterparts—many of these companies filled the most urgent gaps in the consumer economy, particularly in the service sector. Repairs of broken domestic equipment and machines like cars were mostly done by private craftsmen. Even the housing program—central piece of Honecker's social policies—was impossible without the help of small private companies from the service sector.[30]

Most of the remaining owners had adapted to life under socialism and most of them enjoyed a decent standard of living. The personal income an entrepreneur could achieve varied from the equivalent of the average salary of a skilled worker for trades like a bicycle shop to twenty times the income of a skilled worker, if he or she was shrewd and owned a business that was in high demand like a repair shop for automobiles.[31] It is interesting to note that black market activity in the GDR seemed to be negatively correlated to the activity of (semi)private companies and therefore in opposition to the developments in other state socialist countries. Black market activity rose in the Honecker era after the expropriation campaign of 1972 and worsened in the 1980s.[32] It could be said that the expansion of black market activity in the GDR was a result of deliberate policies by the Honecker regime that weakened the domestic economy and gave West German currency and West German a semi-official role as East Germans could buy Western goods with Western currency in state-run stores.

The state of the Mittelstand that was expropriated in 1972 is still a matter of debate and played a large role in the political and scholarly debates of the 1990s. While some authors—like Rainer Karlsch—have argued in microstudies[33] that most of the companies were in a bitter state after twenty years of socialist rule, others—like Jörg Roesler—have pushed for the opposite position in their works and regarded the expropriation of the Mittelstand as the worst economic decision the SED ever made.[34] It is clear, though, that many of the almost twelve thousand companies that were nationalized in 1972 had mostly produced valuable consumer goods for export and domestic consumption.[35] Exceptions from this rule existed e.g. in the area around Chemnitz in Saxony, where a sizeable share of mid-sized machine-building companies was in operation. It is remarkable that many of the former private company owners that were expropriated in 1972 regarded the 1960s as their most glorious decade in interviews that were conducted in the 1990s.[36] Their personal sentiments were therefore in strange unison with the advocates of reformed socialism in the late GDR.[37]

The reasons for this were manifold, some of them lay in human nature, others were unique to the GDR: many of the former owners who were given a chance to reclaim their former property were more than twenty years younger in the 1960s seen from the point of 1990. Furthermore, the human mind tends to remember only good events and to suppress negative experiences that happened in the distant past. The policies of the SED meant that East German entrepreneurs were threatened from inside the GDR but rarely from the anonymous forces of the world market. When some of them tried to start anew in the early 1990s, the tables had turned and they glorified the GDR period in oral history projects.[38] A very specific reason for this positive picture of the 1960s in the mind of the former entrepreneurs could have been the unintended consequences of the economic reforms undertaken in the GDR in the 1960s. The reforms of the industrial pricing mechanisms increased the profits of the (semi)private sector in the second half of the 1960s by 14.6 percent to an average rate of return of 12.4 percent. This effect was based on a miscalculation by the economic reformers inside the planning commission.[39] The reformers themselves neither wanted to support private entrepreneurs in the GDR nor did they want to nationalize their companies in the short or mid-term.[40]

Peculiarities of East German 'entrepreneurship'

It has been argued by some economists like Werner Abelshauser that there were no entrepreneurs under state socialism. He argues that entrepreneurs are individuals who have to make decisions under the condition of uncertainty. They rely on elaborated networks to gather information and anticipate future developments. Since state socialism in its (Central) Eastern European form was a system where everything was meticulously planned, there was no space for entrepreneurs left. When strategic planning and resource allocation are outsourced to the state planning commission and branch ministries, why then should one need any visionary engineers and businessmen as company heads in state socialism? According to Abelshauser, there may have been managers in state socialism but no entrepreneurs.[41]

This point of view is buying too much into the narrative of the planning bureaucracy itself. It is a top-down perspective of how things should have worked on paper. In reality, communication between the state bureaucracy and the (state-owned) companies was not one-sided. Company offices occasionally found ways to lobby their own interests and to circumvent orders from the central bureaucracy.[42] They competed with their peers for scarce resources like material and labour, but on the other hand had to cooperate with them to thwart orders from the center they considered inappropriate and to anticipate future developments in the state planning agencies and technological developments in their field. Although they could not technically go bankrupt, it was often unwise for the leadership of a state socialist company to remain idle. Production facilities could be relocated, careers disrupted, privileges revoked, if one did not choose his or her moves wisely.

This applied in an amplified way to (semi-)private companies and their leadership. As they were—in the case of the GDR in the 1960s—superficially integrated in the planning system, they stood on the lower end of the planning hierarchy. Large state combines commanded greater lobbying power and privileged access to scarce input factors. Furthermore, the former owners of private enterprises were more susceptible to state prosecution than their peers who had started their careers as party appointees without a capitalist past. Although the system was far from being rigged in their favor, a sizeable number of private entrepreneurs accomodated to the new situation and prospered. Some of them survived till 1989. This achievement was not due to their passivity or being merely 'managers' or administrators, it was rooted in their entrepreneurial skills.

Andrei Yudanov made the point for the USSR that the Soviet economy knew only one single type of company, large volume-producers.[43] Even technically small enterprises with a few hundred or less employees in the former Soviet Union behaved like large enterprises.[44] They pursued a volume strategy, just with smaller batch sizes and therefore even less efficiently than their larger brethren. Yudanov states that a company can pursue four different strategies to be successful: volume strategy, niche strategy, customized strategy, and innovative strategy. For an economy to prosper, all strategies have to be present on the macro level. Companies that produce goods of average quality cheaply and in large numbers are as much needed as highly innovative companies which push the giants of industry into the future and companies that focus on small batches of highly specialized products or that offer customized products and services on short notice.

The small and medium sized companies that remained (semi-)private in the German Democratic Republic could not be called innovative. The innovative entrepreneurs of the East German Mittelstand had either emigrated to Western Germany before 1961 or transformed their companies' character under state socialism.[45] Most companies of the Mittelstand in East Germany had not been of a particularly innovative character before the advent of state socialism, as well. The bulk of these enterprises consisted of family-run companies with artisanal traditions, deeply rooted in their region. However, what some of them retained under socialism was a preference for niche and customized strategies. They performed these strategies quite well in the 1960s in cohabitation with the large state combines. The nationalization campaign of 1972 decimated the Mittelstand and lowered its ability to excel in the respective strategies, but it did not annihilate the entrepreneurial spirit completely; nor did the events of 1972 completely disrupt the functions performed by private companies in the GDR. Compared with Yudanov's statements on the Soviet Union, the East German economy in 1989 was thus in a much better structural position, as East German companies performed more than one function.

The road to reformed socialism

On November 17, three days after his election by the East German Parliament (Volkskammer)—Hans Modrow delivered his first comprehensive policy statement. Reunification was at that time not on the table. As it became clear that the authority of the SED had taken a serious blow in the course of 1989, the Modrow government decided to incorporate parts of the opposition in December 1989, at first in informal round table discussions. Parts of the opposition, particularly of the dissident movement in East Germany, were sympathetic to ideas of reformed socialism and of a 'third way' that avoided the mistakes of Stalinism and Capitalism alike. On November 17 Modrow stated the following on his plans for the economy:

> "This government is committed to the people who want a good form of socialism [...] Such kind of socialism, which can only develop into a performance-oriented society through the labour of its citizens, can provide for the social security of its members within the frame of its economic results [...] We will utilize this substance, the great public property in the industrial and in other sectors of the economy, and make it increasingly powerful [...] We commit ourselves to socialist entrepreneurial spirit. This does not only apply to the company and combine directors of the socialist sector, but to all private companies, independent craftsmen, down to the retail and restaurant sector. We consider the acquisition of small companies by private entrepreneurs in the consumer goods industry—but not only there—possible. We all together have to think about the size of such companies."[46]

By the accounts of its own state bureaucracy, the economic output of the GDR had started to decline in October 1989. In its projection for 1990 the Council of Ministers expected a sharp recession with an annual decline in output by up to five percent. The output of some key sectors like the construction industry was expected to slump to the levels of the early 1980s. However, there were some bright spots in the reports from early 1990, as well. A decline in output did not necessarily equate to a decline in productivity, as the population base was shrinking and thus the need to supply the same quantities of consumer goods as in 1989. Furthermore, imports declined more than exports, so that the economic planners could report a monthly export surplus to the non-socialist world of 150 million US-$ for January 1990.[47]

A draft version the task force for economic reform presented to the Council of Ministers called for a multi-layered framework of short- and medium-term reforms to be enacted in stages from early 1990 to 1994.[48] The authors of the document related their work to the public statements Hans Modrow had made on 17 November in the East German Volkskammer. The short-term aims for reform were to stabilize the economy and to lay the groundwork for rising productivity and increasing global competitiveness of East German companies, thereby maintaining the level of social security achieved in the late GDR. Interestingly, this should be achieved by closer cooperation within the CMEA—the survival of which was taken for granted in early 1990—as well as by some form of cooperation of the GDR with the European Community and the Bretton Woods institutions.[49]

When it came to ownership reform the paper called for equal opportunities for all forms of ownership by granting freedom of trade, equal tax and wage regulations as well as equal access to capital, labour, and material resources for private companies, cooperatives, and state combines. Rewarding and nurturing personal merit in any form 'should encourage the entrepreneurial spirit of all workers and give way to free their productive forces'.[50] All companies should gain legal independence. As Christa Luft had stated in West Berlin in February

1990, the paper called for a transition to a 'social and ecologically oriented market economy'. The economic reform paper defined as 'decisive steps' for such a transition:

> "the immediate opening up of space for entrepreneurship in all forms of ownership and the creation of an independent development of the relations between producers, commerce, and consumers on the domestic market accompanied by a sizeable increase in number of independent companies [...] Establishing forms of broad democratic participation of the public in economic policy making and in the company decisions by the respective employees [...] Besides state-owned property a multitude of different forms of ownership is to be established to develop production for a market economy."[51]

The authors of the paper explicitely called for the creation of possibilities to re-privatize the small and medium-sized companies that were incorporated into the state combine system in 1972. Doing so was part of the short-term goals to be achieved in 1990. This included creating the prerequisites for joint ventures between state combines and Western companies to acquire modern technology. The possibility of joint ventures between Western and East German companies had already drawn attention in late November 1989, as the documents on a meeting between Christa Luft and William Roth, US Senator from Delaware, in East Berlin on 28 November 1989 show.[52] Senator Roth was not the only American interested in the policy ideas of the new SED leaders. When the Chairman of the House Small Business Committee, John J. LaFalce, together with thirteen members of Congress visited East Berlin in January 1990, he was briefed on the plans to create a system of equal opportunities for all forms of ownership and to foster the growth of (semi-)private small businesses.[53]

These meetings did not take place solely for economic reasons. The East German leadership thought it could use other Western powers like the US to become less dependent on economic cooperation with West Germany and thereby less susceptible to political blackmail.[54] For this strategy to work, Western leaders—apart from the government in Bonn—had to regard the preservation of the territorial status quo in Europe as being in their own interest. The time table for economic reform in East Germany laid out in early 1990 went up to the mid-1990s. The mid-term goals set for the time period 1991–94 focused on full convertibility of the East German Mark and a gradual liberalisation of prices and wages.[55] However, by calling for equal opportunities for all forms of ownership, the language of the economic reform document resembled the promises made by the SED in the late 1940s when its leaders had stated the same.[56]

The question was, if they were serious this time, and if they had enough time left. To gather support for economic reform, the government had to build up trust. On 11 January 1990, the Volkskammer had passed an amendment to the constitution of the GDR allowing private ownership of resources, factories and means of production. The minister of economic affairs, Christa Luft, did not dodge public debate. Her statements from February 1990 were no outlier. Two days after the Volkskammer had passed the amendment, she stood in front of a mixed East-Western audience at the prestigious Institute for Business Management[57] on the outskirts of East Berlin and explained:

> "Property reform forms the basis of economic reform by pushing back common phenomena of alienation of work, of anonimity of property, of passivity as well as of irresponsibility. Unjustified limits and constraints of private initiative as well as private and cooperative forms of ownership—which were common and are still common today—are rectified [...] Next to

securing and strengthening state ownership which will continue to remain strong—particularly in the sectors of heavy industry, energy, transportation, and other key sectors—other forms of ownership will experience significant development:

- cooperative property in its current and in new suitable forms;[58]

- private property, including the ownership of industrial companies;

- mixed property in a national and international context"[59]

Jump-starting the private economy

It was clear to the East German politicians in charge that such unprecedented but still gradual reforms would 'free up' a sizeable part of the workforce currently employed in the large state combines. Increasing the productivity of the state sector meant a higher output per employee. This could be done by modernizing the technologies used in the production process and by laying off workers that were not directly needed on the factory floor after the introduction of new machines and technology or had belonged to the group of the 'hidden unemployed' beforehand. A sizeable part of the economic reform proposals focused on maintaining social security while at the same time relocating a large part of the workforce to different economic sectors. A booming infant private sector could allow the large state combines to regain competitiveness, while absorbing the social costs associated with economic reform. In late January 1990 the Modrow government calculated with 100,000 workers and office clerks who would immediately lose their jobs at the beginning of the reform process with more to come.[60] The primary goal was therefore not to rapidly build up 'hidden champions' trying to replicate West German reality but to buy time for the large state combines and support their restructuring by more efficient supply chains.

The basic laws that had decimated the East German Mittelstand in the early 1970s were the tax laws of December 1970 and the set of laws that allowed for an easy nationalization in 1972. The road to a rejuvenated Mittelstand had to tackle these two obstacles. The draft version for a new tax code dealt with the events of 1970 and explicitely referred to them. Self-employed freelance work was taxed at thirty percent. The cooperatives of craftsmen[61] that had thrived during the 1960s should experience a jump-start by explicitly restoring the tax code of 1962 and declaring the changes of 1970 void. No legal nor natural person should be taxed at a higher rate than 75 percent, if all taxes were added up. Property taxes were to be lowered from 2.5 to 1 percent. In general, the marginal tax rate on profits of corporations and business partnerships was to peak at 60 percent. What may still sound like confiscatory taxation from today's point of view was a huge tax cut. For most parts of the 1970s and 1980s the marginal tax rates for (semi-)private businesses and corporations had peaked at 95 percent.[62]

Under the old tax code an annual private gross income of 30,000 Mark—a sum that was in reach for a high-ranking state-employed professional, as well –faced a marginal tax rate of 56 percent, if the person in question was a craftsman, and 84 percent, if the respective person happened to be the owner of a corporation. The aim of this unprecedented and probably largest 'tax cut' in the history of the GDR was as follows:

> By lowering taxes we are creating incentives for the small and medium-sized businesses to fully utilize their capacities and to unlock their reserves.[63]

The tax cuts were estimated to dent state revenues by 3.24 billion Marks with the largest revenue losses on income taxes of highly skilled professionals with university degrees and craftsmen, as the taxes of ordinary factory and unskilled workers remained untouched. Interestingly, there were at least a few hundred persons in the GDR who had officially earned close to or even more than one hundred thousand Mark in annual income, many of them were self-employed artists, writers or acclaimed physicians.[64]

In February 1990 the Council of Ministers started to debate a set of laws that would allow the reprivatization of the companies expropriated in 1972. As was the case with the reformed tax code, the new law explicitely referred to the events of the early 1970s, this time to February 1972. The former owners and their heirs could file a motion to regain their former company within a time period of six months after the law had passed. A decision had to be made by the respective regional administration within three months.[65] The law applied to the former cooperatives of craftsmen[66] and (semi-)private industrial companies alike.[67] It was passed in early March 1990 just before the parliamentary elections under the name 'law on founding and running private companies and on shares in companies'[68]

This law was of a very peculiar character. Although it implicitely acknowledged that the expropriations of 1972 were wrong, it presented them as ordinary business transactions, as reprivatization came attached with a price tag. The former owners were not simply given back their property but they had to buy it back from the state and could only buy back the stakes that changed hands in 1972 not the parts the government had acquired prior to 1972. The involuntary character of the nationalization campaign of 1972 had been masked by 'sales agreements' which forced the private owners to sell their stakes at artificially low prices. The sum was then transferred to a trustee account at the state bank from which the 'seller' could only draw a limited sum annually. This sum was then also taxed according to the new tax code of December 1970.

This meant that the 'spirit' of the law was to recreate the situation of the 1960s by pretending that 1972 did not happen. This led to a series of angry letters to the Volkskammer and Council of Ministers. At least a sizeable part of the potential reprivatizers considered the terms of the law inappropriate. Some demanded compensation, others feared that even if they could pay the sums demanded they didn't command the financial resources to modernize the companies and invest in new technology.[69]

The past that never was

As the Modrow government was ousted following the parliamentary elections in March 1990, the economic reforms envisioned by the last socialist government of the GDR remained vague and were never fully enacted. Christa Luft had talked repeatedly about creating a market economy in East Germany. She made clear in her speeches that any reform should go further than what had been discussed in the CMEA before 1989. Yet, how far, remained unclear. There was no shock therapy planned that foreshadowed later approaches. Neither was there any reference to Deng Xiaopings's reforms in China. When the reform proposal of January 1990 was discussed, the Council of Ministers cautioned on emphasizing the term market economy in the reform proposals—even if always used with the attributes social and ecological—and warned that 'market economy is no social order'.[70]

The reforms that were enacted and laws passed by the Modrow government point at a particularly 'reactionary' character with relation to private entrepreneurship. As the laws of the early 1970s that had led to the expropriation of large parts of the East German Mittelstand were declared void, the economic structure of the 1960s was to be recreated. The laws on taxes and reprivatization either implicitely or explicitely refered to this 'golden age' of East German socialism. The goal was not to find a smooth way for transition to capitalism. The goal was to maintain the essence of socialism. This is not to say that the last socialist government of the GDR was not serious about transforming East Germany into a much less repressive state with free elections and a marginalized security apparatus. However, the search for a past that never was, was the essence of a sizeable part of the reform program.

The point of reference for such an endeavor was unique and due to the particular twists and turns of GDR history. At least implicitly, this meant the end of Marxist teleology and the approach of communism. The search for a 'good' socialism and for a point in the past, where socialism diverged from the right way, however, was not unique to the reform-oriented wing of the SED represented by Hans Modrow and his government. Gorbachev and his political allies looked mainly for the Leninist heritage of Soviet culture and politics and tried to identify the fundamentals for 'good' socialism in the 1920s. Only with the advent of Stalinism did socialism in the Soviet Union take the wrong turn. It is interesting that terms like NEP,[71] or references to more recent Polish, Hungarian, and Yugoslav policy experiments never turn up in the internal documents on reform proposals of the Modrow government.

This does not necessarily prove that East German reform socialists never looked East but it hints at a rather narrow mind map. There is evidence for several meetings between Christa Luft and Hungarian representatives to discuss matters of economic cooperation. However, economic reforms and issues of learning from each other's experiences had to be discussed alongside urgent trade issues at these bilateral East German-Hungarian meetings. Both sides were interested in maintaining their level of economic exchange. The GDR and FRG were two of the biggest trade partners of Hungary and the ambassador of Hungary wanted his country to profit from increased cooperation between the two Germanies.[72] In mid-February 1990, Christa Luft traveled to Hungary herself, where she met with the Prime Minister Miklós Németh and his deputy Péter Medgyessy among others.[73] The archival evidence shows that Christa Luft and her colleagues from the Council of Ministers took the Hungarian leadership more seriously than their Polish neighbor that underwent painful socio-economic change at the same time.

Christa Luft claimed in the books she published after reunification that reform-minded East German economists like her were actively looking for inspiration outside the GDR, particularly when it came down to ideas to reform public ownership and 'democratize the economy'. The attitude of the workers to the large public combines had to change according to her account. What she characterized as an attitude of anonimity was to become a more lively and intimate relationship. Workers should identify with the publicly owned factories and recognize that they were stakeholders of socialism. Luft claimed that the East German debates were inspired by the Yugoslav example and the Kibbuzim in Israel.[74] However, there is no archival evidence that such discussions had any influence on the planned legislation and reform debates inside the cabinet in early 1990. As Christa Luft and other important actors in the last SED government like Hans Modrow published their memories and thoughts on politics with considerable delay, there is no clear link. Although the GDR reestablished working relations with Yugoslavia after Stalin's death, this did not apply to Israel. The SED entertained close relations with the Baathist regimes in Syria and Iraq but not with Israel. This makes it unlikely that Kibbuzim could be studied and discussed by East German scholars.

The term 'social market economy' that was often used by Christa Luft and appears in several documents, as well, is misleading. On a first look it either sounds like a marketing trick to find a more sympathetic audience in West Germany or as if the last socialist government of the GDR had planned to simply copy the West German 'success model'. Neither is true. Christa Luft later called the market 'a historic achievement of human civilization', a means of consumer emancipation and the liberation of productive forces.[75] At the center of her vision of a social market economy was competition combined with a right to work for everyone. Private ownership played only a marginal role in this variant of 'social market economy'. That was the basic reason why privatizations were only part of the reform program of early 1990 and not at the heart of reform.[76] The term was a shell for a varety of meanings in East Central European politics in 1990. József Antall, who became prime minister of Hungary in April 1990, used the term in his speeches, as well, but with more direct and positive references to the West German economic model.[77]

Legacy

There is no comprehensive political legacy of the last socialist East German government when it comes to the socio-economic reforms enacted in late 1989 and early 1990. The notable exception is the Mittelstand. By bringing up the topic which it did not need to do despite mounting political pressure, the Modrow government set the frame for future debate and political action. Defining the group of company owners expropriated in 1972 as a special group, thereby privileging them, and distinguishing them from other groups of entrepreneurs that were forced out of business or forced to leave the country by the SED's policies between 1949 and 1989, was to a certain extent quite arbitrary.

This prominence can only be explained by taking two things into account: the nationalization campaign of 1972 was not the only one that had occurred in the GDR but it was the last one that could be pinned down to a certain date. Most often expropriations had occurred in regional nationalization campaigns or on a small-scale but continuous basis. This made it easier to frame the citizens affected by the events of 1972 as a comprehensive social group. Second, and more important, the nationalization campaign of 1972 was accompanied by the notion that this was to be the final economic sin of the GDR that will eventually lead to its downfall. At least with hindsight, even leading figures of the regime, like Gerhard Schürer, the head of the state planning commission, claimed to have harbored strong negative sentiments for the nationalization campaign.[78] Such statements at the time of the East German transformation contributed to the myth of a somewhat glorious past, the prospects of which were cut off by events like the nationalizations of 1972.

Even the newly formed East German 'Association of Entrepreneurs'[79] focused on the group of 1972. In a letter to the president of the newly elected East German parliament, the head of the association, Rudolf Stadermann, wrote on 12 April 1990:

> The Association of Entrepreneurs of the GDR feels indebted to those members whose companies were nationalized in 1972 and who demand—within the realm of their newly acquired freedom—compensation for the lost profits, interest, and other ownership rights. We support

> the conditions of the law passed on 7 March 1990 to transform the formerly expropirated private companies, companies with public interest, and cooperatives of craftsmen, into private property in accordance with the conditions that led to their transformation to public property in 1972.[80]

This nurtured excessive expectations on a reemergent East German Mittelstand that were unrealistic to begin with, because they were based on a highly idealized past. East German entrepreneurs had proved surprisingly resilient during 40 years of socialism. Despite all attempts to expropriate all forms of private companies the GDR leadership had to accept that it could not do without some form of private entrepreneurship to stabilize its rule and to supply the populace with urgently needed consumer goods and services the state sector was unable to provide on a sustainable basis.

However, this relationship went both ways. The expectation of many East German citizens, Western politicans and privatizers of the Treuhandanstalt alike was that freed from its shackles, the surviving Mittelstand would rise up again and become the core engine of growth, much the way it historically had been up to the Second World War.[81] Measured by the high expectations of 1990 the Mittelstand rather imploded, particularly the reprivatized companies. In 1997, only 2,700 of the companies that were nationalized in 1972 and reprivatized after 1989 were still active and only 500 of them were not on the brink of bankruptcy.[82] The reasons for this relative underperformance were manifold, most of them related to the way economic reunification was organized. However, there is one cultural argument made by Andreas Pickel in the early 1990s that deserves further scrutiny.

He argued—quite convincingly—that the GDR would have been the socialist state best suited to adopt a gradual reform program to a market economy, because it had been the only country in the former socialist bloc with a strong legacy of legal private entrepreneurship that was accepted by large parts of party and society and functioned relatively smoothly with comparatively low levels of corruption. Although a black market economy existed in the GDR as well, its scale was not as large and its consequences not as disruptive as in other state socialist countries. Black market activity was not generally associated with entrepreneurship or small-scale enterprises. Managers and former owners of (semi) private companies and managers of state combines were used to a decades-long history of mutual cooperation. The shock therapy that was imposed with reunification had doomed the remaining East German Mittelstand, because most East German entrepreneurs had adopted many cultural and business norms of state socialism in order to survive in some kind of cohabitation with the state sector. Leaving them no time to adopt to their new life in capitalism, they went down together with the particular form of society they had managed to exist in for fourty years.[83]

Notes

1. Hochschule für Ökonomie Bruno Leuschner.
2. The correct translation of her position is 'Deputy of the Head of the Council of Ministers for the Economy.' For all practical purposes her position equaled the post of a minister of economic affairs.
3. Deutscher Industrie- und Handelstag (DIHT) in German.
4. „Dem Mittelstand kommt eine Schlüsselrolle zu.'
5. Luft, 'Dem Mittelstand Kommt Eine Schlüsselrolle Zu,' 17.
6. See on West German economic policies towards small- and medium-sized companies Ritschl, 'Soziale Marktwirtschaft.'

7. See Böhm, 'Bedeutung Des Mittelstands'; Röpke, 'Funktion Des Klein- Und Mittelbetriebes'; Rüstow, *Zwischen Kapitalismus Und Kommunismus*. Mittelstand and Mittelschicht are overlapping yet different concepts. The focus in this paper is on Mittelstand in the sense of businesses run by owner-managers.
8. Piore and Sabel, *The Second Industrial Divide*, 17, 258.
9. See on the economic reforms in the GDR between 1962 and 1970 Steiner, 'Reformen in Der DDR.'
10. See e.g. Sobell, *The Red Market*, 30; Ambrosius, 'Sozialistische Planwirtschaft,' 20–24; Brabant, *Economic Integration in Eastern Europe*, 76–81.
11. Pickel, *Radical Transition*, 12.
12. Ebbinghaus, *Ausnutzung Und Verdrängung*, 345.
13. Ebbinghaus, 10.
14. Ebbinghaus, 90–91.
15. Although the output of the state sector was larger than the output of the private sector, due to the large size of state companies, the number of fully state-owned companies was smaller than the one of (semi)private companies throughout the 1960s.
16. See Winkler, 'Stabilisierung Durch Schrumpfung.' There were, of course, notable exceptions like Telekom, Post, Volkswagen and the Preussag Holding.
17. See on the ambiguities of SED policies in the late 1950s/early 1960s Ebbinghaus, *Ausnutzung Und Verdrängung*, 114–19.
18. See as an example on this kind of surveillance – apart from what the secret service did – the reports by the SED regional committee (SED Kreisleitung Gotha) in Gotha in Thuringia, in: Landesarchiv Thüringen – Hauptstaatsarchiv Weimar, SED Kreisleitung Gotha IV A/4.05/074.
19. Müller, *Wiederbegründung Der Industrie- Und Handelskammern*, 35.
20. Ebbinghaus, *Ausnutzung Und Verdrängung*, 24–25.
21. Atkinson and Lind, *Big Is Beautiful*, 12–14.
22. Åslund, *Private Enterprise in Eastern Europe*, 2, 19–20. The revitalisation of the private sector was much less linear than in Hungary and its reemergence threatened again at roughly the same time the last nationaliaztion campaign occurred in the GDR:
23. Steiner, 'Re-Kapitalisierung Oder Sozialisierung,' 250–51.
24. Müller, *Wiederbegründung Der Industrie- Und Handelskammern*, 39–40.
25. Pickel, *Radical Transition*, 12–13. The numbers are a bit fuzzy, as one can find statements in the research literature ranging from 8,500 to 12,000 companies that were nationalized in 1972.
26. Müller, *Wiederbegründung Der Industrie- Und Handelskammern*, 36.
27. Pickel, *Radical Transition*, 101–4.
28. Pickel, 12–13.
29. Müller, *Wiederbegründung Der Industrie- Und Handelskammern*, 39.
30. Müller, 38–39; Pickel, *Radical Transition*, 12.
31. Pickel, *Radical Transition*, 165–66.
32. Zatlin, *The Currency of Socialism*, 172–81.
33. Karlsch, 'Die Kapitalistischen Betriebe.'
34. Gerlach, *Mitverantwortlich*, 133; Roesler, *Zwischen Plan Und Markt*, 90; Ebbinghaus, *Ausnutzung Und Verdrängung*, 9–10.
35. Steiner, 'Re-Kapitalisierung Oder Sozialisierung,' 244.
36. Pickel, *Radical Transition*, 188.
37. Pickel, 188.
38. See Arp, *Vaters Ehemaliger Betrieb*.
39. Steiner, 'Re-Kapitalisierung Oder Sozialisierung,' 217.
40. Steiner, 264.
41. Abelshauser, *Deutsche Wirtschaftsgeschichte*, 405–6.
42. See Germuska, 'Business History of Communist Enterprises'; Scranton, 'Managing Communist Enterprises.'
43. Yudanov, 'USSR,' 414.
44. Yudanov, 416.

45. The success of the West German 'Mittelstand' after 1945 is closely linked to the brain drain of East German management and engineering know-how.
46. 'Hans Modrow: Regierungserklärung Am 17.11.1989.'
47. „Mitteilung zur wirtschaftlichen und sozialen Entwicklung der DDR im Januar 1990,' dated 13 February 1990, Bundesarchiv Berlin, DE 10/135.
48. „Zielstellung, Grundrichtungen, Etappen und unmittelbare Maßnahmen der Wirtschaftsreform in weiterer Verwirklichung der Regierungserklärung vom 17.11.1989,' dated 29 January 1990, Bundesarchiv Berlin, DA/3/93.
49. Ibid.
50. Ibid.
51. Ibid.
52. „Vermerk über ein Gespräch der Genossinnen Prof. Dr. Christa Luft, Stellvertreter des Vorsitzenden des Ministerrates der DDR und Uta Nickel, Minister der Finanzen und Preise der DDR, mit USA-Senator William Roth, Republikanische Partei, am 28. November 1989 im Hause des Ministerrates der DDR,' Bundesarchiv Berlin, DC 20/17987.
53. „Gespräch mit einer Delegation des Repräsentantenhauses des USA-Kongresses unter Leitung des Abgeordneten John J. LaFalce, Vorsitzender des Ausschusses für das Klein- und Mittelunternehmertum, am 11.1.90, um 17.00 Uhr,' Bundesarchiv Berlin, DC 20/17987.
54. Ibid.
55. „Zielstellung, Grundrichtungen, Etappen und unmittelbare Maßnahmen der Wirtschaftsreform in weiterer Verwirklichung der Regierungserklärung vom 17.11.1989,' dated 29 January 1990, Bundesarchiv Berlin, DA/3/93.
56. Boldorf, *Governance in Der Planwirtschaft*, 178; Ebbinghaus, *Ausnutzung Und Verdrängung*, 33.
57. Institut für Unternehmensführung in Rahnsdorf.
58. This refers to the PGHs.
59. „Vortrag von Frau Professor Dr. Christa Luft Stellvertretende Vorsitzende des Ministerrates für Wirtschaft auf einer Beratung führender Vertreter aus Wirtschaft und Politik der Bundesrepublik Deutschaldn und der Deutschen Demokratischen Republik im Institut für Unternehmensführung Berlin am 13. Januar 1990,' Bundesarchiv Berlin, DC 20/11379.
60. 'Vorschläge für auszuarbeitende Maßnahmen und Regelungen zur Lösung der mit volkswirtschaftlichen Strukturveränderungen verbundenen Arbeitskräfte- und sozialen Fragen,' dated 23 January 1990, Bundesarchiv Berlin, DE 10/135. The government that followed after the parliamentary elections in March 1990 immediately publicized the quantitative aim of 500,000 new jobs in small and medium-sized enterprises by the end of 1990 in its first address to parliament in early April. By coincidence or on purpose this number equaled the size of the workforce incorporated into the combine system in 1972.
61. Produktionsgenossenschaften des Handwerks (PGH).
62. „Gesetz zur Änderung der Rechtsvorschriften über die Einkommen-, Körperschaft- und Vermögenssteuer sowie die Lohnsteuer,' early 1990, Bundesarchiv Berlin, DC 20/11378.
63. Ibid.
64. Ibid.
65. Bezirksverwaltung.
66. PGH.
67. „Gesetz über die Gründung und Tätigkeit privater Unternehmen und über Unternehmensbeteiligungen zur Förderung privater Initiativen zur Entfaltung des Unternehmertums,' dated 23 February 1990, Bundesarchiv Berlin, DE 10/135.
68. Gesetz über die Gründung und Tätigkeit privater Unternehmen und über Unternehmensbeteiligungen.
69. See e.g. the petitions in: Bundesarchiv Berlin, DE 10/156 and DE 10/326.
70. „Festlegungsprotokoll der Beratung des Wirtschaftskabinetts am 22.1.1990 unter Leitung des Stellvertreters des Vorsitzenden des Ministerrates für Wirtschaft, Frau Prof. Dr. Luft,' Bundesarchiv Berlin, DC 20/9126.
71. The New Economic Policy (NEP) was introduced in 1921 after the failed experiments with War Communism. NEP allowed for market elements as well small as small-scale private entrepre-

neurship and led to a recovery of the economy after the civil war. NEP was ended by Stalin in favor of forced industrialization programs.

72. This included interest in some kind of „Gastarbeiterprogramm'between Hungary and the GDR where young Hungarians would go to the GDR for work. Furthermore, Hungarian companies should serve as suppliers for the East and West German automotive industries in case of a closer cooperation between the two. „Vermerk über ein Gespräch mit dem Botschafter der Republik Ungarn am 18.1.1990,' dated 18 January 1990, Bundesarchiv Berlin DC 20/17987.
73. Christa Luft also met with members of the liberal opposition from SZDSZ. Medgyessy, who became Prime Minister of Hungary himself in 2002, was her main negotiating partner. 'Information über den Besuch des Stellvertreters des Vorsitzenden des Ministerrates für Wirtschaft in der Republik Ungarn am 23. Februar 1990, dated 26 February 1990, Bundesarchiv Berlin DC 20/17987.
74. Luft, *Lust Am Eigentum*, 19.
75. Luft, 19–20.
76. Luft, 21–23.
77. Ákos, 'A szociális piacgazdaság Antall József programjában—Antall József közelről.—Így történt.hu.'
78. Ebbinghaus, *Ausnutzung Und Verdrängung*, 9.
79. Unternehmerverband der DDR.
80. Letter by Rudolf Stadermann to Dr. Bergmann-Pohl, dated 12 April 1990, Bundesarchiv Berlin DE 10/155.
81. Pickel, *Radical Transition*, 196–97.
82. Karlsch, 'Die Kapitalistischen Betriebe,' 30.
83. Pickel, *Radical Transition*, 190–91.

Disclosure statement

No potential conflict of interest was reported by the author(s).

References

Abelshauser, W. (2011). *Deutsches Wirtschaftsgeschichte: Von 1945 Bis Zur Gegenwart* (2nd ed.). C.H. Beck.

Ákos, B. P. A szociális piacgazdaság Antall József programjában—Antall József közelről.—Így történt.hu. Retrieved December 7, 2018, from https://antalljozsef.igytortent.hu/szolgalatban/kormanyfokent/gazdasagpolitika/107-a-szocialis-piacgazdasag-antall-jozsef-programjaban.html

Ambrosius, G. (2006). Sozialistische Planwirtschaft' Als Alternative Und Variante in Der Industriegesellschaft—Die Wirtschaftsordnung. In André Steiner (Ed.), *Überholen Ohne Einzuholen. Die DDR Als Fußnote Der Deutschen Geschichte?* (pp. 11–32).

Arp, A. (2005). *VEB, vaters ehemaliger Betrieb: Privatunternehmer in Der DDR*. Militzke.

Åslund, A. (1985). *Private enterprise in Eastern Europe: The non-agricultural private sector in Poland and the GDR, 1945–83*. St. Martin's Press.

Atkinson, R. D., & Lind, M. (2018). *Big is beautiful: Debunking the myth of small business*. MIT Press.

Böhm, F. (1956). Die Bedeutung Des MIttelstands Und Die Ursachen Seiner Gefährdung. In *Der Mittelständische Unternehmer in Der Sozialen Marktwirtschaft. Wortlaut Der Vorträge Auf Der Vierten Arbeitstagung Der Aktionsgemeinschaft Soziale Marktwirtschaft e.V. Am 17. November 1955 in Bad Godesberg* (pp. 9–20). Martin Hoch.

Boldorf, M. (n.d.). *Governance in Der Planwirtschaft: Industrielle Führungskräfte in Der Stahl-Und Der Textilbranche Der SBZ—DDR (1945–1958)*. De Gruyter Oldenbourg.

Brabant, J. M. V. (1989). *Economic integration in Eastern Europe: A handbook*. Routledge.

Ebbinghaus, F. (2003). *Ausnutzung Und Verdrängung: Steuerungsprobleme Der SED-Mittelstandspolitik 1955–1972*. Duncker & Humblot. https://opacplus.bsb-muenchen.de/search?isbn=3428108663&db=100.

Gerlach, M. (1991). *Mitverantwortlich: Als Liberaler Im SED-Staat*. Morgenbuch.

Germuska, P. (2018). What can we learn from the business history of communist enterprises? *Enterprise & Society*, *19*(3), 538–545. https://doi.org/10.1017/eso.2018.14

Hans Modrow: Regierungserklärung Am 17.11.1989. Retrieved November 27, 2018, from http://www.glasnost.de/hist/ddr/89regerkl.html

Karlsch, R. (2016). 'Die Kapitalistischen Betriebe, Die Sich Halbstaatlich Nennen, Müssen Wir Liquidieren': Der Letzte Schlag Gegen Den Dresdner Mittelstand Im Frühjahr 1972 (Justus H. Ulbricht, Ed.). *Dresdner Hefte 34*(4), 24–31.

Luft, C. (1990). Dem Mittelstand Kommt Eine Schlüsslrolle Zu. In Deutscher Industrie- und Handelstag (Ed.), *DIHT-Kongreß Deutsch-Deutscher Marktplatz 13. Februar 1990 in Berlin (West)* (pp. 16–21). Deutscher Industrie- und Handelstag.

Luft, C. (1996). *Die Lust Am Eigentum: Auf Den Spuren Der Deutschen Treuhand*. Orell Füssli.

Müller, J. (2017). *Die Wiederbegründung Der Industrie- Und Handelskammern in Ostdeutschland Im Prozess Der Wiedervereinigung. Vierteiljahreschrift Für Sozial-Und Wirtschaftsgeschichte*. Franz Steiner. https://opacplus.bsb-muenchen.de/metaopac/search?isbn=9783515115650&db=100

Pickel, A., et al. (1992). *Radical Transition: The Survival and Revival of Entrepreneurship in the GDR*. Westview Pr.

Piore, M. J., & Sabel, C. F. (1984). *The second industrial divide: Possibilities for prosperity*. Basic Books.

Ritschl, A. (2016). Soziale Marktwirtschaft in Der Praxis. In Werner Abelshauseret al. (Eds.), *Das Bundeswirtschaftsministerium in Der Ära Der Sozialen Marktwirtschaft. Der Deutsche Weg Der Wirtschaftspolitik* (Vol. 4, pp. 265–389). Wirtschaftspolitik in Deutschland 1917–1990. De Gruyter Oldenbourg.

Roesler, J. (1991). *Zwischen Plan Und Markt: Die Wirtschaftsreform in Der DDR Zwischen 1963 Und 1970*. Haufe.

Röpke, W. (1947). Die Funktion Des Klein- Und Mittelbetriebes in Der Volkswirtschaft. In *Handwerk Und Kleinhandel in Der Modernen Volkswirtschaft. Entwicklungsmöglichkeiten Und Rechtsgrundlagen* (pp. 19–40). Fehr.

Rüstow, A. (1949). *Zwischen Kapitalismus Und Kommunismus*. Helmut Küpper.

Scranton, P. (2018). Managing communist enterprises: Poland, Hungary, and Czechoslovakia, 1945–1970. *Enterprise & Society*, *19*(3), 492–537. September https://doi.org/10.1017/eso.2018.13

Sobell, V. (1984). *The red market. Industrial co-operation and specialisation in comecon*. Gower.

Steiner, A. (2006). Reformen in Der DDR Der Sechziger Jahre: Planwirtschaft Auf Dem Weg Zum Markt. In Christoph Boyer (Ed.), *Sozialistische Wirtschaftsreformen in Der Tschechoslowakei Und DDR Im Vergleich* (pp. 125–190). Vittorio Klostermann.

Steiner, A. (2006). Re-Kapitalisierung Oder Sozialisierung? DIe Privaten Und Halbstaatlichen Betriebe in Der DDR-Wirtschaftsreform Der Sechziger Jahre. In Christoph Boyer (Ed.), *Sozialistische Wirtschaftsreformen in Der Tschechoslowakei Und DDR Im Vergleich* (pp. 191–266). Vittorio Klostermann.

Winkler, H. A. (1983). Stabilisierung Durch Schrumpfung: Der Gewerbliche Mittelstand in Der Bundesrepublik. In Werner Conze and Rainer M. Lepsius (Eds.), *Sozialgeschichte Der Bundesrepublik Deutschland. Beiträge Zum Kontinuitätsproblem* (pp. 187–209). Klett-Cotta.

Yudanov, A. Y. (1997). USSR: Large enterprises in the USSR—The functional disorder. In Alfred D. Chandler Jr. (Ed.), *Big business and the wealth of nations* (pp. 397–432). Cambridge University Press.

Zatlin, J. R. (2009). *The currency of socialism: Money and political culture in East Germany*. Cambridge Univ. Press.

Losing the global: (Re)building a Bosnian enterprise across transition

Anna Calori

ABSTRACT
This article charts the rise and fall of Yugoslavia's global economic project through the case of Energoinvest, a large enterprise in Bosnia and Herzegovina. This company was the protagonist first of a 'leap outwards', embedded in Yugoslavia's economic partnerships with the Global South. After a brief phase of reforms, its operations were halted abruptly by the outbreak of the war in Bosnia. Afterwards, the company was at the centre of two clashing visions of post-war economic development, and two different sets of notions about what the future configuration of Bosnia's post-socialist economy should look like. Should the country rely on its previous socialist-global giants, or should it turn to SMEs development? This debate reveals a complex and long-term discussion about the prospects of post-socialist semi-peripheries in the global economy, about notions, visions, and expectations of 'globality', and about the legacies of socialist globalisation after the collapse of state socialism.

Introduction

This article takes the case of a Yugoslav large exporting company embedded in global production and trade networks, and illustrates that a business environment was not only existing in the socialist semi-periphery, but also that it was – and to a certain degree still is –'global; in its actions, narratives, and imaginaries. By doing so, it sketches the kinds of imperatives that doing business in the global market (and particularly in developing countries) created on enterprises functioning at the domestic level, and illustrates the afterlives of this entrepreneurial culture and organisational identity in the context of post-socialist transformation. This global orientation, the article contends, was entrenched within the local entrepreneurial ethos and brought to a clash with new/different models of reconstruction and development in the post-socialist context.

This article speaks to some of the themes outlined in this special issue as it delineates the notions and practices of a globally-oriented business environment in socialist (and post-socialist) Yugoslavia. It sits within contemporary debates in business history scholarship, by bringing together the study of socialist globalisation, Non-Alignment, and business history to show how global economic entanglements shaped a domestic business environment in late- and post-socialist Bosnia and Herzegovina (Águeda et al. 2016; Amatori, 2009). In doing so, this article positions Southeast European history in dialogue with the literature that increasingly views business history as global history (Lubinski & Wadhwani, 2017).

The history of global socialism and socialist globalisation has analysed the multiple ways in which the socialist camp sought to expand its sphere of influence in the Global South through development projects and trade agreements (Mark et al., 2018; Mark & Rupprecht, 2017; Westad, 2005; Karkov 2018). Recent research historicising development as a global phenomenon has produced innovative work on the intellectual exchanges and encounters that challenged established economic orders in the long 20th century (Bockman, 2015; Macekura & Manela, 2018; Unger, 2018). In addition, this historiography has analysed the multiple ways in which the socialist camp sought to create alternative projects of 'globalisation' or 'modernization', by expanding its sphere of influence in the Global South through development projects and trade agreements (Mark et al. 2018, 2019). By mapping East-West, East-South and South-South connections, studies have outlined the contribution of the socialist world in forging hegemonic ideas about processes of globalisation, development, interdependency, (neo)liberalism and the global market (Bockman, 2011; Slobodian, 2018).

Yet, only a small number of contributions highlight the role of enterprises (and even a smaller number has looked at Yugoslav companies) as simultaneously sites of, and actors in, multiple processes of economic entanglement between East, West, and South (Spaskovska, 2018). Most studies have looked at these companies in a profoundly national context, if indeed they looked at them at all (Wilkins, 2010). As this article illustrates, these companies were not isolated and domestic, but thought and acted global. A focus on Yugoslavia not only completes the geographical breadth of recent research on the global socialist entrepreneurship, but also shows the significance that the 'Third' or Non-Aligned Bloc, and Yugoslavia's self-positioning as an 'alternative' to established world orders, had onto local managerial cultures even after the collapse of the socialist regimes. This aims to complicate further the narrative of Eastern European enterprises as abiding to the 'capitalist' rules of the game, or operating in a distinctively 'socialist' fashion (Scranton, 2018; Vinsel, 2018).[1]

While compelling, an analysis of Yugoslav companies' entanglement within the global market would be incomplete if it were to halt at the country's collapse. Often, the historiography of socialist globalisation misses a longue durée perspective that transcends and surpasses the historical threshold of 1989–1991 and the Cold War framework (see Lee 2010; Jakovina, 2016; Mišković et al., 2014). What was the fate of this globalist and outward gaze as the socialist regimes and their project of internationalism crumbled during the long 1990s? This article proposes to go beyond such a chronological break, and to analyse the long-term (re)configuration of a Bosnian socialist enterprise's spatial horizons through transition. This allows to trace the upwards and downwards trajectory of a 'global' gaze as it was configured in a company situated simultaneously in the European semi-periphery, and within a web of Non-Aligned trade partnerships.

Relying on the specific case study of a globally embedded Yugoslav enterprise, it showcases the complex representations of 'the global' which underpinned the operations of this company. As we shall see, a growing push towards doing business in the Global South was driven simultaneously by a profit-oriented motive to compete on the market as a 'global business'; by an understanding of Non-Alignment as a business environment that granted Yugoslav companies privileged avenues for technical cooperation and the establishment of joint ventures in the Global South; and, finally, by an embeddedness within a broader discourse of (socialist) global development, where Yugoslavia's model of third-way self-managed market socialism posed a potential alternative to the Soviet and North-American development models (For a discussion on alternative development models in the Global Cold War, see Ekbladh, 2009; Engerman, 2018; Lorenzini, 2019).

The first section of this article presents the case study, and illustrates how a 'global' organisational identity and business orientation developed within a large enterprise in the Yugoslav semi-periphery, and how this was embedded in Yugoslavia's development projects for the Global South (for a discussion on organisational identity in late- and post-socialist enterprises, Clark and Soulsby, 2012). The second part briefly sketches the company's history throughout the collapse of the Yugoslav Federation and the ensuing war of 1991–1995. The third section analyses the shift from a global to a local orientation of this company, introduced because of privatisation reforms during transition. It outlines how peacebuilding and economic reconstruction efforts from international donors implied a repositioning of Bosnia and its enterprises from agents to subjects of development, and a reconfiguration of their spatial horizons from 'the global' to 'the local'.

Part 1 – Non-Alignment as a business opportunity?

The Non-Aligned Movement (NAM) was officially established in Belgrade in 1961 as a strong alliance between India, Egypt and Yugoslavia which brought together developing and post-colonial countries of the 'Third World' in a political, economic, and military neutralist alliance that challenged the bipolar logic of the Cold War. Josip Broz Tito, leader of Yugoslavia's socialist revolution and partisan resistance during WW2, and president of the Socialist Yugoslav Federation until his death in 1980, was a strong promoter of the principles and ideals of nonalignment, particularly in the decolonised world.

Partly drawing upon the Third-Worldist visions of neutrality, racial equality, and Afro-Asian alliances which had already emerged at the Bandung Conference of 1955, and partly an outcome of President Tito's fears of international isolation and internal de-legitimation after the expulsion from Cominform in 1948, the NAM grew into a complex framework of alliances which loosely tied the foreign policies of developing and newly de-colonised countries (Laron, 2014; Niebuhr, 2011; Životić & Čavoški, 2016).[2] Beyond a 'provocative, yet inclusive concept of Third World neutralism', Non-Alignment also established a set of economic alliances and principles that sought to challenge North-South trade imbalances, as well as the 'spectre' of the industrialised world reaching trade agreements that would exclude the Global South after East-West rapprochement in the early 1970s (Byrne, 2015). Together with other Non-Aligned Countries, Yugoslavia was particularly active within UNCTAD (UN Conference on Trade and Development) and was a strong supporter of a more equal organisation of the global economy, demands that took the form of New International Economic Order, discussed and proposed in the UN in the early 1970s (Murthy, 2013).

According to the Yugoslav Federal Council for International Technical Cooperation, Yugoslavia was to be considered a 'developing' and even a 'half-colonial' country.[3] Its approach to aid and development was one that focused on technical cooperation, rather than the establishment of development funds, financial aid, or major industrialisation/infrastructure projects. Since its resources were limited, the solution was to 'be found in the linking of technical cooperation with current interests of the [Federal] economy. [...] Economic organisations [i.e. companies] should take up a significant part of securing resources for financing of such cooperation, and become the integral element of all economic relations and business ventures with developing countries, as part of long term political orientation towards economic relations with these countries'.[4] Thus, the role of large and internationally-oriented Yugoslav companies was envisioned as simultaneously 'agents' of development, competitors in the international arena, and central actors in the country's modernisation.[5]

That internationalisation was a precondition for economic progress and modernisation was a common view amongst the Yugoslav Communist leadership at the Federal and national level. Since the late 1960s, the Central Committee of the Bosnian League of Communists, advised by local economic experts, encouraged economic policies fostering the development of local large industrial conglomerates, which rapidly grew to be amongst the ten largest companies in Yugoslavia (Barjaktarević, 1989). The export sector was viewed as the most profitable and competitive part of the Yugoslav economy, one that could ensure a rapid growth of production and revenues.[6] Economists and researchers concluded that it would be the most likely to use new technologies, and to become a push-factor for economic growth and development.[7] While these companies were organised according to the Yugoslav principle of workers' self-management, managers and general directors played an increasingly crucial role in processes of decision-making regarding investments, as well as in liaising with party structures and institutions. As the Yugoslav companies grew in size and complexity, so did the interest in rationalising their internal organisation and management. Throughout the 1970s and 1980s, courses in management and business organisation-related disciplines were held at universities, and specialist magazines for entrepreneurship, management theory and practice were published.[8]

The industrial milieu of a country like Bosnia, a middle-developed Yugoslav Republic,[9] grew around large self-managed enterprises – each comprising of a research and engineering core, a branch for import-export, and several smaller factories that produced for both the domestic and foreign markets. Bosnia's biggest trade partners were developing countries in North Africa, the Middle East as well as the USSR, where Bosnia exported key components for civil and hydro-engineering.[10] Export-oriented companies like Energoinvest (engineering and power plants construction), Unis (metal processing and engineering), and Šipad (wood and furniture manufacturer) quickly rose to third, sixth and tenth biggest producers in Yugoslavia in terms of revenue respectively, and together employed an overall of 190 thousand workers across the country.[11]

Alone or in cooperation with other Yugoslav enterprises, these companies relied upon credits from the Yugoslav Bank for International Economic Cooperation (Jugoslovenska Banka za Medjunarodnu Ekonomsku Saradnju – JUBMES), established in the late 1970s to finance joint ventures with foreign firms, deal with export credits, as well as raise foreign credits (Četković, 2015).[12] With a small internal market, Yugoslavia had to produce for foreign markets in order to achieve certain economies of scale; furthermore, it was deemed more efficient to attract foreign capital in the form of joint business ventures, also in view of reducing its foreign debt in the form of credits (Adamović, 1982). These companies benefitted from Yugoslavia's preferential orientation towards developing countries, anchored upon strong diplomatic and commercial ties with the Non-Aligned members. As the construction of the Non-Aligned project was also driven by economic cooperation, they became sites of bilateral technical cooperation, and agents of development. Economic development of the Global South (construction and electrification projects) was understood as an opportunity for growth, profit-making and increased competitiveness at the national level.

The focus of this study is the company Energoinvest, a large electrical engineering enterprise with a central branch in Sarajevo and more than 100 daughter companies spread around Bosnia and Herzegovina (henceforth Bosnia), as well as joint ventures and partnerships across the globe. Most prominently, it was involved in major development projects and technical cooperation with developing countries, from the electrification of villages in Bangladesh, Pakistan and Myanmar, to the construction of electrical switchgears, electric power lines and refinery components in the Middle East.

In the 1960s and 1970s, the company progressively assumed a leading role as the centre of a web of economic contacts and exchanges between the Global South, Western Europe and the Soviet Bloc. It rapidly became the largest exporter in Yugoslavia, with a yearly contribution to the Federation's export of roughly 4%.[13] In this period, Energoinvest consolidated its global presence, establishing joint ventures in Mexico (EnergoMex), Libya (ELPCO), the USSR (ENHA) and Pakistan (EnergoPak).[14] It was the recipient of loans from JUBMES to establish joint venture in Libya, as well as for the implementation of electrification of villages in Bangladesh, and the constructions of dams in Ethiopia.[15] It also had partnerships in Western Europe (such as IterEnergo in France and Germany) and the United States. By 1988 its yearly revenue from exports was of over 440 million US dollars, and the company had a workforce of 55,000 (roughly 40 thousand in Bosnia), with over 10 thousand expert cadres;[16] this made it the third largest company in Yugoslavia in terms of both overall revenue and number of employees.[17] Energoinvest was part of a pool of engineering and construction enterprises that were considered very successful at the international level. In 1981, the US Magazine 'Engineering News Record' listed Energoinvest, Energoprojekt, and other three large Yugoslav enterprises amongst the top 250 most prominent in the world.[18]

Crucial for their competitive advantage was the fact that such technical cooperation was grounded upon the exchange of expertise and know-how. Engineers and experts – trained in the companies' research centres across Bosnia – would often travel on site and provide technical assistance. The relative cheapness of their expert workforce (particularly white collar workers and engineers) as well as their preferential commercial avenues with developing countries granted them a comparative advantage over other international competitors. Amila Omersoftić, one of the few women engineers in Energoinvest, then president of the management board in the late 1990s, recalls:

> Yugoslavia was at the centre of the Non-Aligned, that means that in all continents, Africa, Asia, the Americas, we made big projects... Mexico, Iraq, Libya, Kenya, everywhere... that means we were the part of the world, we were open, we had connections ... I travelled a lot and enjoyed working in such diverse environments...[19]

These expert networks, global entanglements, and competitive advantage not only placed the company in the top five Yugoslav producers, but also granted it international visibility as a 'fierce capitalist competitor'.[20] The global consulting firm McKinsey, engaged by Energoinvest to support its internal management restructuring in the late 1960s and early 1970s, reportedly acknowledged that the company's competitiveness lay in the modernity of their production facilities, the relatively low labour costs, as well as their ability to deliver on the production of very specific components – such as pressure vessels employed in nuclear power-plants across the Soviet Union (Filipović, 2002).

In dialogue with the company's top management, McKinsey proposed an internal re-organisation that would facilitate management and investment, whilst maintaining the core structures of socialist self-management such as workers' councils.[21] This was in line with the entrepreneurial ethos and corporate culture that took shape within the company: an orientation towards profit-making, combined with the paternalistic features of a socialist enterprise (investment in research and training, but also in workers' housing and off-work socialising activities), and an understanding of self-management as a system that, if steered correctly, could promote workers' motivation and entrepreneurial spirit.[22]

News of international trade deals and contacts always accompanied details of production and development of factories and companies across the country. For example, in 1988 the then President of the Federal Executive Council Branko Mikulić went on a visit at Energoinvest's Egyptian plant EVACO – which produced cast carbon steel gate valves, components used in crude oil- and steam-operated machines. President Mikulić declared that the factory, which employed Yugoslav technology in partnership with Egyptian producers, was 'the best and most concrete manifestation of the idea and concept of Non-Alignment.[23]

This kind of praise galvanised Energoinvest's managers, branch directors, and cadres, into viewing the fate of their company as entwined with its global ties. Interviews conducted with the company's former managers highlight the extent to which this global business ethos was perceived to be a central, defining feature of this company. For example, Žarko Primorac, Energoinvest's Director of Finance during the 1980s, noted:

> Tito gave us access to many markets, we had access to many countries, the Yugoslav companies then used that political capital...for example let's say Iraq and Iran, Syria, Central African countries, Zambia, Congo, Tanzania, Ethiopia etcetera...when you came from Yugoslavia, regardless what company, they would have more open doors than other countries. This is one thing. But the other thing, of course, is that you would not arrive at such a privileged position if you weren't competitive. Even in those friendly countries like Lybia and Iraq, you had to be competitive.[24]

Managers, engineers, and cadres viewed Yugoslavia's geopolitical leading position in the Non-Aligned movement as instrumental to Energoinvest's global development, and their company's success as a consequence of its global orientation. The 'corporate culture' or organisational identity that developed within the company emerged from the complex relation of three dimensions: Non-Alignment as a business environment conducive of possibilities for technical cooperation; Yugoslavia's turn to developing countries as partners – rather than recipients – of development; and ultimately a competitive advantage and a chance for further profit.

Part 2 – The Bosnian War and the destruction of production sites

At the beginning of the 1980s, Yugoslavia was shaken by an increasingly serious economic crisis. Its international debt grew dramatically, and inflation spiralled out of control. This was a decade of profound transformations, which saw repeated attempts from the side of the political leadership at implementing economic reforms that would gradually introduce private ownership (through workers' shareholding) and market liberalisation (Bartlett, 1991; Uvalić, 2001; Young, 1998). The last two Yugoslav governments, and particularly that of Ante Marković and his team of Yugoslav economic experts gathered in the Commission for Reforms, envisioned a gradual privatisation of Yugoslav enterprises.[25] These experts, exposed to intellectual circles in both East and West, were familiar with corporate governance theories and the shareholders' value paradigm that was debated in management studies throughout the 1980s, and envisioned workers' shareholding as a gradual step towards the transformation of social ownership into private (Jackson, 2010; O'Sullivan, 2001). Scholars of management and company directors made sense of the transformations that market reforms required by interpreting self-management as potentially stimulating of workers' productivity, motivation, entrepreneurship, and business initiative – in particular if employees were rewarded with shares of their companies (Radunović, 1989). While this implied a partial opening towards privatisation, it also constituted a significant attempt at reconciling a market environment conducive of entrepreneurship with a (reformed) version of self-management.

The late 1980s were also a moment of reconfiguration of established economic spheres of influence, and geopolitical bipolarism was crumbling fast. Non-Alignment was in itself becoming a looser political and economic alliance, as East-West and North-South divisions were increasingly blurred in the globalised economy (Pant, 2017). Bosnian officials viewed this as an opportunity to strengthen further the country's position 'in between' East and West, as well as its orientation towards developing countries.[26] At the beginning of 1989, for example, the leadership of the Bosnian League of Communists started looking into increasing trade with China, Kazakhstan, Iraq and Malaysia, as well as Italy and Germany.[27] Within Energoinvest as well, the crisis of the 1980s did not bring about a rejection of this globalist model. While there was talk about enterprise restructuring, as well as about the development of the private sector, the idea for large enterprises was not to scale down, but to transform structures into holdings, in preparation for a further 'leap outwards' and into the newly formed common European market. The top management at that time included economics professors engaged in drafting and promoting privatisation reforms at the Federal and national level.[28] They envisioned a transformation of large Bosnian self-managed enterprises into holdings – owned through a form of managers' and employees buy-outs.

However, with the collapse of the socialist system, and the ensuing wars, Yugoslavia lost its prominent position within the Non-Aligned. Economic and commercial ties were lost, joint ventures and partnerships halted as Yugoslav companies quickly became unreliable business partners (Dizdarević, 2009; Jović, 2009).[29] Energoinvest's central branch in besieged Sarajevo was hardly able to maintain its global contacts, or to deliver on its agreements, as production for the foreign market was discontinued. Its factories, as well as research centres were often destroyed or looted by different warring factions.

In 1994, by government decree, the company was re-nationalised and passed under the direct control of the Ministry of Industry. While some of the old managerial group maintained a position within the company, the main jurisdiction over its reconstruction, privatisation, and overall business direction now pertained the government directly. After the end of the war, a first attempt at voucher privatisation meant a partial sell-off of the company, a series of bankruptcies and a loss of property value as vouchers were sold cheaply on the black market (Bayliss, 2005).

Part 3 – A shrinking global space? From agents to subjects of technical assistance

After the Dayton Peace Agreement was signed in 1995, peacekeeping operations took the form of reconstruction assistance and peacebuilding. In the early 2000s, international organisations started moving towards a focus on economic development, growth and employment. This was dependent on donations and loans that international financial institutions such as the IMF and the World Bank granted to the government, in cooperation with international organisations, foreign embassies and donors (Donais, 2005; Pugh, 2005, 2011).

Large international institutions like the OECD and UNCTAD had set up models of development for transitioning countries based on growth of the small and medium private sector, while until then there had been a propensity to favour large (private) businesses (OECD, 2004). This was a tendency that had been growing since the 1980s, where economic policy-makers – particularly in Western capitalist countries – 'were more than usually concerned to encourage the growth of SMEs [Small and Medium Enterprises]. Research at the time, since refuted, seemed to point to this sector as the most dynamic in terms of job creation in times of recession' (Coopey, 2005).

Donors and international institutions involved in economic reconstruction in Bosnia shared this rationale for transformation: in an increasingly globalised economy, the focus was on the quick growth of those enterprises that could attract foreign direct investment, rather than the restructuring of older companies and the development of employment capacity (Coopey, 2005, p. 14; UNCTAD, 2001). Hence, institutions such as the OHR, the OECD, and the EBRD put together a variety of analyses and policy recommendations on the development of a small private sector, more likely to attract private capital and develop local entrepreneurship (OECD, EBRD, 2005; Tchalakov & Jouko, 2013).[30]

Privatisation was introduced as a solution to the lingering 'communist' legacy that was affecting the Bosnian economy. The understanding of Bosnia's large companies as forming the last stronghold of an outdated communist mentality was widespread amongst advisors at the IMF, World Bank and Office of the High Representative (OHR, the UN special envoy tasked with the implementation of the Dayton Peace Agreement). Top officials from the World Bank, OHR, and USAID agreed that 'the motto of growth for Bosnia should not be in large companies but in SMEs.'[31] By its own admission, the World Bank in the 1990s did not hold a great deal of specialist knowledge on the workings of centrally planned economies, nor did it employ specialists to take part in advisory missions in transitioning countries (Nellis, 2002).

While it was true that these companies were at the time much less profitable than other large Western firms, the fact that they covered market niches in the developing countries was not considered to be an asset – possibly because the 'Global South' was itself considered needing of development and so was not reputed a reliable economic partner.[32] Bosnia was not a member of the formerly globally engaged, industrialised centre of the Non-Aligned world, but rather, part of a state-led obsolete system that had to be Europeanised.

In 2001, the World Bank issued a Privatisation Technical Assistance Credit of the amount of 19.8 USD million to the Bosnian government. This aimed at supporting private investors and SMEs, accelerating privatisation of large-scale enterprises, and finally reforming the labour market. Within this framework, first the USAID, and then the World Bank, were tasked to advise and guide the privatisation of Energoinvest.[33] A major objective in the privatisation of big corporations was of 'unbundling', i.e. splitting them into smaller business units (de facto SMEs) and subsequently selling them through tender.

An Advisory Group for Privatisation, which included most international agencies and donors (EBRD, EU, GTZ, IMF, OHR, USAID, WB) had a strong mandate to coordinate and proceed with the privatisation of strategic enterprises across the countries, i.e. companies of 'significant importance for the Bosnian economy', which would be sold to strategic partners and investment funds.[34] International experts specialised in tender privatisation ('dealmakers') were hired to assist the governments in selling State Owned Enterprises to strategic local and foreign investors.[35]

Although Energoinvest was structured in a way that each daughter company or factory would produce for the foreign market under direct coordination of the central branch and other research units, the new privatisation framework envisioned that they would be privatised as separate entities, and function as private small enterprises. Furthermore, the privatisation agreement entailed the sale of all foreign partnerships, joint ventures, and capital. The proposed privatisation agreement deemed the core engineering central branch as most attractive to the foreign partners, whilst its established global connections were expendable.

This created friction with the 'old guard' of the company's management, many of whom had now academic posts from where they sought – often unsuccessfully – to steer the privatisation debate back to questions of global business and employment. Recalling his experience as a minister and first contact for the international community experts, Hasan Muratović, governor for Bosnia at the World Bank between 1995 and 1998 and former manager at Energoinvest, commented:

> 'the so-called international community told us we needed micro and small businesses. [But] we had, let's say, four companies that had more than 30 thousand workers each, so what small business will employ 150 thousand people? And who would they sell to, if there are no large enterprises to buy their product?'[36]

Economic experts in prominent political positions saw international advisors as ill-informed about the characteristics of the Bosnian economy, and criticised the rationale for privatisation and development of SMEs as ineffective for the restoration of large industries.

This conflict entered the doors of Energoinvest, with its Management Board vehemently critical of the privatisation programme proposed by international advisors and accepted by the national government. A detailed report of the Energoinvest's Board, motivating its opposition to the plan, stated:

> 'the restoration of sectors took place under the existence of a full embargo on investments into state-owned companies before privatisation. The embargo is an imposed factor of the international community. This has led to the under-capitalisation of Energoinvest, which in turn has prevented from activating big businesses, founding new markets, and returning to some former markets necessary for modernisation.'[37]

That local managerial and economic expertise was disregarded in this context is not just specific to this case study, nor in fact of the former Yugoslavia alone. Studies conducted at the time of transition in Central and Eastern Europe highlighted how foreign partners and international donors saw 'local knowledge of companies in transition as insignificant in strategic terms, creating a balance of dependency of the local on the foreign partner (Clark & Geppert, 2006).' Although the pre-existing culture of management was found to be crucial in shaping how enterprises worked during transition, donors were unable to incorporate local cultures of management in their transition programmes across the post-socialist world (Kouzmin & Korac-Kakabadse, 1997).

Experts and former management in Bosnia often lamented this lack of dialogue and engagement. For example, Professor Anto Domazet, Dean of the Economics Faculty and former manager in Energoinvest, worked in close proximity with both local governments and international advisors (UNDP). On the matter of 'failed' negotiations, he commented:

> 'There was a group of 15 economists from across the country and we worked and we prepared a [...] strategy for economic development of Bosnia and Herzegovina, but it was not in harmony with the policies of the World Bank, and it was an anti-neoliberal approach, and they rejected all that [laughs].'[38]

Indeed, a group of economists from the Universities of Sarajevo, Banja Luka and Mostar – some of whom had previously held prominent positions in Energoinvest – were rather vocal in criticising Bosnia's development strategy based on the fall of employment, stimulation of export, privatisation and financial liberalisation, which in their view was 'based on the failed concept of neoliberalism, which the World Bank represents.'[39]

The globally oriented organisational identity that experts and former managers had hoped would be the basis for returning Energoinvest to its pre-war splendour could find little room in a geopolitical context where preferential links with Non-Aligned developing countries had been severed, where the project of global socialism had run its course, and where no viable alternatives to the 'failed concept of neoliberalism' were on sight. Ultimately, they had envisioned a different path of post-war reconstruction, one grounded upon their active participation in shaping the economic development of a semi-peripheral country in the global economy.

Despite the reported clashes with international advisors, and the privatisation or bankruptcy of most of production sites in Bosnia and across the former Yugoslavia, the core engineering company of Energoinvest continues operations in the Global South.[40] Relying upon the business contacts it established in the 1970s, it was able to strike new electro-engineering construction contracts in North and Central Africa throughout the late 2000s and early 2010s.[41] Albeit on a smaller scale, these renewed ties are illustrative of a surviving corporate culture embedded within the legacy of past notions, visions, and expectations of 'globality'.

Conclusions

This article has traced the history of a Yugoslav company positioned simultaneously at the semi-periphery of Western global trade, and at the centre of an alternative web of economic connections. Its trajectory reflects, in small, wider processes of global transformation, in terms of reconfiguration of global alliances, networks, and visions of development.

Different notions of 'development' and of expertise factored in the inability to mediate between local knowledge, business and managerial cultures and international visions during transition. Managers and experts in Energoinvest were socialised in a spatial and temporal context where 'global development' through technical cooperation was mostly associated with business in developing Non-Aligned countries.

From the perspective of a small country in Europe's semi-periphery, the advantages of Bosnia's 'in-betweenness' amongst Europe, the middle East, Africa and the rest of the Non-Aligned world, was lost on the post-communist country's path to economic transition. In the name of a further engagement in the expanding globalised economy, and in order to attract Foreign Direct Investment, large socialist enterprises in Bosnia were to re-orient their global gaze towards the domestic and, at best, regional markets. Here, privatisation meant de-globalisation, a shrinking of the operational space of a large company that had built its raison d'être on the globalist vision of its management. The debate and friction that lays at the basis of Energoinvest's transition trajectory reveals a broader history of tensions in the globalising semi-periphery – a history of clashing ideas of where innovation is (in large or small enterprises) and what is understood as global horizons, spheres of influence, or business opportunities.

The development path that international experts and donors envisioned for the former Yugoslavia was embedded within a different vision of global spatial orders. After the wars and the collapse of Yugoslavia's geopolitical prominence within the Non-Aligned, the region was placed back on the periphery, and made an adjunct to the West with the rest of the (post)socialist world. As such, the destiny of large enterprises like Energoinvest was not that of being re-integrated as competitors in the world market, but being restructured and privatised as smaller companies of a small-size economy in the European semi-periphery.

The long-term trajectory illustrated in this article will hopefully be propaedeutic to opening towards new avenues of research and debate: How can an actors' based history of global business entanglements contribute to achieve new understandings of development and globalisation? What forms of entrepreneurship and business models emerged from the engagement of socialist semi-peripheries in the Global South? What notions, visions, and configurations of 'the global economy', and the role of semi-peripheries in it, underpinned the different visions of development brought forward by local and international experts? What can a longue durée history of transformation tell us of how business ideas and practices transformed as spatial constructs and regional alliances were reconfigured through time? Fostering the dialogue between business historians, historians of globalisation, and historians of the (post)socialist world will further research in this direction.

Notes

1. In relation to this, see the recent exchange between Scranton and Vinsel (2018) and Vinsel (2018).
2. Josip Broz Tito, leader of Yugoslavia's socialist revolution and of the partisan resistance during WW2, was president of the Socialist Yugoslav Federation until his death in 1980.
3. 'Yugoslavia's pre-WW2 economic and political position is factually half-colonial, with low economic development and under the yoke of western political powers; its conditions were similar to those of the newly freed countries'. This view was expressed on a report on Yugoslavia's technical cooperation, issued for the Federal Executive Council and compiled at the Meeting of Directors of the Federal Council for International Technical Cooperation and Directors of Republican Councils for Technical Cooperation, 1968 [Savetovanja Direktora Saveznog Zavoda za Međunarodnu Tehničku Saradnju i Direktora Republičkih Zavoda za Tehničku Saradnju, 1968.] Arhiv Jugoslavije, Fond 130, fasc. 607, p. 14.
4. See footnote 3.

5. 'Tito bez protokola Energoinvest', 17.11.1966. Available at: https://www.youtube.com/watch?v=AWnl8CQpGa8
6. 'Consensus for Market Economy, Legal State and Democratic Society', Statement by Ante Marković on the occasion of the review of the Programme of economic reform and measures for its implementation in 1990 at the joint session of the Federal Chamber and Chamber of Republics and Provinces of the SFRY Assembly on December 18, 1989, in: Federal Executive Council Secretariat for Information, ed. *Yugoslav Changes*, p. 94
7. Šavić, N. (1990). Prestrukturiranje, Razvojni Ciklus i Privatizacija u Jugoslaviji. In Šavić, N (Ed.) *Prestrukturiranje, Razvojni Ciklus i Privatizacija [Restructuring, Development Cycle and Privatisation]* (pp. 1–15). Zbornik Radova Jugoslovenskih Ekonomista Za Savetovanje, 8–10 Maj 1990, Brioni. Beograd: Savez Ekonomista Jugoslavije, 1990, p. 5.
8. Such as the magazine Direktor: časopis za teoriju i praksu rukovođenja i upravljanja [Director: Magazine for the theory and praxis of leadership and management].
9. Within Yugoslavia, Republics were categorised according to their level of development, based on calculations of GDP pro-capita and growth rate. Slovenia and Croatia being the most 'developed', whilst the autonomous region of Kosovo and Macedonia were considered 'underdeveloped'. In this categorisation, Bosnia stood somewhat in the middle.
10. Republički Komitet za Odnose sa Inostranstvo, Izvještaj o Radu u 1988. Godini [Republican Committee for Foreign Relations, Report on Works of 1988], Sarajevo, Januar 1989 godine, pp. 14-15. Folder 47 Zapisnici sa sjednice RSMO (1-6), Državni Arhiv Bosne i Hercegovine. Here, Energoinvest is mentioned together with UNIS as the largest company responsible for cooperation and export.
11. '140 Najvećih proizvodnih preduzeća industrije i rudarstva, poljoprivrede, šumarstva i građevinarstva prema ukupnom prihodu u 1989. Godini' [140 Largest companies of indutrial, mining, agriculture, forestry and construction sector according to total income in 1989], *Ekonomska Politika*, num. 2008, 24 September 1990, p. 4.
12. As Četkovic shows, however, this Bank, like most of the financial institutions in Yugoslavia, became increasingly reliant on foreign credit, especially throughout the 1980s.
13. 'U reformu – bez odlaganja', *Energoinvest List*, num. 944, November 21 1988, p. 2.
14. Of these, Energoinvest was the owner of at least 51% of the overall capital.
15. Agreements between JUBMES, Fond solidarnosti sa nesvrstanim zemljama i zemljama u razvoju [Solidarity Fund for non-aligned countries and developing countries], and the Bangladesh Power Development Board for the electrification of villages, to be carried out in Bangladesh by Energoinvest. JUBMES, Fond 782, fasc 1209, 1968 (Arhiv Jugoslavije). Fond 782, fasc 1215; Agreements between the Bank, Energoinvest and the Ethiopian Electric Light and Power Authority for the construction of hidroelectric plants in Ethiopia. JUBMES, Fond 782, fasc 1217, 1983-1988 (Arhiv Jugoslavije).
16. Svijet cijeni poslovnost i kvalitet. *Energoinvest List*; num. 946, December 12 1988, p. 2. In 1981, the US Magazine 'Engineering News Record' listed Energoinvest, Energoprojekt, and other three large Yugoslav enterprises amongst the top 250 most prominent in the world. Yugoslav News, Yugoslav Press and Cultural Centre, New York, December 10 1982, p. 2.
17. '10 Najvećih proizvodnih Organizacija Udruženog Rada u oblasti industrija i rudarstva poljoprivrede i šumarstva i građevinarstva' [10 Largest companies in the area of industry, mining, agriculture, forestry and construction], *Ekonomska Politika*, num. 1849, 7 September 1987, p. 5, p. 45.
18. *Yugoslav News*, Yugoslav Press and Cultural Centre, New York, December 10 1982, p. 2
19. Amila Omersoftić, Interview with author, Sarajevo, 02.07.2014.
20. 140 Najvećih proizvodnih preduzeća industrije i rudarstva, poljoprivrede, šumarstva i građevinarstva prema ukupnom prihodu u 1989. Godini», *Ekonomska Politika*, No. 2008, September 24 1990; Burck, Gilbert. 'A Socialist Enterprise That Acts Like a Fierce Capitalist Competitor', *Fortune Magazine*, January 1972.
21. On this cooperation, and on the strategies Yugoslav enterprises employed to reconcile 'market' and 'socialism', see Calori and Spaskovska (forthcoming, 2020). While it is beyond the purpose of this paper to evaluate the functionings of the Yugoslav system of self-

management, it should be noted that frictions between workers and management board became increasingly strong throughout the late 1970s and 1980s, and thus the internal re-organisation proposed by McKinsey was no necessarily viewed by workers as a solution to such imbalances.

22. 'Otkloniti sve što samoupravljanje čini neefikasnim', *Energoinvest List*, num. 973, July 3 1989, p. 5.
23. 'Praktična primjena ideje nesvrstanosti.' *Energoinvest list*, no. 884, July 13 1987, p. 2
24. Žarko Primorac, Interview with author, Zagreb, 16.03.2016.
25. Marković, A. 'Changes in the Yugoslav Social System to Meet the Needs of Society', statement at the joint session of the Federal Chamber and the Chamber of Republics and Provinces of the Assembly of the SFRY on the occasion of the election of the President of the Federal Executive Council on March 16, 1989, Federal Executive Council Secretariat for Information, ed. *Yugoslav Changes*, p. 37.
26. Magnetofonski Snimak Sjednice Republickog Društvenog Savjeta za Međunarodne Odnose [Recording of the Assembly of the Republic Social Council for Interanational Relations], 3 March 1989, p. 73. Folder 47 Zapisnici sa sjednice RSMO (1-6), Državni Arhiv Bosne i Hercegovine.
27. Rezime osnovnih mišljenja, stavova i ocjena iznesenih u raspravi o Aktuelnim Kretanjima u Socijalističkim Zemljama Evrope i Njihovom Uticaju na Savremene Međunarodne Odnose na Sjednici Savjeta [Resume of the basic opinions, views and evaluations presented at the discussion on the Actual developments of socialist countries in Europe and their impact on contemporary internaitonal relations], 25 April 1989. Godine, pp. 16–17. Republički Društveni Savjet za Međunarodne Odnose [Republic Social Council for Interanational Relations], Folder 47 Zapisnici sa sjednice RSMO (1-6), Državni Arhiv Bosne i Hercegovine.
28. 'Ni u svijetu nije med i mlijeko', *Energoinvest list*, num. 980, September 18 1989, p. 2.
29. Manoharan, M. Non-Aligned Movement at odds over Yugoslavia, *Independent*, Monday 31 August 1992 (Available at: https://www.independent.co.uk/news/world/europe/Non-AlignedNon-Aligned-movement-at-odds-over-yugoslavia-1580470.html last access 24 November 2019).
30. 'Enterprise Policy Performance Assessment and Herzegovina.' OECD, EBRD, Stability Pact for South Eastern Europe, March 2005, pp. 7–8; 'Bosnia and Herzegovina: Poverty Reduction Strategy Paper—Mid-Term'. *IMF Country Report*, April 2004. IMF, pp. 62–63; on entrepreneurship in East and Central Europe, see Tchalakov and Jouko (2013).
31. 'Ralph Johnson, prvi zamjenik Visokog Predstavnika u BiH'. *Privatizacija. Stručni Časopis Agencije Za Privatizaciju u Federaciji Bosne i Hercegovine*,num. 10/11, July 2000, p. 5; see also Speech by Principal Deputy High Representative Donald Hays at the USAID-sponsored SME Donor Roundtable, Sarajevo, 7 April 2004, OHR Archive. http://www.ohr.int/?p=46231; "Ohrabren sam, ali ne i zadovoljan. *Privatizacija. Stručni Časopis Agencije Za Privatizaciju u Federaciji Bosne i Hercegovine*, num 10/11, July 2000, p. 8; Special credits were provided for this purpose, see *OHR Economic Newsletter*, Vol. 2, No. 1, February 1999.
32. For a detailed discussion of North-South imbalances and the construction of development policies, see Escobar (1995).
33. "Project Appraisal Document on a Proposed Credit in the Amount of SDR 15.6 Million (US$19.8 Million Equivalent) to Bosnia and Herzegovina for a Privatization Technical Assistance." Private and Financial Sectors Development Unit South East Europe Country Unit Europe and Central Asia Region. 31 May 2001: The World Bank, Table 2, p. 5.
34. *OHR Economic Newsletter*, Vol. 3, No. 6, October 2000.
35. 'Implementation Completion and Results Report on a Credit in the Amount of SDR 15.60 Million (US$19.80 Million Equivalent) to Bosnia and Herzegovina for a Privatization Technical Assistance Credit.' IDA-35310. World Bank Private and Financial Sector Development Unit South East Europe Country Unit Europe and Central Asia Region, March 21, 2007, p. 8.
36. Hasan Muratović, Interview with author, Sarajevo, 13.12.2016.
37. 'Visok ugled u zemlji i svijetu', *Energoinvest List*, Num. 1098, March 2000, p. 2.
38. Anto Domazet, Interview with author, Sarajevo, 05.04.2016.
39. 'Cetiri bh. koraka do prokletstva', *Oslobođenje*, January 1 2004, p. 7.

40. Recently, the company signed an agreement with the Tanzania Electric Supply Company Limited for the construction of a transmission network linking Tanzania and Kenya. https://www.sarajevotimes.com/new-business-energoinvest-tanzania-worth-53-million-dollars/ (Accessed on 24 November 2019).
41. 'Nastavak uspješnog poslovanja', *Energoinvest List*, Num. 1155, June 2010, p. 3.

Disclosure statement

No financial interest or benefit has arisen from the direct applications of this research.

References

Adamović, L. S. (1982). The foreign trade system of Yugoslavia. *Eastern European Economics*, *20*(3–4), 144–165. https://doi.org/10.1080/00128775.1982.11648261

Águeda, G., Zozimo, R., Román, E. S., & Jack, S. (2016). At the crossroads. Management and business history in entrepreneurship research. *Journal of Evolutionary Studies in Business*, *1*(2), 156–200.

Amatori, F. (2009). Business history: State of the art and controversies. *Revista de Historia Industrial*, *1*(39), 17–35.

Bartlett, W. (1991). Economic reform, unemployment and labour market policy in Yugoslavia. *MOCT-MOST Economic Policy in Transitional Economies*, *1*(3), 93–109. https://doi.org/10.1007/BF01102300

Bayliss, K. (2005). Post-conflict privatisation. A review of development in Serbia and Bosnia-Herzegovina. *Overseas Development Institute*, London, ESAU Working paper 12.

Bockman, J. (2011). *Markets in the name of socialism: The left-wing origins of neoliberalism*. Stanford University Press.

Bockman, J. (2015). Socialist globalization against capitalist neocolonialism: The economic ideas behind the new international economic order. *Humanity: An International Journal of Human Rights, Humanitarianism, and Development*, *6*(1), 109–128. https://doi.org/10.1353/hum.2015.0010

Byrne, J. J. (2015). Beyond continents, colours, and the Cold War: Yugoslavia, Algeria, and the struggle for non-alignment. *The International History Review*, *37*(5), 912–932. https://doi.org/10.1080/07075332.2015.1051569

Calori, A., & Spaskovska, L. (2020). A non-aligned business world?—The global socialist enterprise between self-management and transnational capitalism. *Nationalities Papers* (2020), 1–15.

Četković, P. (2015). *The role of banks in economic development in the former SFR Yugoslavia*. The WIIW Balkan Observatory Working Papers, Num. 114, pp. 1–20.

Clark, E., & Geppert, M. (2006). Socio-political processes in international management in post-socialist contexts: Knowledge, learning and transnational institution building. *Journal of International Management*, *12*, 340–357.

Clark, E., & Soulsby, A. (2012). Constructing post-socialism: Organisational identity and the experience of international joint ventures. *Europe-Asia Studies*, *64*(2), 257–280. https://doi.org/10.1080/09668136.2011.646496

Coopey, R. (2005). Venture capital and enterprise. In Y. Cassis & I. P. Minoglou (Eds.), *Entrepreneurship in theory and history* (pp. 127–148). Palgrave Macmillan.

Dizdarević, R. (2009). *From the death of Tito to the death of Yugoslavia*. TKD Šahinpašić.

Donais, T. (2005). *The political economy of peacebuilding in post-Dayton Bosnia. Contemporary security studies*. Routledge.

Ekbladh, D. (2009). *The Great American mission: Modernization and the construction of an American world order*. Princeton University Press.

Engerman, D. C. (2018). *The price of aid. The economic Cold War in India*. Harvard University Press.

Escobar, A. (1995). *Encountering development: The making and unmaking of the third world*. Princeton University Press.

Filipović, I. (2002). *Emerik Blum. Monografija*. Šahinpašić.

IMF. (2004). Bosnia and Herzegovina: Poverty Reduction Strategy Paper—Mid-Term. Country Report. April.

Jackson, G. (2010). *Understanding corporate governance in the United States*. Working paper. Dusseldorf: Hans-Boeckler Stiftung.

Jakovina, T. (2016). *Treća Strana Hladnog Rata*. Fraktura.

Jović, D. (2009). *Yugoslavia: A State that withered away*. Purdue University Press.

Karkov, N. R., & Valiavicharska, Z. (2018). Rethinking East-European Socialism: Notes toward an anti-capitalist decolonial methodology. *Interventions, 20*(6), 785–813. https://doi.org/10.1080/1369801X.2018.1515647

Kouzmin, A., & Korac-Kakabadse, N. (1997). From phobias and ideological prescription: Toward multiple models in transformation management for socialist economies in transition. *Administration & Society, 29*(2), 139–188. https://doi.org/10.1177/009539979702900202

Laron, G. (2014). Semi-peripheral countries and the invention of the 'Third World', 1955–65. *Third World Quarterly, 35*(9), 1547–1565. https://doi.org/10.1080/01436597.2014.970859

Lee, C. J. (2010). *Making a world after empire: The Bandung moment and its political afterlives*. Ohio University Press.

Lorenzini, S. (2019). *Global development: A cold war history*. Princeton University Press.

Lubinski, C., & Wadhwani, R. D. (2017). *New entrepreneurial history and international entrepreneurship: Exploring the intersections* [Paper presentation]. *Paper Presented at the 33rd EGOS Colloquium 2017*, Copenhagen, Denmark.

Macekura, S. J. and Manela, E. (Eds.). (2018). *The development century: A global history*. Cambridge University Press.

Mark, J., Iacob, B., Rupprecht, T., & Spaskovska, L. (2019). *Global 1989: Eastern Europe and the making of the modern world*. Cambridge University Press.

Mark, J., & Rupprecht, T. (2017). Europe's '1989' in global context. In J. Fürst, S. Pons, and M. Selden (Eds.), *The Cambridge history of communism* (pp. 203–223). Cambridge University Press.

Mark, J., Slobodian, Q., & Thompson, A. (2018). Eastern Europe. In M. Thomas (Ed.), *The Oxford handbook of the ends of empire*. Oxford University Press.

Mišković, N., Fischer-Tiné, H., & Boškovska, N. (Eds.), (2014). *The non-aligned movement and the cold war. Delhi – Bandung – Belgrade*. Routledge.

Murthy, C. S. R. (2013). Non-aligned movement countries as drivers of change in international organizations. *Comparativ, 23*(4/5), 118–136.

Nellis, J. (2002). *The World Bank, privatization and enterprise reform in transition economies: A retrospective analysis*. Operations Evaluation Department, The World Bank.

Niebuhr, Robert. (2011). Nonalignment as Yugoslavia's answer to bloc politics. *Journal of Cold War Studies, 13*(1), 146–179. https://doi.org/10.1162/JCWS_a_00072

O'Sullivan, M. (2001). *Contests for corporate control: Corporate governance and economic performance in the United States and Germany*. Oxford University Press.

OECD, EBRD. (2005). Enterprise Policy Performance Assessment and Herzegovina. Stability Pact for South Eastern Europe, March.

OECD. (2004). *Promoting SMEs for development. In Promoting entrepreneurship and innovative SMEs in a global economy: Towards a more responsible and inclusive globalisation*, Istanbul, Turkey.

Pant, H. V. (2017). The end of non-alignment? *Orbis, 61*(4), 527–540. https://doi.org/10.1016/j.orbis.2017.08.004

Pugh, M. (2005). The political economy of peacebuilding: A critical theory perspective. *International Journal of Peace Studies, 10*(2), 23–42.

Pugh, M. (2011). Local agency and political economies of peacebuilding. *Studies in Ethnicity and Nationalism, 11*(2), 308–320. https://doi.org/10.1111/j.1399-6576.2011.01113.x

Scranton, P. (2018). Managing communist enterprises: Poland, Hungary, and Czechoslovakia, 1945–1970. *Enterprise & Society, 19*(3), 492–537. https://doi.org/10.1017/eso.2018.13

Slobodian, Q. (2018). *Globalists. The end of empire and the birth of neoliberalism*. Harvard University Press.

Spaskovska, L. (2018). Building a better world? Construction, labour and the pursuit of collective self-reliance in the 'Global South', 1950–1990. *Labor History, 59*(3), 331–351. https://doi.org/10.1080/0023656X.2018.1429185

Tchalakov, I., & Jouko, N. (2013). *Innovations and entrepreneurs in socialist and post-socialist societies.* Cambridge Scholars Publishing.

UNCTAD. (2001). *Improving the competitiveness of SMEs in developing countries. The role of finance to enhance enterprise development.* United Nations Conference on Trade and Development.

Unger, C. R. (2018). *International development: A postwar history.* Bloomsbury.

Uvalić, M. (2001). Privatisation and Corporate Governance in Serbia (FR Yugoslavia). Florence.

Vinsel, L. (2018). The Scrantonian Worldview Gazing East, 1970. *Enterprise & Society, 19*(3), 561–569. https://doi.org/10.1017/eso.2018.16

Westad, O. A. (2005). *The global cold war. Third world interventions and the making of our times.* Cambridge University Press.

Wilkins, M. (2010). Multinational enterprises and the varieties of capitalism. *The Business History Review, 84*(4), 638–645.

Young, B. (1998). Nothing from nothing is nothing: Privatisation, price liberalisation and poverty in the Yugoslav successor states. In C.-U. Schierup (Ed.), *Scramble for the Balkans: Nationalism, globalism and the political economy of reconstruction*. Macmillan.

Životić, A., & Čavoški, J. (2016). On the road to Belgrade: Yugoslavia, third world neutrals, and the evolution of global non-alignment, 1954–1961. *Journal of Cold War Studies, 18*(4), 79–97. https://doi.org/10.1162/JCWS_a_00681

OPEN ACCESS

Varieties of capitalism or variegated state capitalism? East Germany and Yugoslavia in comparative perspective

Gareth Dale and Vladimir Unkovski-Korica

ABSTRACT
This essay is a contribution to comparative capitalism studies. We begin with a critique of the 'Varieties of Capitalism' school, before presenting the 'variegated' alternative. We note difficulties of both schools in characterising statist challengers to the dominant market order. The rise of China has made this a pressing issue, one that raises questions: Is China capitalist, and since when? And how should one analyse the communist world, which has since the 1920s represented a substantial swathe of the global economy? We next present an account of capitalism that explains étatiste variants as the product of late development, and the 'communist' economies as a state-capitalist model geared to catch-up industrialisation. This obliges us to consider how to account for their differences. In the second half we take up this challenge, via comparative analysis of two state-capitalist economies: the GDR (representing the orthodox Soviet model) and Yugoslavia (a maverick, market-friendly variant).

1. Introduction

Although universal and universalising, capitalism is anything but homogenous. It takes radically different forms through time and across space. This raises questions: how to relate capitalism in general to particular institutionally-bounded capitalist societies, how to define and taxonomise the latter, and how does the institutional variation help us understand the whole? This article begins with a critical literature review, in which we identify the origins and pre-suppositions of the 'Varieties of Capitalism' (VoC) school and draw attention to three shortcomings: its firm-centric focus, its lack of a theory of capitalism, and its tendency to misrepresent the global economy as an aggregate of national units. We then turn to the concept of *variegation,* an alternative to VoC that offers better tools for understanding global capitalism. Variegation emphasises the interconnectedness and hierarchies in the world economy which elude the VoC literature.

Comparative capitalist research has traditionally focussed on 'advanced' market economies, but some contributions within both schools—VoC and 'variegated'—have recently turned their attention to China's state-capitalist model and its major role in the world economy today. We review and critique these studies, arguing that they obscure the historical origins of Chinese state capitalism. Their assumption that Soviet-style societies, including Mao's China, should be understood as non-capitalist and cut off from the world capitalist system requires revision. Using the concept of uneven and combined development (UCD), we extend, in time and space, the use of the concept of variegation. We argue that the USSR and its derivatives in the Cold War (and to some extent after) represented not 'state socialism' but a distinct variety of state capitalism, a 'variety' that enjoyed its heyday in the middle decades of the twentieth century. Turning to our case studies, East Germany and Yugoslavia, we show that these societies were integral parts of a variegated global capitalist system, as was the state-capitalist firm. There is a strong case, we will conclude, for bringing the largely neglected communist-run states of the Second World into the study of business history, with significant implications for understanding business history as such.

2. Origins of a debate

Theorisation of capitalism and its 'varieties' goes back to the nineteenth century.[1] Karl Marx's approach centred not on national institutions but on capitalism as a system defined by two axes of conflictual social relations: the separation of producers from the means of production and the competitive relationship among the owners of the means of production. The compulsive connection between the two processes, competition and exploitation, provide the capitalist epoch with its core dynamics. Marx paid attention to the sharply divergent evolution of various nations, for example of colonised Ireland vis-à-vis colonial Britain, and he was interested in the articulations between different modes of production. Nevertheless, his analysis was of capitalism as a universalising and tendentially global system; his focus was not the institutional complexes of capital accumulation. In his day, he believed, all countries of Western Europe were transitioning to the capitalist mode of production. England figured centrally in his work not because he regarded it as an instance of a particular institutional complex but, rather, as an illustration of his theory of capitalism as such. 'If', he added, one of his German readers, 'pharisaically shrugs his shoulders at the condition of the English industrial and agricultural workers, or optimistically comforts himself with the thought that in Germany things are not nearly so bad, I must plainly tell him: *De te fabula narratur!* ... The country that is more developed industrially only shows, to those that follow it on the industrial path, the image of its own future' (Marx, 2004).

'That story is *not* about us!', replied Germany's school of *Nationalökonomie*. Marx's contemporaries (roughly speaking), they have a stronger claim to have inaugurated the study of comparative capitalisms (Marx & Reitmayer, 2019). Their antagonists were not only Marx and Engels but above all the British classical economists. Against the tendency of the latter to postulate the market economy as a natural phenomenon they stressed its constructedness. They rejected the naturalist-positivist quest to discover transhistorical laws of social behaviour, emphasising instead historical specificity and the variability of national economies. From Friedrich List onward, this school of German institutionalism defined its position against the laissez-faire model of 'Manchester capitalism'.[2] Troubled by the threat to social cohesion that the free market posed, they warned of the 'casino speculation mentality' that it spawned, and advocated welfare measures and state regulation (Schmoller in Peukert, 2001, p. 99).[3] As institutionalists, the accent—shared by Wilhelm Roscher (of the 'Older' school), Gustav Schmoller, Albert Schäffle and Adolf Wagner (of the 'Younger') and Werner Sombart and Max Weber (of the 'Youngest')—was on the social construction of markets, the centrality of states in coordinating them, and the cultural and psychological rootedness of national economies.

Weber played his part in establishing institutionalism, including comparative political economy, on a firmly orientalist platform, with western capitalism seen as uniquely liberal, rational, and 'growth permissive' (Hobson, 2004, p. 15). The East, and the ancients, by contrast, were held back by non-capitalist institutions, or by forms of capitalism that were less properly capitalist.[4] The Eurocentric ethic of this position need not detain us. Rather, we are interested in the image it projects of the formation of global capitalism and its 'varieties'. Modern capitalism, for Weber (2019, p. 373), developed in the West thanks to particular institutional and ideological innovations (cities, Calvinism, corporate agencies capable of checking princely power, and suchlike). The effect of the West on 'the rest', both directly (e.g. imperial powers erasing and creating institutions in colonies) and indirectly (e.g. the very different conditions that confronted non-Western businesses and states following the initial carve-up of the world-market by colonial states and firms) is occluded. Weber takes care to sequester his rational occidental capitalism from its history of brutality, despotism and genocide. He does this by locating its 'spirit' in commercial practices that are at least one remove from centres of power (Rehmann, 1998).

3. A 'diversity of planning regimes'

Rich in institutionalism but poor in theorisation of capitalism, these threads from early comparative capitalisms scholarship extended forward to the 1960s, at which point systematic research in this field was born. Its initial focus, invariably forgotten (except by Wolfgang Streeck), was on the onward-marching power shift 'from private capitalism to interventionist nation-states and their—*highly diverse—planning regimes*' (Streeck, 2010, p. 13, emphasis added). We are speaking here of the Hungarian-British economist Andrew Shonfield. He lays claim to have been *the* seminal thinker in the field of comparative capitalisms. It was only following *Modern Capitalism,* his magisterial study of national political-economic systems, published in 1965, that, in the judgement of Søren Etzerodt and Jesper Eriksen (2017, p. 2), it became 'conventional wisdom that there is more than one viable road to economic growth'.

Shonfield's (1965) method is institutionalism; his subject is the 'evolution of institutions'. His book sets up the British and French systems as the core polarity: Britain with its 'arms-length government' contrasted with French *dirigisme*. He links France's statism to its history of centralised absolutism, but also to its eighteenth and nineteenth-century relative backwardness vis-à-vis Britain, to which governments responded by steering economic innovation. His comparison between Britain and France does not foreground how they market but how they plan. The focus on planning is striking. It dominates the book's early chapters. One chapter, on Austria and Italy, is titled 'The State as Entrepreneur'[5] and includes a sub-section on 'state capitalism'. Equally striking is that Shonfield classes the USA and Germany as 'exceptions'—albeit ones that, given their size, may one day become the mainstream. Whereas the section on Britain and France is entitled 'The Approach to Planning', the USA and Germany are relegated to a later section: 'Market Ideologies'. The US is introduced as the only country in which capitalism is considered 'an OK word'. The US and Germany, in Shonfield's lofty summary, are 'out of the mainstream of modern capitalism', for they 'show no enthusiasm for the increasingly organised pattern of economic behaviour. … Their official doctrines continue to carry a high content of simple traditional capitalist folklore'.

The focus on planning apart, Shonfield's book has much in common with the VoC literature of our century. It is institutionalist and methodologically nationalist. It builds its argument upon a polarity posited between a traditionally liberal and a less liberal state. It ignores the economic effects of militarism. Its geographical focus is parochial, with Europe and the USA receiving a monopoly of attention. (As one reviewer (Kidron, 1966) snorted at the time, 'to pretend that this Handbook of Contemporary Planning Practice in Some Major Developed Orthodox Capitalist Countries is an analysis of modern capitalism is nonsense. … 450-odd pages on *capitalism* could not ignore the arms economy and its effect on the system; or the Cold War; or the colonial revolution. Yet this is what Shonfield has done'.) Finally, it is technocratic, equating success with economic growth. Its broad theme is simple enough, writes the same reviewer: 'growth now requires planning; only governments can plan on a national scale' (Kidron, 1966). Planning, for Shonfield, was 'not only essential for growth but also essentially for growth'—as such, he was a purveyor of 'growth fetishism' (Kidron, 1966).

Shonfield was writing during an age of rapid growth, state capitalism and national planning. Comparison between types of capitalism appeared straightforward: study the various national institutions that shape economic activity. But the return of recessions, the demise of planning, the neoliberal ascendancy, regionalisation, and above all the juggernaut of globalisation unsettled that, and comparative capitalisms research swerved in a new direction.

First, the turbulent 1970s saw the birth of the regulation school. It braided threads from Polanyi,[6] Marx, and institutionalism in its theorisation of regimes of stable capital accumulation ('modes of regulation'). Simultaneously, economic sociology was turning to the study of regional clusters of industrial production (Marx & Reitmayer, 2019), and brought Japan within its purview. This shift was associated above all with Ronald Dore, who happened to be a leading member of the Andrew Shonfield Society (yes, it existed), and who was to play a pivotal role in the renaissance of comparative capitalisms research.

Next, in the 1980s, and especially the 1990s after the collapse of the Soviet bloc and the spectacular implosion of the Japanese miracle, the question of convergence appeared with redoubled force. Were national economies being dissolved by globalisation? Would capitalist diversity disappear altogether?

The 1990s, although commonly recalled as the decade of neoliberal globalisation, in which pressures to institutional homogeneity—the Washington Consensus—reached their zenith, had begun with an explosion of comparative capitalisms research. US-Soviet bipolarity was dead; long live the new bipolarity of the Rhine model versus the Neo-American model!—to borrow Michel Albert's terms. In *Capitalism Against Capitalism* (1991), Albert proposed that there exists a Rhine model of capitalism (Germany, Netherlands and, oddly perhaps, Japan) that is institutionally pitted against, and boasts superior efficiency and welfare potential to, the less organised and coordinated Anglo-Saxon variety.

A similar approach was being developed by Dore. Dore (1996) co-edited one of the defining comparative capitalisms books of the 1990s, *National Diversity and Global Capitalism*, and contributed a chapter on Japan to one of the others, Colin Crouch and Wolfgang Streeck's (1997) *Political Economy of Modern Capitalism: Mapping Convergence and Diversity*.[7] Dore located Japan's distinctive model in its cooperative industrial relations, obligated relational contracting in intermediate goods sectors, mutually protective stock cross-holdings, and a muscular role for the state in industrial policy and distributional issues. Japan and West Germany (which after Willy Brandt was now suddenly re-theorised at the 'corporatist' pole), he argued, exemplified 'welfare capitalism' in contrast to the 'stock market capitalism [of the] Anglo Saxons'. The former tended to value social cohesion; the latter to facilitate greed. (That Dore (2000, p. 8) cites Donald Trump and Robert Maxwell as exemplars of Anglo greed caught our eye, for we are writing this on the day when Trump is giving his benefactions to Maxwell's jailbird daughter, Ghislaine.)

4. Varieties of capitalism?

The dominant colour of comparative capitalisms research in the 1980s and 1990s was 'old institutionalism', exemplified by Polanyians such as Streeck, Boyer and Esping-Andersen. At the start of the new century that changed. A growing body of Marxist scholarship entered the field, notably David Coates (2000), and these were joined, more influentially, by Peter Hall and David Soskice (2001). From this moment on the centre of gravity of research on comparative capitalisms shifted decisively.[8] Hall and Soskice's volume popularised a New Institutionalist research programme centred on the study of clusters of institutions that are most propitious for economic growth, and the development of institutional taxonomies. The central argument is that 'institutional complementarities' enable efficiency improvements and successful growth, while hybrids do not. Firms, understood as institutions, either fit with the broader institutional framework in which they're embedded, or they sit uneasily within it and economic performance suffers.

Here is not the place to discuss the VoC literature in detail. Instead, we shall draw attention to the ways in which the research programme has branched out since its beginnings in the Hall/Soskice volume. Initially, it focussed exclusively on two 'varieties' of economy in the Global North: the liberal market economy (LME) of which the US and UK are paradigms, and the coordinated market economy (CME) found in Germany and Japan. Since then it has branched out in several directions. (i) The 'varieties' have proliferated, taxonomically and geographically. Some identified a 'State-influenced market economy' (SME) that comprises France, other European Mediterranean countries, South Korea and Taiwan, while Bruno Amable distinguished five varieties: market-based, Continental European, Asian, Social-democratic and Southern European. Others have extended the scope to include countries of the Global South (in which category we are including Eastern Europe), although this remains a tiny fraction of the VoC corpus (Bohle & Greskovits, 2012; Feldmann, 2019; Schneider, 2013). (ii) The historical scope has expanded. Here, Martha Prevezer merits mention. In *Varieties of Capitalism in History* (2019), she argues that to comprehend the functioning of the 'meso-institutions' on which VoC theory focuses requires a historical orientation on 'primary' capitalist institutions (property rights, legal systems, state apparatuses) and how they have evolved historically in each nation. Also important is *Business History's* special issue on VoC, in particular the introduction by Marx and Reitmeyer (2019) which seeks to 'integrate historical institutionalism and a theory of institutional change' into the VoC framework. (iii) Some researchers affiliated to the VoC paradigm have trained their lens on the role of the state. Notably, the Institute of World Economics of the Hungarian Academy of Sciences sponsored a series of conferences on 'The Role of the State in Varieties of Capitalism'.

As a consequence of these developments within the research programme, in combination with resurgent interest in state capitalism (Kurlantzick, 2016), VoC theorists have extended the model to include 'communist' countries, notably China. At first blush, China appears a prime candidate for VoC analysis. Its growth has been stellar and, with its institutional hybrid of planning and markets, it tests the VoC thesis that mongrels underperform. In fact, however, there exists only a small literature, and with no common findings. For example, Christopher McNally (2007, p. 196) theorises China as 'a distinctly new variety of capitalism, incorporating aspects of the East Asian model of state-led capitalism, "network capitalism" and the "new global capitalism"'. In another essay, by Joachim Ahrens and Patrick Jünemann (2010), China is seen as a hybrid of LME and CME, albeit closer to the latter. Michael Witt, by contrast, presents China as an LME. In its industrial relations, for example, although *de jure* it exhibits high levels of employment protection, in practice, workers can be fired as easily as in LMEs such as Britain, and there is no possibility of collective bargaining along CME lines because independent trade unions are outlawed (Witt, 2010).[9]

5. Variegation, not variety

The lack of consensus on China's 'variety' relates to a broader criticism that has been levelled at the VoC literature, namely that, despite the name, VoC has no theory of the 'C'. It has, Jonas Pontusson (2005, p. 164) observes, 'a great deal to say about "varieties," but surprisingly little to say about "capitalism"'. Streeck has made the point with particular force: 'Ultimately, the functionalist make-up of the Hall and Soskice conceptual schema would seem to be most apparent in, and perhaps to derive from, the way it equates its main concept, "capitalism," with that of "market economy." The very problems of distribution and exploitation that are centrally emphasised when a socioeconomic formation is referred to as capitalist are thereby submerged in, or redefined as, problems of efficient production' (Pontusson, 2005). In its predilection for firm-centric analysis of a technocratic kind, it tends to downplay the antagonistic relations inherent to capitalist society. Instead it stresses cooperation and coordination, offering a functionalist perspective that conceives of countries as 'tightly coupled interactive systems of "complementary" institutions'. In short, it assumes stability, and downplays crisis tendencies; it depicts the two main varieties of capitalism in 'homeostatic equilibrium as they adjust to external economic pressures' (Schmidt, in Hay, 2005).

A related critique is that in its methodological nationalism VoC tends 'to privilege typological classification', (Peck & Zhang, 2013, p. 362) according only secondary significance to 'origin, history, agency, conflict, and change' (Streeck, 2010, p. 28). It portrays the global economy as an aggregate of national units, marginalising or altogether neglecting questions of imperialism and of uneven and combined development (UCD). As David Coates (2014, p. 174) puts it, the British and US economies 'are best thought of, not as LMEs but as imperial capitalisms, at different stages on a standard imperial trajectory'. In contrast to VoC approaches, UCD, as Nick Taylor (2014, pp. 131–132) describes, conceives of the world economy as 'a single entity in which the systemic logic of capital accumulation draws together its component parts into an overarching structure. States play an important constitutive role in this latter conception of the world economy. But so too do finance, inter-capitalist rivalry, the productivity of labour and a hierarchy of nations, or what Trotsky called an "imperialist chain"'.

In another notable contribution, Ingrid Wehr (2015, p. 134) has advanced a trenchant critique of VoC that links its lack of a relational understanding of global capitalism to its Eurocentrism. VoC leaves under-theorised 'the relational character of capitalism—that is, the fact that national forms of production and social regulation are influenced by international competition, predominant (global) modes of capital accumulation and transnational (inter-)dependencies'. It suffers from a 'blindness concerning the colonial and imperialist foundations of capitalist expansion and their repercussions for "postcolonial" societies' (Wehr, 2015, p. 135). Wehr (2015, p. 140) identifies in the VoC literature a widespread orientalist tendency to label economic regimes in the Global South 'patrimonial' (or 'crony') capitalism, centred on informal rules and authoritarian interests and thus 'not fully capitalist or not capitalist to the same degree as the United States, France or Germany'. This, she goes on, neglects the increasingly patrimonial features of Northern capitalisms and it ignores 'the fact that the dependence on subsistence production and unpaid domestic work is not an exclusive feature of "peripheral" societies but equally characteristic—not least through the gendered division of labour—for supposedly "fully developed" capitalist countries in the North'. What most comparative capitalisms research forgets, she concludes (Wehr, 2015, p. 142), is that 'capitalism from its very beginnings has been a global enterprise, not only in the sense of establishing contacts between geographically distant regions through trade but also by linking diverse geographical spaces and forms of production, consumption and social regulation. For instance, the breakthrough of industrial capitalism in England cannot be explained without the intimate entanglement of wage and slave labour'.

The above criticisms are most closely associated with left Polanyians and Marxists (Coates, Streeck, Jamie Peck, Bob Jessop) who have developed an alternative nomenclature: 'variegated capitalism'. The concept, Streeck (2010, p. 39) explains, has been advanced 'in explicit criticism of the VoC approach, not in an attempt to deny differences, but in order to place them in a context of economic and political interdependence'. Where 'varieties' connotes difference among units, 'variegated' presents the world economy as a hierarchically ordered space of flows, with multiscalar, differentially imbricated patterns of power. The concept draws attention to the role of the overall dynamics and steep hierarchies of the global system in driving institutional differentiation at the national level. Thus, a dominant 'variety', such as Britain in the nineteenth century and the US in the twentieth century, exerts enormous influence over the 'varieties' within their camp, and also, through commercial interdependence and geopolitical rivalry, on those without. Exemplary of the latter is China, which Tobias Ten Brink (2013) theorises as 'a variegated form of state-permeated capitalism', deeply shaped by its integration into the capitalist world system. Similarly, Peck and Zhang (2013, p. 266) highlight the dialectic of coexistence and competition with extant 'varieties of Western capitalism' that has moulded the Chinese model, intricately integrated as it is with the wider world economy through 'global value chains'.

6. Uneven and combined development

For Peck and Theodore (2007, pp. 733, 761), the idea of variegated capitalism shifts us away from VoC's reified taxonomy of institutional varieties in favour of a 'more expansive concern with the combined and uneven development' of capitalism 'and the polymorphic interdependence of its constitutive regimes'. They do not expand on the meaning of UCD, however.

They use 'combined' simply to mean 'systemic interdependence'. In our reading, the UCD of capitalism is a more complex concept that knits together the following ideas:

(i) Capitalism is a universalising mode of production. It undermines and usurps others. All corners of the world become in a sense 'combined': shaped by international economic and political rivalries and domination. These processes are *radically* uneven in that the development of the early colonial-capitalist powers forcefully and dramatically altered (and alters) the terrain for the rest. Seeking to keep up and to catch up, late developers adopt elements from the dominant powers: technologies, norms, institutions. These cannot be adopted wholesale; they are necessarily combined with existing structures and social relations.[10] To understand capitalism's institutional forms, one should not study only those that have evolved in the rich and former colonial powers but, equally, those at the margins and frontiers. To understand the system as a whole, the periphery has to be centred.

(ii) Capitalist market competition itself is radically uneven. Businesses operate in a framework of antagonistic interdependence: innovation in one threatens the viability of others. 'Far from establishing a harmonious equilibrium', as John Weeks (1997, p. 105) puts it, 'capitalist competition disrupts, eliminates the weak, challenges the strong, to force upon industry a new standard of efficiency and cost. The movement of capital to equalise profits across industries is the process of generating uneven development: equilibrium in exchange (a single price in a market) hides the generation of uneven development in production'. Just as innovation and high tech form the cutting edge of some capitalist sectors, crime, sweated labour, and repression are competition by other means that are forced on those in weaker positions—yet they are no less capitalist for that. Being subject to the same field of capitalist competition leads not to a homology of institutional forms but to difference, reflecting the different endowments and capacities of the various actors.

(iii) The early-developing bourgeois-colonial enterprises and states exploited their first-mover advantages, accruing wealth and power. Since then, in the Western heartlands a liberal institutional model has tended to prevail, with central state power balanced by decentralised political authority and market economy. Such structures facilitate economic globalisation and relatively flexible international political arrangements. Virtuous circles ensued, ensuring that capitalism's Western heartlands, home to the most profitable structures of accumulation and the most successful colonial domination, consolidated their global influence, while sovereignty was denied or limited for much of the rest (Dale, 1999; Van der Pijl, 2005). But the liberal capitalism of the heartlands co-constituted its 'others', through emulation and contestation. States outside the core engaged in catch-up industrialisation, which mostly relied on high levels of political mobilisation of populations and resources, dirigiste and mercantilist economic regimes and illiberal political forms.

(iv) Late development faces high hurdles. Funds for accumulation come from savings from current and future consumption, 'and if the level of current livelihood of the population is low, and the political and administrative machine weak', in Nigel Harris's words (1971, p. 140), 'then any surplus from this source is likely to be small. If the population is simultaneously growing, what surplus there is may only provide a basis for standing still rather than actually improving the situation. On the other hand, only a very powerful army and police force can snatch the surplus for national investment between the peasant's hand and mouth'.

(v) Later developers may also discover advantages of backwardness, enabling them to leapfrog developmental stages and industrialise rapidly. These include the forms of 'combination' that Trotsky identified: the availability of technology and techniques developed elsewhere, and institutional emulation.

(vi) The *loci classici* of UCD were late nineteenth-century Russia and Japan. Here, absolutist states, under pressure from military competition from Western powers (the Crimean War; Commodore Perry's black ships), launched modernisation programmes. Just as innovations in the pooling of capital through banking and the joint stock company had enabled US and German capitals to match their British rivals, in Russia and Japan the state was deployed to push through land reform, construct infrastructure, marshal resources and siphon them to 'national champions'. 'The more backward a country', observed Gershenkron, 'the more likely its industrialisation was to proceed under some organised direction; depending on the degree of backwardness, the seat of such direction could be found in investment banks, in investment banks acting under the aegis of the state, or in bureaucratic controls' (Selwyn, 2011, p. 429). In Russia, he notes, the government *substituted* for the weak domestic bourgeoisie (Gerschenkron, 1962). Highly advanced and traditional forms of production were integrated (or 'combined') within a new national amalgam, with socio-politically explosive results. Japan, as Paul Kennedy (1988, p. 266) puts it pithily, 'had to be modernised not because individual entrepreneurs wished it, but because the state needed it'. Stages of development, and institutional forms gathered by emissaries from all around the world, were combined by the newly centralised Meiji state into a new structure, with 'archaic' and 'advanced' elements side by side. In their state-capitalist trajectory, Russia and Japan were followed by China.

7. Bureaucratic state capitalism as 'variety' and 'era'

Even if China is now widely analysed as a form of state capitalism, with transnational economic processes and domestic state or private capitals folded together in different ways,, even the most sophisticated of theoretical approaches, including the 'variegated capitalisms' research programme and Steven Rolf's UCD approach (2021), still lack an explanation of the *origins* of China's capitalism. The act of transubstantiation from 'state socialism' to state capitalism is implicitly attributed to the ability of the leadership of a supposedly workers' state—Deng Xiaoping and his comrades—to leap from one mode of production to another without encountering any major social struggle or resistance. While we find much of value in the 'variegated capitalisms' research programme, we propose to solve the apparent historical conundrum of the supposed transformation under Deng by proposing a different understanding of Mao-era China. In this section, we argue that the communist-run societies, built in the image of the Soviet Union, are best understood not as 'state socialism' but as bureaucratic state capitalism, a variant of a general trend to state capitalism in the middle decades of the twentieth century that was never as insulated or alien as implied by labels like 'state socialism'.

Indeed, to make sense of the institutional variegation of capitalism, one needs to compare across space and through time. Institutionalists tend to focus on the former, asking 'which institutional complex favours rapid growth?', radicals on the latter, asking 'what transformations are global capitalism undergoing and will they hasten its demise?' During each phase of capitalism, most 'varieties' tend to trend together. In the literature on variegated capitalism there is acute awareness of this in respect of our current era, neoliberalism. But there has been little or no attempt to theorise the varieties that prevailed during the previous phase. For the purposes of this article we call the previous phase 'state capitalism'. From the 1910s, it flourished worldwide in a variety of forms (war economies, corporatism, import-substitution industrialisation (ISI), Stalinism, Keynesianism), before yielding in the final third of the twentieth century to neoliberal globalisation.

The state-capitalist trend was widely noted in the late nineteenth century, and already back then it was identified with 'state socialism'. In 1880 Prussia's railways were nationalised. It was essentially a war measure, but a school of Listian institutionalists, the Kathedersozialisten, saluted it as 'state socialist'. All governmental regulation of the economy is socialist, they maintained. Socialism is simply 'the transformation of private and competing capitals into a united collective capital', explained Albert Schäffle, a prominent Kathedersozialist (Schäffle quoted in Draper, 1989, p. 81).

Marx scoffed at this—as if 'a new society can be built through state loans, much as the building of a new railway!' Friedrich Engels, too, wrote withering critiques of the Kathedersozialisten 'who see in the nationalisation of something a half-way or preparatory measure' towards a socialist order. 'The term "state socialism"', he went on, 'expresses no clear idea whatsoever ... it is "a pointless bit of twaddle"' (Engels quoted in Draper, 1989, p. 73). 'The modern state in whatever form', he went on to argue, 'is an essentially capitalist machine, the ideal collective capitalist. The greater the productive forces it takes ownership of, and the more it becomes in reality a collective capitalist, the greater the number of citizens it exploits. The workers remain wage workers, proletarians; the capital relation is not *aufgehoben*, rather, it is intensified'.[11] Rudolf Hilferding and Nikolai Bukharin took the case further, theorising the distinctive features of 'organised capitalism' and state capitalism in the age of imperialism and world war.

Several drivers lie behind the trend to state capitalism. Firstly, as the production process becomes more sophisticated, the provision of physical infrastructure and the equipping and management of the workforce becomes complex, and likewise the education and social reproduction of the workforce. States tend to take responsibility for, if not direct control of, these tasks. A second factor is the scale of organisation of leading industries. To caricature only a little, the dominant scale of ownership, production and marketing in most firms in the eighteenth was local; in the nineteenth and early twentieth centuries it was national, and this was conducive to the rise of 'national' variants of state capitalism. A third is geopolitical competition, including arms races and war. During the First World War, capitalist states assumed muscular coordination roles, notably of the arms industry and other strategic sectors—and it was this that inspired the work of Otto Neurath on administered economies, and Nikolai Bukharin on state capitalism. Nazi Germany, with its 4-Year-Plans, is another salient case. It is no accident that the most extreme forms of state capitalism emerged during the era bookended by two world wars. Fourth is deglobalisation, by which we refer to the breakdown of international trade and capital flows, most strikingly during the Great Depression, to which states tend to respond through greater intervention, and fifth is economic crisis, to which some states respond by bailing out firms and reorganising industrial sectors. The 1930s is the paradigm here, although there has been renewed interest in state capitalist theory since the 2008 crash, including in the internationalisation of state owned enterprises (SOEs) like Germany's Deutsche Bahn AG or Russia's Gazprom. The sixth and final driver is uneven development and steep-ascent industrialisation. Meiji Japan and Tsarist Russia were discussed earlier. They were followed by the 'developmental states' of East Asia (Johnson, 1999), and by a host of postcolonial countries that aspired to state-led industrialisation, including India, North and South Korea in the 1950s, Egypt under Nasser, and Brazil under Kubitschek, Goulart and Geisel—during which time the state controlled roughly half of all investment (Dale, 2020).

Taken together, these factors explain why state capitalism prevails at certain times and in certain places. It thrives in societies geared to war and in conditions of de-globalisation. Its heyday was the interwar period. It would be misleading to see the proliferation of command-economic forms in that era as the result of political elites selecting a particular model as we might choose chocs from a box. Rather, they were well adapted to mobilising economies for military conflict and for orchestrating the conditions for capital accumulation in relatively backward economies during a period of trade involution.

The state-capitalist trend was not localised but global. It included Keynesianism and corporatism in the West, and ISI in the South.[12] So profound was the transformation that towards the end of the 1930s, E.H. Carr (1939, p. 117) could declare that the old liberal belief in the 'separation between politics and economics has ceased to correspond to any aspect of current reality'. The further generalisation of *étatisme* during World War Two only confirmed Carr's observation, as war economies were constructed even in the liberal heartlands, notably the United States and Britain. In the middle of the century, subsequent to decolonisation, many more countries followed suit, and this period also saw the beginning of the rise of Newly Industrialising Countries (NICs) such as South Korea, Taiwan and Singapore, with high levels of state planning and ownership of key industries, government manipulation of currencies, trade protection and directed credit. Under the aegis of repressive regimes, state officials were often directly involved in the running of businesses, and promulgated conformist ideologies that stressed the need for hard work and deferred gratification. As Harris (1987, p. 145) notes, the growth of the NICs was 'just as much a triumph of state capitalism as [were] the achievements of the first Five Year Plans in the Soviet Union or the People's Republic of China'. In all these cases, governments supervised the catch-up drive, they acted to protect or even insulate domestic industry from the world market, and they acted as 'binding agents' between the ('political') interests of stability and security and the ('economic') interests of accumulation, as well as repressing workers' struggles and other social movements. Today, state capitals are found disproportionately in particular economic sectors (where natural monopolies exist, e.g. transport, and/or deemed strategic, e.g. arms and energy) and in a variety of hydrocarbon economies (UAE, Russia) as well as in such rapidly-industrialising countries of the Global South as China and Indonesia (Büge et al., 2013). In the OECD states, despite neoliberalism, average government expenditure as a percentage of GDP has for several decades remained roughly level, at around 40 percent—several times greater than in the interwar period.

8. State capitalism, Soviet-style

If state capitalism could be measured by the proportion of national output produced by state-owned firms and farms, its limit would have been reached in the Soviet-style societies. Our stance here is unorthodox, since the Soviet Union is normally referred to as 'socialist' or 'state socialist'. Early Soviet leaders and theorists, though, drew a distinction between the creation of a revolutionary-democratic state power in the form of soviets that had sprung up in 1917 and inherited economic structures that could not be revolutionised overnight. As Lenin (1922) saw it, a form of state capitalism existed in early 1920s Russia, albeit shaped and constrained by the workers' government. With the evisceration of the soviets in conditions of civil war, however, and with the ebbing of the revolutionary wave that had ricocheted around Europe to Latin America before finally ending in defeat in China (1926–1927), soviet power lost its social basis at home and the potential for international extension. Political power was increasingly shaped by forces of geopolitical and geo-economic competition. In the mid-1920s a burning question was where to source the surpluses needed for new investment. In a context defined by a growing fear of external military threat, Joseph Stalin acted to violently create a new social system, based around forced industrialisation and collectivisation. In the decade that followed, investment more than doubled while consumption fell drastically as a proportion of national product. This was a 'modernising counter-revolution', undertaken by the state bureaucracy around Stalin, in the interests of capital accumulation and global competition (Cliff 1948/1974; Dale, 2017; Haynes, 2002). This moment marked the beginning of a new 'variety of capitalism'.

The state capitalism that characterised the Soviet Union from 1928 to 1991 was of a distinctive kind. This is fundamentally because the already weak forces of private business had been crushed in the aftermath of 1917, and because *all* other factors conducive to state capitalism were simultaneously present: economic backwardness, the legacy of tsarist *étatisme*, the intensity of the arms race against powerful and revisionist neighbours to the East and West, the nation's vast natural resource base (and hence its potential for autarky), and its repressive state apparatus. In addition, Cold War competition brought powerful pressures to autarky through sanctions on international transactions, notably via the CoCom list.[13]

The Soviet Union continues to be seen as the defining model of 'Communism', although we should recall that by now (2022) the North Korean CP has been in power longer than the CPSU, and the Chinese CP for roughly the same duration. While in cold-warrior fantasies all 'Communist' societies were painted with the same brush, in fact there were very striking differences, through time and among states. The extension of the bureaucratic state capitalist model after the Second World War was closely tied to the Red Army's advance, but, even so, some communist parties relied completely on Soviet power, others did not. The formation of the GDR through conquest was a different prospect to the relatively autonomous takeover of power by the Yugoslav and Albanian communist parties. Moreover, there were very different degrees of industrialisation, urbanisation, education, and so on across the region. Another variable was the immediate experience of war: some had sided with the Allies, others the Axis. And then the onset of the Cold War placed some countries, notably the GDR and Czechoslovakia, to the fore in the inter-camp rivalry while others remained peripheral, like Yugoslavia and Albania. The latter two states ended up outside the bloc, looking elsewhere for allies, the former to the Third World, the latter to China.

Indeed, the model spread globally, with China, Cuba and Vietnam evolving diverse new adaptations. The different historical legacies, economic eras and geopolitical challenges faced by 'communist' states outside Europe dictated that the adoption of bureaucratic state-capitalist institutions would bring diverging results. Their role in shaping global and regional institutions, their effects on such global processes as de-colonisation, and their mutual cooperation, coexistence or even conflict, reminds us that the Soviet experience is not the only prism through which to view the history of bureaucratic state capitalism. As James Mark and Tobias Rupprecht observe (2019, p. 82), these states were not 'inward-looking, isolated and cut off from global trends', but were 'engines' of globalisation. Our argument is a contribution in this direction, in that it integrates the stories of the GDR and Yugoslavia in a global capitalist setting, a task undertaken in the next section.

9. Variegated capitalism and state capitalism: the GDR and Yugoslavia

Following the 'variegated capitalism' method discussed above, in this final section we sketch a comparative study of two very different state-capitalist entities, the GDR and Yugoslavia, with case studies of industrial sectors. Common to both was communist ideology, their origination following the Second World War when global capitalism was predominantly nationally organised, and they both confronted economic decline when a renewed globalising shift was under way. Salient differences include their level of industrialisation, their relationship to the great powers, their national composition and their origination: one was born of revolution, the other of military occupation. The GDR was the most statist and Yugoslavia the most market-oriented of the Soviet-type economies in the 1949–1989 period.

That East German and Yugoslav political-economic institutions were similar in some ways and different in others is well known. But a systematic comparative analysis has not been attempted. This is our task in this section, drawing on the theoretical discussion above. In contradistinction to the methodological nationalism of VoC, our 'variegated capitalism' approach analyses institutional formation and differentiation as it is constituted, shaped and constrained by geopolitical and geo-economic competition within a steeply hierarchical world system. Such an approach dictates that the terms of comparison are linked to the eras of capitalist development during which the two models we are studying were constituted and functioned. The periodisation we adopt identifies three sub-phases, namely (i) the post-war and early Cold War period of national capitalisms and centralised planning in the context of sharp superpower conflict, ca. 1945–1961; (ii) a subsequent period of reform, within the context of the global great boom, which featured, across Central and Eastern Europe, periods of market experimentation with enterprises given greater autonomy, ca. 1961–1975; (iii) a new context brought about by two major factors, globalisation and deep and protracted crises, both of which posed problems for the continuation of state-capitalist structures, ca. 1975–1990. We begin the comparison on the large canvas then narrow the scope to individual industries.

9.1. An era of national capitalisms (1945–1961)

The GDR and the Federal People's Republic of Yugoslavia were established in a turbulent conjuncture characterised by revolutionary uprisings, economic deglobalisation, war devastation and post-war reconstruction. In East and West alike, the economies emerging from the war were 'war economies' characterised by muscular state intervention and planning, economic nationalism, an emphasis on armaments and heavy industry, and shortages of consumer goods. It was a period of dramatic international change, as empires fell away and the national form triumphed, and fraught with geopolitical tension, as post-war spheres of influence were hammered into place.

Pace the Cold War historians who treated Moscow and Washington as the capitals of symmetrical superpowers, the US and its allies were militarily and economically vastly stronger. Setting the terms of global competition, the US strove to construct a liberal world market, with the rest of the world integrated on its terms. The Soviet Union, having been a wartime ally of the US, emerged as its chief rival, and it simultaneously offered itself to the developing world as the model of state-led industrialisation. Its economic growth in the 1930s and its defeat of Nazi Germany provided triumphant proof that relatively 'backward' nations could deploy state-capitalist methods to leverage competitive success. These two facets of Soviet prowess—its leadership of an imperial bloc and its status as the model of state-capitalist industrialisation—were connected but not synonymous. The GDR, set up by Soviet occupying forces, followed Moscow's geopolitical leadership and adopted its economic model; post-war Yugoslavia adopted the economic model but, following a brief spell in the Soviet bloc, broke away.

Both economies were geared to post-war reconstruction through state-directed resource mobilisation. Both exhibited a strong bias towards heavy industry, in keeping with world trends at the time and that sector's military-strategic importance (Dale, 2011). Both initially favoured a Soviet form of enterprise, that is, vertically integrated and with strong backward integration into component manufacturing, which itself was a variation on the classic Fordist model (Czaban & Henderson, 1998, p. 591). The management of labour encompassed measures to muzzle the workforce, such as the suppression of independent union organisation, as well as the subsidisation of basic consumer goods to assure at least minimal welfare and social stability. The Party's task was to bind each economic unit, and each element of society, behind the overarching project of state-capital accumulation, lashing individuals and institutions into a national corporate unity and promoting a 'siege ideology' to encourage greater sacrifice.

Initially, plans were set deliberately taut in both states, particularly in capital goods and military sectors, with the aim of forcing up growth rates. The planning process centred on competitive bargaining. At the central (ministerial, federal and republic in Yugoslavia), sectoral, and enterprise levels, competition for inputs occurred on the labour market, over the allocation of investment resources (notably by managers currying favour with officials during the process of 'plan-bargaining'), and on 'grey markets' of inter-enterprise barter. Planning was reactive, not *ex ante*, and was undertaken with one eye on world markets. Planning officials were continually comparing their economies' performance against western benchmarks, and introducing successive waves of reforms—sometimes market reforms—in the attempt to 'catch up and overtake' the West. Yugoslavia abandoned taut planning in the mid-1950s but planning remained an important economic coordinating mechanism.

With these structures in view, the GDR and Yugoslavia appear as two instances of the same basic 'variety' of state capitalism. Yet in other respects they were quite distinct. The GDR was the rump of a major industrial power defeated in war; its Soviet-type institutions were directly imposed by the hegemon that brought it into being. Yugoslavia, by contrast, was a largely rural economy that had belonged to the victorious alliance. Its Soviet-type institutions were imposed by a popular party that, although looking to Moscow for inspiration and support, had led a peasant-based resistance movement during the war and came to power largely through its own forces. The GDR was the creature of conquest, Titoist Yugoslavia was born from revolution.

While both states were defined by their low productivity vis-à-vis the dominant centres of the world economy, the reasons were quite different. The GDR had been occupied by a war-devastated and economically backward power which was exacting reparations on a titanic scale. Already in 1947, gross capital industrial assets in the Soviet zone had declined to 75% of the 1936 level, in contrast to the British-occupied zone where they had risen to 111% (Ciesla, 2013, p. 65). The difference was due largely to the dismantling and removal of plant; some sectors never recovered (Ciesla, 2013, p. 67). Major industries were transferred, including, either in their entirety or large majority, aluminium, chemicals, electrical, engineering, iron and steel, locomotives, optical, and tyres. Aviation and aeronautics are another case. Having been (notoriously) a world leader during the war, with firms such as Junkers and Messerschmidt that benefitted from vast supplies of skilled slave labour in Germany and Austria, following the war most plant was removed, and most of the Soviet-occupied zone's aeronautical engineers, scientists, and technicians were removed to the USSR, too, where they worked until the early 1950s. Or consider the auto industry. The zone included plants run by Audi, BMW, and Mercedes-Benz, among others, that had produced over a quarter of Germany's pre-war automobile output. During the war much of this plant was damaged or destroyed, and then the Soviet authorities asset-stripped most of the remainder. In one typical factory in Chemnitz they removed 3800 machines—98% of the capital stock (Ciesla, 2013, p. 64). Of plants where production did restart, many were Soviet-run, with most product shipped as reparations to the USSR, at least until the early 1950s. None of this is to say that East German industries were not innovative. Even the Trabant, when introduced in 1957, was pioneering in several technology and design aspects (Koscs, 2021). But it did place them at a disadvantage vis-à-vis counterparts across the Cold War border. Such 'domestic' disadvantage was exacerbated by economic warfare from the western powers, notably the Battle Act (1951) and the CoCom list—which the SED leadership regarded as a 'productivity-embargo and therefore a factor in the worldwide competitive struggle' (Mittag, in Dale, 2004, p. 164).

At one level, East Germany's adoption of the Soviet economic model was rational: the USSR had proven itself, in terms of industrialisation and growth, in the preceding two decades. A strictly centralised economy would ward against economic encroachment from the West. However, as a resource-poor and plundered economy, geared to rapid industrialisation and squeezed living standards and attempting to replicate, within a fragment of German territory, the sort of industrial breadth that had existed within Hitler's Reich and its *Mitteleuropa* extensions, inevitably bred contradictions. These initial adverse conditions dominated GDR economic history. A significant example was the semi-forced collectivisation of agriculture. Although aimed at releasing labour-power for the industrial towns and squeezing the rural population for industrial investment, in fact it led less to an intended movement of labour-power into the factories than to an uncontrolled flight of farmers to West Germany that resulted in food shortages and consumer discontent.

In Yugoslavia, by contrast, low productivity is explained principally by the backward, agrarian character of much of the country. By some accounts, interwar Yugoslavia had the largest rural overpopulation in Europe and, despite an ISI drive, half of its exports were made up of just five primary products (timber, corn, wheat, iron and copper ores), while four fifths of its imports were finished or semi-finished goods (Aldcroft, 2006, pp. 83–84). War reversed much of the economic progress of the inter-war period, destroying up to two-fifths of industrial facilities (Lampe, 2000, p. 239). The post-war regime hoped to radically change the country's economic base by launching a Soviet-inspired five-year industrialisation plan in 1947, based on a gigantic value transfer from the countryside, support in terms of equipment and materials from the USSR, Czechoslovakia and Hungary, and imports from the West. Its plans proved over-ambitious, badly timed given the onset of the Cold War, and partly resulted in the Soviet-Yugoslav split in 1948, as Moscow and Belgrade clashed over development policies. Soviet leaders viewed Yugoslav leaders as acting too independently, while the Yugoslav side rejected the self-serving terms under which Moscow sought to form Yugoslav-Soviet joint stock companies (Perović, 2007, p. 57).

While Yugoslavia's agrarian character contrasted with industrialised East Germany, it too experienced significant economic dislocation on account of the changing geopolitical situation, which in some ways paralleled the East German experience, and impaired its firms' international competitiveness. To protect against the Soviet military threat and to promote economic equality between the republics, entire factories were stripped and moved to mountainous or coastal areas of Bosnia and Herzegovina or Montenegro. New industrial plant, ranging from machine tools to locomotives, tractors and trucks, was often built in poorly connected areas, sometimes without adequate sources of supply and with few industrial traditions (Bombelles, 1968, p. 34). Significant proportions of the new investment related to defence, and, from the mid-1950s, with Yugoslav-Soviet rapprochement in full swing, military production branched out. Military-industrial capacity began to be used on a dual track to produce for non-military purposes as well, and for exports of military hardware (Pezo, 1983, pp. 38–93). Thus, as with the GDR, economic dislocation had long-term economic consequences, albeit for different reasons. The GDR was asset-stripped by the USSR, while Yugoslavia relocated industries to less developed areas in face of the Soviet threat. Both economies experienced long-term disadvantages as a consequence, even though particular industrial sectors in both states did exhibit innovation and dynamism. Even though it ultimately became a bone of contention between those Yugoslav republics that gained more from it and those that gained less (Lampe, 2013), the military-industrial complex was at the centre of some of Yugoslavia's key diplomatic and economic gains in the Third World (Lazić, 2021).

After 1948, Yugoslavia re-designed its developmental institutions with a view to leaning on the West to maintain national independence. The shift involved abandoning the command economy and the harsher elements of Stalinist rule in favour of enhanced market mechanisms and socio-political freedoms. In performing this manoeuvre, the party-state had to toe a careful line. To prove itself to the West, it had to underline its dissimilarity with the Soviet bloc, which is why it emphasised 'de-centralisation', 'de-*étatisation*' and 'democratisation'. At the same time, to justify its rule and to deflect Soviet accusations that it had abandoned its ideology, it developed the doctrine of the withering away of the state, of which workers' self-management was the basic building block. The commitment to 'withering' was on paper only, but self-management involved a real attempt at decentralising state power and devolving investment to economic units operating on a market basis. Workers participated in enterprise decision-making through elected workers' councils. In these ways, Yugoslav institutions reflected the regime's attempt to adopt a non-aligned, Third Way course between East and West (Unkovski-Korica, 2014).

The Yugoslav system of workers' self-management became a *cause célèbre* among sections of the global left, even spawning an academic school of thought which studied what it called the 'labour-managed' or 'Illyrian firm', which was presumed to maximise profits per worker while operating on the market. Although proponents of the school later accepted that the self-managing firm on the market existed more on paper than in reality (Estrin & Uvalic, 2008), and although up to two thirds of investment at the time was still disbursed by federal institutions, 1950s Yugoslavia appeared sufficiently unlike the Soviet bloc to ensure that it maintained its most-favoured-nation status in the US and friendly trade relations with Western Europe (Unkovski-Korica, 2016, pp. 116–123). The Yugoslav government at this time developed an ISI strategy based on the protection of domestic industries, administered international trade (through import and export licenses), production using imported Western capital goods, cheap primary and intermediate inputs from the CMEA and/or Third World states, and cheap domestic labour (Czaban & Henderson, 1998, p. 591). Thanks to Western aid, Yugoslavia was also able to chart a strategy of accumulation without peasant dispossession. Put differently, aid enabled it to avoid agricultural collectivisation and thereby the sort of damage wrought by the Soviet collectivisation drive in the 1930s. This allowed for a less confrontational transfer of value from countryside to towns, which was achieved instead through price policies. Western aid and loans amounted to seven percent of Gross Social Product in 1952–1966, which underwrote the transfer of fully eight percent of GSP from agriculture in the same period (Dyker, 2011, p. 59). Despite this, the frenzied tempo of Yugoslav investment in finishing the central heavy-industry projects of the first five-year plan led to a squeeze on consumers, with consumption per head not returning to pre-war levels until 1960 (Sirc, 1979, p. 51). Although it avoided open rebellion, as occurred in East Germany in 1953 or Hungary in 1956, Yugoslavia did experience a strike wave that lasted several years starting in 1958, which deeply shook its political leadership and intensified the struggle between proponents and opponents of deeper market reform (Unkovski-Korica, 2016, pp. 165–219). The bilateral trade and financial arrangements with Western economies, meanwhile, had led to a spiralling trade deficit and increased sovereign debt problems, which heralded a growing dependency on Western states (Woodward, 1995).

The history of the Yugoslav automotive industry illustrates the above points. The *Zastava* factory in Kragujevac was not built under Tito but had a long prehistory as an armaments producer since 1853, with a brief attempt at Chevrolet truck assembly in 1939–1941. Sustaining heavy damage during the war, it faced a further crisis when the Tito-Stalin split forced the relocation of military-related production and experts to the mountainous and more defendable terrain of Bosnia (Stankovic, 2018, p. 239). Here Yugoslavia's position outside the blocs provided an outlet for Yugoslav enterprises not immediately available to the GDR. Able to find partners in Western companies, *Zastava* attained a FIAT licence to produce vehicles in 1954 and undertook major modernisation on the basis of Italian know-how in 1958 (Palairet, 1992, p. 900). As early as 1955, *Zastava* underwent an early change in management that characterised the later generational shift in much of Yugoslav industry in the 1960s, as the loyal, political partisan director and former worker gave way to an expert manager and a team of highly trained experts who went on a two-month tour of Western Europe (Stankovic, 2018, pp. 240–241). Under pressure to produce quickly for the domestic market under an ISI strategy, however, *Zastava* relied on local suppliers who did not find it profitable to produce parts with specialised tools given *Zastava*'s small size. Enterprise management complained about the high costs, unreliable quality and intermittent supply of parts (Palairet, 1992, p. 900). Moreover, the company struggled, as did much of Yugoslav industry, to turn peasants into workers. Raising production from 1,000 vehicles in 1956 to 26,000 in 1964 required more workers, more training in response to the demands of mechanisation, and careful negotiation of high absenteeism rates, as worker-peasants shuttled between city and country following the agricultural seasons (Stankovic, 2018, p. 242). For a time, though, firms like *Zastava* in the automobile industry enjoyed a captive local market, and domestic competition was still in its infancy, guaranteeing sales growth despite costly production. By the early to middle 1960s, though, there were signs of market saturation across Yugoslav industry (Musić, 2021, p. 35). This was a problem commonly encountered by states that adopted ISI in Latin America too: despite—or because of—the limits of selling to the small, domestic market, firms had few incentives to compete for new markets abroad (Schwartz, 2000, p. 244).

While Soviet-style ISI had charted some success in lifting the GDR and Yugoslavia out of wartime devastation contradictions were piling up. In the initial phases of ISI, overall accumulation was emphasised over firm-level profitability, leading to the infamous problem of soft-budget constraints. The resulting waste and inefficiency have parallels with the major banks in our own era, which can accrue gargantuan bad debt because they know they are 'too big to fail'. Soft budget constraints and taut planning generated a distinctive business cycle. As each new investment cycle opened, there were shortages of inputs; debt and balance of payment deficits grew; these resulted in disruption and bottlenecks; and finally consumer goods grew scarce, exacerbating worker dissatisfaction. Planners had to slow the pace of investment in order to get priority projects going again, which would then release resources, and economic growth could once again resume. A peculiar cycle of stop-go policies characterised these societies as a consequence, as the state tried to brake and then re-start accumulation. Enterprises in turn hoarded, bartered, engaged in 'storming', and produced low-quality goods to meet formal or informal targets (Dale, 2004, pp. 85–89). Despite abandoning taut planning and increasing market operation from 1950, some of these symptoms persisted, a concern that Tito explicitly decried in the early 1960s (Dyker, 2011, pp. 60–61). These afflictions of the Soviet model provided the context, in Yugoslavia and the GDR alike, for the market reform experiments that we consider in the next section.

9.2. Dilemmas of globalisation (1961–1975)

Through the 1950s, and into the 1960s, the economies of 'communist' Eastern Europe, including the GDR and Yugoslavia, posted growth rates at or above the European average (Good & Tongshu, 1999, p. 114). But the world-economic shift from post-war national reconstruction to internationalisation began to signal problems ahead. Pressures to economic reform resulted from a contradiction inherent in the state-capitalist institutional arrangement. It had achieved some success in promoting 'modernisation' and trade expansion. In so doing, it contributed to forms of economic integration and internationalisation, which in turn would accelerate competitive pressures (Haynes & Husan, 2002, p. 279). Both regimes experimented with business reform and pursued greater internationalisation, but the GDR remained at the statist end of the spectrum, while Yugoslavia pushed the bounds of market reform, passing over temporarily to an export-led growth model.

For the GDR, reform was facilitated by several background conditions: the SED regime's enhanced confidence following the building of the Berlin Wall in 1961, the Soviet Union's own reform debates of 1962–1965, and the slight but significant relaxation of the Soviet grip that followed from Khrushchev's destalinisation, from the shocks of the 1953–1956 upheavals in the GDR and Hungary, and from the Sino-Soviet split. Beginning in 1967, the GDR enacted reforms to business organisation and incentive structures. Larger business units were created, in emulation of the Western multi-divisional corporation, and were given greater managerial autonomy with respect to allocation of resources for investment, collection of income, borrowing, and wage determination (Swain & Swain, 1998, p. 119). Incentives were adapted to encourage quality over quantity, productivity enhancement and intensive growth. Planning criteria were adapted to favour indicators based on efficiency rather than brute output, and prices were accorded an enhanced role in determining resource allocation, with the aim of forcing inefficient methods out of use. Raw materials prices were raised, and managerial reward systems were redesigned to encourage the introduction of new technologies. The SED leader Walter Ulbricht (in Przybylski, 1992, pp. 164–165) even spoke of the need for a 'symbiosis of plan and market', adding that those that fail to meet 'the requirements of the market cannot live up to society's requirements either'.

Simultaneously, attempts were made to expedite international cooperation. Khrushchev's call for greater CMEA integration was embraced by the East German regime. 'The great monopoly groups of Western Europe', warned Ulbricht in 1964, 'have spread across national barriers due to pressure from American competitors, in their search for technical progress' (Marsh, 1973, p. 54). His successor, Eric Honecker, believed, likewise, that West European integration should act as a spur to closer integration in the East, and indeed as a model—and he communicated these beliefs to the CMEA Secretary, Nikolai Faddeev (Graf, 2020, p. 123). The GDR's strategy was to capitalise on its position within the CMEA, promoting its industries as the ones that could supply high-value products in exchange for primary and intermediate inputs from other CMEA states. Some movement on intra-CMEA cooperation was charted, but the going was slow, and conflict among member states over the distribution of costs and benefits was endemic.[14]

To illustrate, let us again take the automotive industry. In the GDR it had not been a strategically prioritised sector, but the car was gaining increasing significance for mobility and as a prized consumer good. Domestic sales brought in substantial revenues to the national treasury due to the high price mark-up on cars (Bauer, 1997), plus there was export potential, at least within the CMEA.[15] However, the industry was becoming increasingly sophisticated. New cars were composed of thousands of parts, many of them complex; each car manufacturer required either ambitious levels of vertical integration or closely coordinated links to networks of suppliers. In order not to be left too far behind global standards, in the 1970s a modernisation programme was initiated. Given the limitations of the domestic engineering industry and pressure on funding in the wake of the economic crisis of 1970–1972, compounded by the financial demands of a housing programme announced by the new SED leader Eric Honecker, a go-it-alone strategy appeared unviable (Bauer, 1997). Instead, planners and auto executives began to explore cooperation with their Czechoslovak counterparts. The Czechoslovaks would develop and produce the engine, with the East Germans taking responsibility for the gearbox, axles, and other parts (Bauer, 1997). The GDR-Czechoslovak joint venture would provide most of the necessary equipment, with the rest to be obtained from the 'non-socialist abroad'. At the time this seemed perfectly rational, in view of the international context of détente and the revival of GDR trade with the West that followed the Federal Republic's 'new Ostpolitik'. Western policymakers and companies also perceived a renewed interest in expanding trade with CMEA partners as a way of rescuing investments and counteracting falling domestic profit rates in the troubled 1970s. Finally, the global financial environment was opening doors. With financial globalisation and the 'oil crisis' of 1974–1975, the world was flush with cheap money. Ultra-low real interest rates were conducive to 'debt-led growth': the import of advanced equipment to modernise industrial plant, the output of which will in part be exported, earning revenues to repay the initial loans. Their good reputation for repaying loans ensured that the East European dictatorships were seen as a safe bet by Western bankers. It seemed, for a time, that the GDR's variant of state capitalism was evolving from a heavily national model towards a new type that would include cooperation with CMEA partners and strengthened trading links with the West. A number of GDR companies commenced collaborative ventures with western counterparts, typically in the Third World, and some of them saw a significant scale of activity (Trecker, 2020). The engineering firm Schwermaschinenbaukombinat 'Ernst Thälmann' (SKET), for example, owned, among many other assets, 350 rolling mills and 1,200 cranes in over forty countries.

Whereas the GDR had scaled back its cautious market reform programme at an early stage, Yugoslavia pressed on. At the turn of the 1960s it embarked on a major market reform programme, with profound implications for its business, societal and political institutions. Market expansion was coupled with a *de jure* strengthening of workers' self-management as ideological cover, as had occurred in the early 1950s. If in the 1950s investment funds had still been centralised, with prices centrally controlled and enterprise income distribution heavily regulated, the 1960s saw investment decisions devolved to enterprises and banks, prices freed except for key raw materials and investment goods, and greater control of income distribution ceded to the enterprises (Granick, 1975, pp. 323–350). In theory, this was happening to allow workers' self-management to realise its full potential. Reforms established the Workers' Assembly, an institution embracing all employees that could, supposedly, take sovereign decisions over and above the elected workers' council, with referendums as a way of making major decisions involving the whole workforce. In practice, however, these bodies were subordinated to the managerial group or the director of the enterprise. Contemporary researchers showed that, in the late 1960s, it was directors who largely made decisions, though they did feel indirectly constrained by the structures of self-management and duly factored in policies which would mollify work forces (Granick, 1975, pp. 351–394). Later research confirmed the increasing power of the managerial elites—*de facto* if not *de jure*. Enterprise managements imported the multidivisional corporate structure from the US (Sacks, 1983). Ljubica Spaskovska and Anna Calori (2021, p. 421) recount the process whereby the Bosnian giant Energoinvest hired McKinsey to advise on its restructuring in the 1960s, with the aim of breaking into global markets. They cite Energoinvest's founder, Emerik Blum, stating his wish for McKinsey to redesign the company's structure, into which he would simply insert the workers' councils wherever he felt necessary. While agreeing that managerial elites in the late 1960s were strengthened in the factories, Goran Musić (2021, pp. 41–49), in his study of two automobile factories in Yugoslavia, has suggested that the extent of the influence of self-management bodies also depended on the standing of individual enterprises on the market, the composition of their workforce, and the political activism of the blue-collar workers themselves through the party, trade unions, workers' councils and higher bodies.

Behind the extensive market adaptations of the self-management system lay the attempt at a much deeper integration in the world economy than that contemplated by the Soviet satellites in the 1960s. Joining GATT in 1961, devaluing the dinar, introducing a single exchange rate, lowering tariffs, allowing foreign direct investment, and bringing most domestic prices in line with world market prices, Yugoslavia began what Diane Flaherty has argued was an export-led growth strategy, which lasted until 1976. While some successes were achieved in terms of productivity gains, the usual stop-go cycle continued, accompanied by rising unemployment, inflation and imports in 1967–1972. Moreover, in the following few years, global growth rates fell, West European protectionism increased and the rate of recruitment of Yugoslav guest-workers, a key source of foreign currency through remittances, decreased dramatically, hampering the export orientation effort. The geography of Yugoslav trade did not follow the expectations of the reformers, who hoped for greater integration with Western markets after the early success of the 1950s and 1960s. In the 1970s, exports began to shift eastwards and southwards, areas where Yugoslav companies could not earn convertible currencies to plug the rising balance of trade deficit and cover the cost of foreign borrowing (Flaherty, 1982).

The Yugoslav auto-industry illustrates some of these tendencies well. The case of *Zastava* is once again instructive, as the company tried to exploit Yugoslavia's position between the blocs to improve its standing in international markets. *Zastava* began domestic vertical integration in the 1960s in order to overcome the obstacles to production described in the preceding section. Then it went a step further, and entered a complex, multi-lateral trading web, spanning the Western and Eastern blocs. With FIAT's help, it developed the capacity to produce the Z-101 model, a variant of a FIAT model. *Zastava* became an exporter of components within a system that united FIAT in Italy, the VAZ plant in the USSR and the FIS factory in Poland. In part payment, *Zastava* took Russian Ladas and Polski Fiats, which it would then sell on the Yugoslav home market. Its income rose from 115,000 clearing roubles in 1969 to 25 million by 1973, and saw *Zastava* devise a plan to ramp up production to 500,000 cars a year in order to supply the CMEA market from 1977. That plan, however, ran into trouble. It is not clear whether there was enthusiasm for it on the Soviet side. What does seem clear is that local political authorities played a role in scuppering it. Following the 1973 oil shock, the Yugoslav government and planners began to shift back towards an ISI model. They wanted to protect local producers, but they also wanted enterprises to seek markets which could lead to earnings in convertible foreign currency, aims which were at odds with the *Zastava* management's plans. Simultaneously, there was resistance to the plans within the factory, as the oil crisis made *Zastava*'s repayment of the debts incurred to produce an earlier model more expensive. There were also reports of a power struggle between the town hall and the firm's historic director, Prvoslav Raković. All that facilitated a politically-engineered coup against Raković in 1974 and the rejection of his plans (Palairet, 1993; Stankovic, 2018). If we leave aside the role of domestic political pressures in this example, the story of *Zastava* reminds us that international forces beyond the control of Yugoslav actors were decisive in enabling and constraining the potential of such ventures.

Deeper market reform in the long 1960s, however, did make it harder for state managers to discipline the population. In his extensive study of labour strikes in the period from 1958 to 1969, Neca Jovanov (1979) concluded that the decreasing influence of workers in the institutions of power in that decade was a prime reason for taking industrial action. Social discontent in the Yugoslav context was, moreover, not easily disentangled from the national question. The various republic leaderships sought to pass the blame to each other or the federal government. After the first post-1948 strike in Trbovlje (Slovenia) in 1958, for example, political leaders from several less developed republics accused the Slovene republic leadership of having encouraged the strike in order to extract from the federal state policy benefits favourable to Slovene industry (Unkovski-Korica, 2016, pp. 165–185). Later, following the 1965 market reforms, there was a further rise in social tensions. This time, the Croatian party leadership prominently rode a wave of popular mobilisation known as the Croatian Spring (1967–1971), which demanded greater liberalisation and republic-level control of resources (Batović, 2017). Given the Soviet-style fusion of political and economic power in the federal party-state, discontent and pressure for greater democratic participation in decision-making threatened to spill over into a threat to the system as such. In the event, Tito and the federal party leadership still had enough room for manoeuvre in the 1960s and 1970s to weather the storm. They gradually reversed the liberalisation of the 1960s, while conceding some national and social demands, including the decentralising constitution of 1974, which strengthened the republics, and the Associated Labour Act of 1976, which promised to strengthen the influence of blue-collar workers relative to managerial and technocratic elites in the institutions of self-management. Increased state spending and debt facilitated a rise in living standards and ensured social peace through the rest of the 1970s, though this would ultimately prove as fleeting as the low costs of borrowing from global financial markets (Duda, 2010; Musić, 2021, pp. 54–59).

In the 1960s and early 1970s GDR and Yugoslavia found themselves torn between relative autarky and world-market integration. The former was expressed as a reliance on protected domestic and regional markets, principally the CMEA. The latter was expressed in trade at world prices, technology imports and debt dependency. The former was attractive because it gave national ruling classes more control over development, but it threatened to suffocate economic growth, given the inefficiencies of protectionism. The latter was attractive because it intensified the competitive edge of some industries, but it also proved destabilising, as it brought dependency on economic fluctuations beyond the control of these states. Worse, from their perspective, their more advanced competitors presided over more resources with which to adapt to, and indeed to shape, these fluctuations. Although the resulting crises and intensified class struggle in the GDR and Yugoslavia could be partially suppressed, they could not be avoided. The unravelling of the two states' attempts at dealing with the dilemmas posed by globalisation is covered in the next section.

9.3. Global shocks and the unravelling of state capitalism (1975–1991)

In the mid-1970s our two regimes faced a suddenly volatile global economic order. The certainties of the long boom, with steadily expanding demand and a predictable low oil price, yielded from 1974 to a rollercoaster decade, with deep recessions and wild fluctuations in oil price and interest rates. In finance, Nixon's dismantling of the Bretton Woods system and the reflux of petrodollars into western banks sparked rapid globalisation and volatility. For Yugoslavia and East Germany, in an exact parallel to the debt crisis that afflicted the ISI economies of Latin America and which led to 'La Década Perdida' of the 1980s, 1979–1983 brought a quadruple whammy in the form of collapsing demand and a soaring oil price, rocketing interest rates and a rising dollar (in which most international debts were denominated). The strategy of debt-led growth now lay in tatters. Both regimes shifted to an emergency footing, centred on desperate attempts to stave off bankruptcy through import controls, additional borrowing, export drives, and austerity measures. Welfare spending was throttled, with knock-on consequences for regime legitimacy.

For East Germany, servicing the interest payments on its existing debt swallowed roughly half of its hard currency earnings by 1980, which made further borrowing inescapable. In 1983 and 1984 the FRG stepped in with two gigantic interest-free loans, each of around 1 billion Deutschmarks. This was merely the most visible aspect of what was becoming a very awkward reliance on West Germany. Already in the 1960s Ulbricht (in Bender, 1995, p. 110) had fretted that trade with the FRG could play the role of a 'trojan horse', leading to an economic dependence that would bring political consequences. By the 1980s, the horse was clearly within the citadel.

Once again we can take the auto industry as illustrative. In East Germany the calculations on which the modernisation plan had been based now suddenly failed to add up. The country's indebtedness to the West was spiralling out of control, and by 1980 its payments for Soviet oil were running at ten times the level of just a decade before (Bauer, 1997, p. 112). The option of self-reliance, with equipment provided by the domestic engineering sector, was vanishing: the share of its output allocated to domestic machine tool production had plummeted to only 16%, with exports prioritised—including of equipment for automobile manufacture (Bauer, 1997, p. 112). In this context, an alternative way of rescuing the joint venture with the Czechoslovaks began to be explored: to buttress it with deals with western auto firms. The method would be barter: the import of complete plant, to be paid for with products from its assembly lines. One such project, a propshaft plant built under licence from Citroën, did go ahead but most others stalled. In consequence, the modernisation plan could not be revived and, despite years of work on its development and substantial preliminary investments, the joint venture with the Czechoslovaks was scrapped (Bauer, 1997). The Ifa conglomerate had little option but to continue to produce the same old models for increasingly dissatisfied domestic consumers, and exports declined. Having once been among Eastern Europe's leading marques, Ifa's Trabants and Wartburgs ceded position to the Fiats and Renaults produced under licence elsewhere in the Soviet sphere and Yugoslavia.

No further CMEA joint ventures were attempted in the auto industry. Ifa's internationalisation initiatives shifted reluctantly but inexorably westward. In the early 1980s, in the context of inter-German détente, a liaison developed with Volkswagen (VW). The Western firm's intention, its president, Carl Hahn (in Dale, 2004, p. 223), explained to East Germany's Minister for Foreign Trade, Gerhard Beil, was to shift production to East Germany due to 'the rising costs in FRG industry'. Or, as VW's director of finance put it, 'why go to Korea when wage levels next door are only a quarter of West German levels?' (Damus, 1990, p. 70). The GDR's well-trained and low-paid workforce, and its proximity to major European markets, then, were obvious attractions. As for the GDR, cooperation with VW was valued as a lever for raising productivity, and a means of earning hard currency through exports to third markets. The SED Economics Secretary Günter Mittag initially hoped that an Ifa-VW joint venture would eventuate (Przybylski, 1992, p. 189). His colleagues, however, concerned about rising dependence on the West and the costs in every-scarcer Deutschmarks, blocked the idea. In 1984 a compromise was reached whereby Ifa would build VW engines under licence; a part of these would be delivered to VW as payment, with the rest to be installed in improved Wartburgs.[16] In short, by the mid-1980s Western TNCs were showing a greater capacity to re-organise the Eastern European division of labour than CMEA-based enterprises themselves. This shift is sometimes viewed as a triumph of private capital over state capital, but the picture was not so neat. Of the three major players in Eastern Europe, Fiat was a private company but Renault was publicly owned and VW was 40% in state hands.

The GDR planners, in the 1980s, were also facing constraints on their ability to manage the domestic population. Following periods of major industrial struggle in the 1940s and the workers' uprising of 1953, a combination of authoritarianism, welfare concessions, and the clampdown on emigration (the Berlin Wall) had succeeded in re-establishing social stability. Following resurgent social discontent in the early 1970s, under Eric Honecker an implicit social contract formed, with industrial relations stabilised in exchange for an improved social wage (including a house-building programme). In the 1980s, a decade of austerity, social discontent returned, and the political limitations of the Soviet-type 'variety' of state capitalism grew more pronounced. Furthergoing economic reform would require the cooperation of classes of the population that were desirous of greater political participation, yet to absorb and channel these demands through liberal democracy was precluded. And because the economy was centralised in state hands, all popular grievances, whether political or economic, zeroed in on the government (Cliff, 1964, p. 319). In earlier decades, when rapid economic growth had brought villagers to the cities and workers into the offices, this vulnerability of the political system mattered less. But the citizenry of the 1980s was more educated and urban and less tolerant of regime hypocrisy and propaganda. When a new political opportunity structure arose, in Gorbachev's reforms and the crumbling of empire, they took the initiative, first through emigration and then through strikes and demonstrations that culminated in East Germany's dissolution in 1990.

Yugoslavia's trajectory from 1970s crisis to eventual dissolution was in some respects similar to that of East Germany. The global economic shocks of the 1970s upset several important calculations of Yugoslavia's reform movement. These were premised on increased trade with the EEC, Yugoslavia's main economic trading partner from the mid-1950s to the mid-1970s onward. To raise productivity, enterprises cut labour, and unemployment was only kept down by mass worker emigration. When migrant labour flows from the GDR dried up in 1961, Bonn sourced replacements in Italy, Greece and Turkey, and then in Yugoslavia. From around 9,000 Yugoslav labour migrants in West Germany in 1960, by 1968 the figure had climbed to 119,000 and to over half a million in 1973 (Dale, 1999; Molnar, 2014). At the height of the guest-worker migration, over a million Yugoslav citizens lived abroad, and the value of foreign-currency remittances, combined with funds raised through foreign tourism in Yugoslavia, helped temporarily finance the country's increasing payments deficit, as imports continued to outpace exports (Bernard, 2019; Schierup, 1990). Then, in the 1970s, rising protectionism in the EEC (including embargos or quotas on Yugoslav beef and textile goods), the 1973 oil shock (Yugoslavia was an oil importer), and the 1974–1975 recession in Western Europe (prompting a sudden drop in recruitment of workers and a rise in returnees) all combined to severely weaken Yugoslavia's economic position. Yugoslav industry in the early 1980s increasingly resembled its East German counterpart: importing Western technology and exporting higher-value products to the Soviet bloc (Artisien & Holt, 1980).

It was in response to these external shocks in the mid-1970s that Yugoslavia returned to ISI. To a degree, the shift was successful in that the economy grew at a respectable pace. Nonetheless, a World Bank document (1983, p. 15) concluded about the five-year plan in 1976–1980: 'Taking the plan overall, in substantial measure Yugoslavia succeeded in achieving its aggregate growth and investment objectives. Yet at the end of the plan its external position was considerably more vulnerable than had been the case at the beginning'. As in previous business cycles, high investment rates across the board, in part the result of a strategy of not disciplining enterprises for fear of provoking national strife, sucked in more imports. This then led to a sudden and unsustainable leap in sovereign debt, given changes in the international economic order at this time (rise in oil price, increase in interest rates, sluggish growth in OECD). In the words of the same World Bank document (1983, p. 15): 'external shocks were to a considerable degree responsible for this outcome'.

The situation deteriorated fast in the 1980s, and Yugoslavia entered economic freefall and institutional breakdown. To deal with its mounting debt crisis, the federal government turned to IMF stand-by arrangements in June 1980. The further deep debt-servicing crisis in 1982, when the sovereign debt exceeded $20 billion, led to a series of painful structural adjustment programmes. The economic plight contributed to inter-republic conflicts over who should pay for the crisis. This expressed itself in part as a struggle between the richer, north-western republics that sought to preserve their powers and the constitutions of 1974, and Serbia, which sought greater centralisation, a demand which dovetailed with the IMF's demand for a clear creditor-borrower relationship (Woodward, 1995). Meanwhile, the IMF programmes in the 1980s contributed to a drastic fall in household income, with one survey showing only 16 percent of Yugoslavs were able to cover their cost of living out of regular incomes in late 1983 (Ramet, 1985, p. 6). Devaluing the dinar repeatedly did little to ameliorate the balance of trade deficit, but hard import restrictions did help overcome the immediate crisis. Yet, on account of import restrictions, the Yugoslav economy found itself on the brink of discontinuing technological transfer altogether in the second half of the 1980s. Policy-makers continued to flounder as export efforts appeared more improvised than strategic, Yugoslav companies found it difficult to beat competition in Western markets, and the end of self-management and the privatisation of the means of production became ever more appealing as a way out of the crisis for increasingly powerful sections of the party leadership (Dyker, 2011, pp. 238–285).

The automobile industry is again illustrative of these trends. The case of *Zastava* in particular is representative, in that every new model it produced saw the need for greater and greater investment, based on imported equipment, and greater debt. Already heavily indebted after 1973 and the Z-100 venture, *Zastava* fell into deeper problems with every new model. Both the Yugo (1979–1980) and Florida (1987–1988) models proved very expensive. Moreover, the company only appeared to invest when new models were designed, and not in the intervening periods, weakening its ability to use the new equipment to rapidly produce new models on a sufficient scale to capture new markets and make sizeable profits. In a desperate bid to earn hard currency, the company was subsidised and egged on by the forex-hungry federal government to push exports to the USA in the second half of the 1980s, even though it could make more profits at home. Producing the Yugo-America for the US market derailed the production of the last run of the still profitable Z-750 for the domestic market, and the Florida was built only in nominal quantities. Michael Palairet estimates that the accumulated losses in the 1980s amounted to $1 billion (Palairet, 1993, pp. 120–126).

As the crisis deepened and living standards plummeted, strike levels rocketed, bringing open class struggle back, after the relative hiatus of the 1970s. The number of strikers was 28.5 times higher in 1988 than it had been in 1980 (Dobrivojević Tomić, 2019, pp. 172–173) In his study of two automobile factories in this period, Music investigates how the crisis was filtered through the institutional framework set up by the Associated Labour Act of 1976. He compares and contrasts the Slovene Maribor Automobile Industry (*Tovarna avtomobilov Maribor*, TAM) and the Serbian Rakovica Motor Industry *(Industrija motora Rakovica*, IMR). In the former, the managerial-technical cadres largely survived the purges and reorganisations of the 1970s, successfully disciplining the organs of self-management to push through their preferred policies. In the latter, the highest organs of self-management, especially the Central Workers' Council, acted as an arbiter for lower-level councils and department directors, blocking decision-making. Unlike in TAM, the lower-level department directors in IMR did not see eye-to-eye, and were constrained by more assertive blue-collar activism in the organs of self-management (Music, 2021, pp. 60–78). The contrast between IMT and TAM allows Music to illustrate the extent to which, contrary to dominant interpretations of the period, the subjective factor, i.e. the conscious activity of ordinary workers, was an important feature of the history of individual enterprises and, indeed, the politics of the country as a whole.

As Musić shows, mounting worker dissatisfaction and unrest fed directly into the legitimacy crisis of the ruling institutions. The higher party echelons of the 1980s, he shows, were reliant on the very same specialists that they had campaigned against in the 1970s, and whom workers actively distrusted. Prompted to discuss their views, however, workers in IMR actively sought figures in the higher party-state officialdom who would take their side against management and specialists, but without success. The sense of being blocked increased dissatisfaction, which kept building as time passed (Musić, 2021, pp. 122–131). While management in TAM used nationalist divide-and-rule tactics consistently in the mid-1980s, that was eschewed in IMR, until after the leaked publication of the excerpts of the infamous Memorandum of the Serbian Academy of Sciences in 1986. The Memorandum was a Serb nationalist diatribe against the paralysed Yugoslav federal state, but, as Musić recounts it, ordinary workers in IMR felt that their own company was paralysed and hobbled like the federal state, a feeling many industrial workers across the country shared. The promise of radical institutional reform sounded like a way out of the impasse, and legitimised the use of extra-institutional mobilisation like strikes (Musić, 2021, pp. 147–185).

The explosion of extra-institutional mobilisation worked itself out differently across the Yugoslav republics in the late 1980s. The nature of workers' self-management played an important role in how these transpired. Slobodan Milošević rose to prominence as a defender of Serb national interests, but also a champion of self-management *and* a market reformer, calling for obstacles to be removed so that the individual and society would 'to be able to enrich themselves' (Musić, 2021, p. 187). This appealed to many workers, but the older generations were less receptive to Milošević's nationalist messaging than younger and more rural constituencies. Milošević's 'Anti-bureaucratic Revolution' in 1988–1989 channelled national and class resentments in a direction that allowed him to attempt to centralise the federation (Musić, 2021, pp. 217–226). He failed, as other republic leaderships and populations preferred to quit Yugoslavia than be subordinated to Belgrade. Indeed, in Slovenia, unlike in Serbia, although there was also an independent strike movement, it resembled an explosion without an impact (Musić, 2021, pp. 226–238). Ironically, though, labour institutions in Serbia were weak compared to Slovenia in the transformation process. Marko Grdešić (2008) points out that Serbia's nationalist fervour through the 1990s wars lasted a comparatively long time, de-centring labour as an important category, preserving the role of trade unions as a conveyor belt for the state, and ultimately resulting in a privatisation process with few insider buy-outs in the 2000s. By contrast, Slovenia, with a short war of independence, saw privatisation occur in a process of insider buy-outs, in which management and labour continued a corporatist coalition, and labour unions developed a certain bargaining power. Yugoslavia's decentralised institutional infrastructure therefore left different, but connected, legacies after the disappearance of the state itself.

10. Conclusion

This paper is a contribution to the field of comparative capitalism studies. To simplify a little, we have delineated two approaches. The first, VoC, has faced criticism, not least for its lack of a theory of capitalism. Serving as little more than an 'empty signifier', capitalism is reduced to a synonym of market economy. This approach masks the exploitative nature of capitalist relations, privileges a functionalist explanatory framework, and cleaves to a methodological nationalism that overlooks global hierarchies of power. It also faces difficulties in assessing statist challengers to the dominant 'varieties'. The rise of China has made this a pressing issue, one that raises questions for comparative capitalism research: What accounts for China's rapid growth? Is China capitalist and, if so, since when?

The other major approach, in which capitalism is presented as 'variegated', overcomes many of the methodological flaws of VoC, as we have detailed above. Yet it too has encountered problems explaining the nature and rise of China. Several accounts treat China as state capitalist but they ignore the pre-Deng period, and the 'communist' system more broadly. This raises a further problem. If the variegated approach is to analyse capitalist development in the round, how does one deal with the so-called communist camp, which has since the 1920s represented a substantial swathe of the world economy?

Our account of capitalism explains its *étatiste* variants not as the result of archaic forces that disrupt a pristine logic of capitalist competition, but as the product of late development in the shadow of the leading liberal powers. We theorise the 'communist' economies as a state-capitalist model geared to catch-up industrialisation. In so doing, we bring them squarely into the purview of comparative capitalisms research, but this then obliges us to consider how to account for their differences. In the second half of the paper we take up this challenge, via a comparative analysis of two state-capitalist economies: the GDR (representing the orthodox Soviet model) and Yugoslavia (a maverick and relatively market-friendly variant). In studying the institutional forms that comprise their economic regimes (state, business, labour relations), with a particular focus on the automotive industry, we emphasise interlinkages with the world market and geopolitics. We explore their joint origins in a Soviet-led post-war transformation to which they related in contrasting ways: one as a creature of occupation, the other of revolution. This contrast, we show, carried implications for the institutions their regimes set out to build. We proceed to analyse their institutional evolution in three phases. In the 1950s, both states constructed command economies, but the GDR, as a client of the Soviet Union, sought to limit its dependence on the West, while Yugoslavia, in a non-aligned position, balanced between the blocs and undertook significant market reforms. The following sections deal with their attempts and ultimate failures to compete in a globalising era. The first phase (1961–1975) saw the two states and their industries attempt to fit into regional and, in Yugoslavia's case, global value chains. They increasingly found themselves caught between reliance on protected domestic and regional markets, principally the CMEA, and world market integration. When the global economic winds turned adverse in the subsequent era of neoliberal globalisation (1975–1990), their small-scale and debt-laden enterprises struggled to cope. The economic crisis of the Soviet bloc helped fuel political demands for national self-determination from Soviet tutelage across the region, leading ultimately to German unification, and accelerating Yugoslavia's dissolution.

In parsing the economic history of these two states with concepts from the variegated capitalism literature, we are heeding Phil Scranton's and Patrick Fridenson's (2013) call for a departure from longstanding assumptions that the West is the paradigm for business history. Business history must be able to bring in the 'Second' and 'Third' Worlds—the

West's Others. Those who take issue with our approach—that the GDR and Yugoslavia are best theorised as state capitalist entities—may instead develop a 'variegated socialisms' analysis, but it must necessarily address the relationship between those states and the world market. From the USSR in the 1930s to China today, 'communist' states have been significant actors within the world economy; for economic history and business history to develop a truly global perspective requires further engagement with that experience.

Notes

1. A case could be made that the physiocrats got there first, in that they advocated the conversion of France's political economy to the English model. Yet they lacked a conception of capitalism, and, except in the dimmest of outlines, of political-economic models/varieties. See Dale (2021).
2. In overstating the difference, they helped to impart the laissez-faire model with a reified status. See Dale, 2019.
3. Translation GD.
4. We leave aside the awkward fact that Weber's much vaunted 'rational capital accounting' drew on sophisticated banking and trading techniques borrowed by Italians from the Islamic world.
5. Italy, we may note, is the country of birth of Mariana Mazzucato, the author of *The Entrepreneurial State, Debunking public vs. private sector myths,* Anthem Press, 2003.
6. Parenthetically, we may note the shared biographies of Shonfield and Polanyi. Both were Hungarian Jews descended from rabbis, both were naturalised in Britain (albeit Shonfield was born there), both were married to Communist Slavic aristocrats.
7. The other two key volumes of this period were Esping-Andersen (1989) and Joseph Rogers Hollingsworth and Robert Boyer (1997).
8. Peck and Theodore (2007, p.766) play down the shift. They follow Fred Block in subsuming all institutionalist comparative capitalisms research under the label 'Polanyian'. This is misleading. Polanyi's method was utterly unlike that of the new institutionalists (Dale, 2016).
9. For similar reasons, Martin Wolf describes China as 'in a sense, the most "capitalist" economy ever'. The reason is simple: its rate of capital accumulation. Between 1997 and 2009, he notes, 'gross investment rose from 32 per cent to 46 per cent of GDP, while household consumption fell from 45 per cent of GDP to a mere 36 per cent. This must be the lowest share of consumption in any significant economy ever'. (Wolf, 2010).
10. The two senses of combined, writes Steven Rolf (2021, p. 4) "are intrinsically linked," in that UCD in the first sense, the pressure exerted by international political and economic competition, drives later developing states to initiate the second form of UCD, the combining of their existing economic elements (technologies, institutions, etc) with borrowings from the advanced economies.
11. Engels (1894 [1878]) *Herrn Eugen Dührings Umwälzung der Wissenschaft,* Stuttgart: Dietz, p.260 (translation GD).
12. And statism in the South cannot be explained in terms of inspiration from Moscow. Indeed, while Moscow at times encouraged the turn to ISI—not least because of the potential it brought for its manufacturing exporters—at other times it actively encouraged an export promotion orientation, with the exports in question almost exclusively primary products (Kidron, 1972, p.12).
13. This point should not, however, be overcooked. In his meticulously documented *Red Globalization*, Oscar Sanchez-Sibony (2014, p.6) goes so far as to claim that the Soviet economy 'became first autarkic and then globalized in roughly the same measure and on roughly the same timetable as the world first became autarkic in the interwar period and then globalized in the postwar'.
14. The CMEA's problems were typical of regionalist projects globally in this same period, many of which collapsed over arguments over distribution of benefits. Jaster, 1963, p.519; Ravenhill, 2005.

15. Full disclosure: One of the authors owned a British-imported Wartburg.
16. Emile Boustani (2019) suggests that VW arrived only in 1990. In fact, its involvement in the Eastern German economy began a decade earlier.

Disclosure statement

No potential conflict of interest was reported by the authors.

References

Ahrens, J., & Jünemann, P. (2010). Transitional institutions, institutional complementarities and economic performance in China: A 'varieties of capitalism' approach. *Ordnungspolitische Diskurse*. https://www.econstor.eu/handle/10419/55399.

Aldcroft, D. (2006). *Europe's third world, the European periphery in the interwar years*. Ashgate.

Artisien, P. F., & Holt, S. (1980). Yugoslavia and the E.E.C. in the 1970s. *JCMS: Journal of Common Market Studies, 18*(4), 355–369. https://doi.org/10.1111/j.1468-5965.1980.tb00852.x

Batović, A. (2017). *The Croatian spring: Nationalism, repression and foreign policy under Tito*. LB. Tauris.

Bauer, R. (1997). Car manufacture in the German Democratic Republic in the seventies: A modernization-project failure. *Icon, 3*, 106–123.

Bender, P. (1995). *Die 'Neue Ostpolitik' und ihre Folgen; Vom Mauerbau bis zur Vereinigung*. Deutscher Taschenbuch Verlag.

Berger, S., & Dore, R. (Eds.). (1996). *National diversity and global capitalism*. Cornell University Press.

Bernard, S. (2019). *Deutsch Marks in the Head, Shovel in the Hands and Yugoslavia in the Heart: The Gastarbeiter return to Yugoslavia (1965–1991). Series: Studien zur Sozial- und Wirtschaftsgeschichte Ostmitteleuropas (28)*. Harrassowitz Verlag.

Bohle, D., & Greskovits, B. (2012). *Capitalist diversity on Europe's periphery*. Cornell University Press.

Bombelles, J. T. (1968). *Economic development of communist Yugoslavia*. Hoover Institution Publications.

Boustani, E. (2019). *Variegated firm finance and global production networks: Car component manufacturers in Hungary and Eastern Germany* [PhD thesis]. Newcastle University.

Brink, T. T. (2013). Paradoxes of prosperity in China's new capitalism. *Journal of Current Chinese Affairs, 42*(4), 17–44.

Büge, M., Egeland, M., Kowalski, P., & Sztajerowska, M. (2013, May 2). State-owned enterprises in the global economy: Reason for concern? *VoxEU*. https://voxeu.org/article/state-owned-enterprises-global-economy-reason-concern

Carr, E. H. (1939). *The twenty years crisis, 1919–1939*. Palgrave Macmillan.

Ciesla, B. (2013). Winner takes all: The Soviet Union and the beginning of central planning in Eastern Germany, 1945–1949. In H. Berghoff & U. Balbier (Eds.), *The East German economy, 1945–2010: Falling behind or catching up?* Cambridge University Press.

Cliff, T. (1948/1974). *State capitalism in Russia*. Pluto.

Coates, D. (2000). Models of capitalism, polity.

Coates, D. (2014). The UK: Less a liberal market economy, more a post-imperial one. *Capital & Class, 38*(1), 171–182. https://doi.org/10.1177/0309816813514816

Crouch, C., & Streeck, W. (Eds.). (1997). *Political economy of modern capitalism: Mapping convergence and diversity*. Sage.

Czaban, L., & Henderson, J. (1998). Globalization, institutional legacies and industrial transformation in Eastern Europe. *Economy and Society, 27*(4), 585–613. https://doi.org/10.1080/03085149800000034

Dale, G. (1999). Capitalism and migrant labour. In G. Dale & M. Cole (Eds.), *The European Union and migrant labour* (pp. 281–314). Berg.

Dale, G. (2004). *Between state capitalism and globalization, the collapse of the East German economy*. Peter Lang.

Dale, G. (2011). The transition in Central and Eastern Europe. In G. Dale (Ed.), *First the transition, then the crash: Eastern Europe in the 2000s* (pp. 1–20). Pluto Press.
Dale, G. (2016). *Reconstructing Karl Polanyi*. Pluto Press.
Dale, G. (2017). After 1917: Civil war and 'modernising counter-revolution'. https://www.rs21.org.uk/2017/10/26/revolutonary-reflections-after-1917-civil-war-and-modernising-counter-revolution/
Dale, G. (2019). Justificatory fables of ordoliberalism: Laissez-faire and the 'third way'. *Critical Sociology, 45*(7–8), 1047–1060. https://doi.org/10.1177/0896920519832638
Dale, G. (2020). Amazon burning. https://www.academia.edu/52935366/Amazon_burning/
Dale, G. (2021). Rule of nature or rule of capital? Physiocracy, ecological economics, and ideology. *Globalizations, 18*(7), 1230–1247. https://doi.org/10.1080/14747731.2020.1807838
Damus, R. (1990). Jenseits von Realem Sozialismus und Kapitalismus. In M. Heine, et al. (eds.), *Die Zukunft der DDR-Wirtschaft*. Rowohlt.
Dobrivojević Tomić, I. (2019). Harbingers of crisis. Labour strikes in Yugoslavia (1958–1974). *Istorija 20. Veka, 1*, 161–174.
Dore, R. (2000). *Stock market capitalism, welfare capitalism: Japan and Germany versus the Anglo-Saxons*. Oxford University Press.
Draper, H. (1989). *Karl Marx's theory of revolution* (Vol. IV). Monthly Review Press.
Duda, I. (2010). *Pronađeno blagostanje. Svakodnevni život i potrošačka kultura u Hrvatskoj 1970-ih i 1980-ih*. Srednja Europa.
Dyker, D. A. (2011/1990). *Yugoslavia, socialism, development and debt*. Routledge.
Esping-Andersen, G. (1989). *The three worlds of welfare capitalism*. John Wiley & Sons.
Estrin, S., & Uvalic, M. (2008). From Illyria towards capitalism: Did labour-management theory teach us anything about Yugoslavia and transition in its successor states? *Comparative Economic Studies, 50*(4), 663–696. https://doi.org/10.1057/ces.2008.41
Etzerodt, S. F., & Eriksen, J. (2017). *Varieties of capitalism and varieties of welfare state capitalism: An empirical assessment of economic growth*. Centre for Comparative Welfare Studies, Institut for Økonomi, Politik og Forvaltning, Aalborg Universitet.
Feldmann, M. (2019). Global varieties of capitalism. *World Politics, 71*(1), 162–196. https://doi.org/10.1017/S0043887118000230
Flaherty, D. (1982). Economic reform and foreign trade in Yugoslavia. *Cambridge Journal of Economics, 6*(2), 105–143.
Gerschenkron, A. (1962). *Economic backwardness in historical perspective: A book of essays*. Belknap Press of Harvard University Press.
Good, D. F., & Ma, T. (1999). The economic growth of Central and Eastern Europe in comparative perspective, 1870–1989. *European Review of Economic History, 3*(2), 103–137. https://doi.org/10.1017/S1361491699000076
Graf, M. (2020). Drifting Westward? East Germany and integrated Europe, in European socialist regimes. In A. Romano & F. Romero (Eds.), *Fateful engagement with the West: National strategies in the long 1970s*. Routledge.
Granick, D. (1975). *Enterprise guidance in Eastern Europe: A comparison of socialist economies*. Princeton.
Grdešić, M. (2008). Mapping the paths of the Yugoslav model: Labour strength and weakness in Slovenia, Croatia and Serbia. *European Journal of Industrial Relations, 14*(2), 133–151. https://doi.org/10.1177/0959680108089187
Hall, P., & Soskice, D. (Eds.). (2001). *Varieties of capitalism: The institutional foundations of comparative advantage*. Oxford University Press.
Harris, N. (1971). Imperialism today. In J. Palmer & N. Harris (Eds.), *World crisis*. Hutchinson.
Hay, C. (2005). Two can play at that game … or can they? Varieties of capitalism, varieties of institutionalism. In D. Coates (ed.), *Varieties of capitalism, varieties of approaches*. Palgrave.
Haynes, M. (2002). *Russia – Class and power, 1917–2000*. Bookmarks.
Haynes, M., & Husan, R. (2002). Whether by visible or invisible hand: The intractable problem of Russian and East European catch up. *Competition & Change, 6*(3), 269–287. https://doi.org/10.1080/10245290215043

Hobson, J. (2004). *The Eastern origins of Western civilisation*. Cambridge University Press.

https://www.hagerty.com/media/car-profiles/maligned-and-misunderstood-east-germanys-tiny-trabant-left-an-outsized-legacy/

https://www.marxists.org/archive/lenin/works/1922/nov/14b.htm

Hollingsworth, J. R., & Boyer, R. (Eds.). (1997). *Contemporary capitalism: The embeddedness of institutions*. Cambridge University Press.

Jaster, R. (1963). The defeat of Khrushchev's plan to integrate Eastern Europe. *The World Today, 19*(12), 519.

Jessop, B. (2007). What follows neoliberalism? The deepening contradictions of US domination and the struggle for a new global order. In R. Albritton, R. Jessop, and R. Westra (eds.), *Political economy and global capitalism: The 21st century, present and future*. Anthem Press.

Johnson, C. (1999). The developmental state: Odyssey of a concept. In M. Woo-Cumings (Ed.), *The developmental state* (pp. 32–60). Cornell University.

Jovanov, N. (1979). *Radnički štrajkovi u SFRJ*. Zapis.

Kennedy, P. (1988). *The rise and fall of the great powers*. Random House.

Kidron, M. (1966). Some trees, no wood. *International Socialism*, No. 24.

Kidron, M. (1972). *Pakistan's trade with eastern bloc countries*. Ardent Media. https://www.marxists.org/archive/kidron/works/1966/xx/nowood.htm

Koscs, J. (2021, October 4). Maligned and misunderstood, East Germany's tiny Trabant left an outsized legacy. *Hagerty*.

Kurlantzick, J. (2016). *State capitalism: How the return of statism is transforming the world*. Oxford University Press.

Lampe, J. R. (2000). *Yugoslavia as history: Twice there was a country*. Cambridge University Press.

Lampe, J. R. (2013). Yugoslavia's foreign policy in Balkan perspective: Tracking between the superpowers and non-alignment. *East Central Europe, 40*(1–2), 97–113. https://doi.org/10.1163/18763308-04001001

Lazić, M. (2021). Arsenal of the global south: Yugoslavia's military aid to nonaligned countries and liberation movements. *Nationalities Papers, 49*(3), 428–445.

Lenin, V. I. (1922/1971). *To the Russian colony in North America. Lenin collected works* (Vol. 42, pp. 425–427). Progress Publishers.

Mark, J., & Rupprecht, T. (2019). The socialist world in global history: From absentee to victim to co-producer. In M. Middell (Ed.), *The practice of global history: European perspectives* (pp. 81–115). Bloomsbury Academic.

Marsh, P. (1973). *The politics of integration in Eastern Europe* [M.A. dissertation]. University of Manchester.

Marx, K. (2004). *Capital* (Vol. 1). Penguin.

Marx, C., & Reitmayer, M. (2019). Introduction: Rhenish capitalism and business history. *Business History, 61*(5), 745–784. https://doi.org/10.1080/00076791.2019.1583211

McNally, C. (2007). China's capitalist transition: The making of a new variety of capitalism. In L. Mjøset & T. H. Clausen (Eds.), *Capitalisms compared* (Comparative social research, Vol. 24, pp. 177–203). Emerald Group Publishing Limited.

Molnar, C. (2014). Imagining Yugoslavs: Migration and the Cold War in postwar West Germany. *Central European History, 47*(1), 138–169. https://doi.org/10.1017/S000893891400065X

Musić, G. (2021). *Making and breaking the Yugoslav working class: The story of two self-managed factories*. CEU Press.

Palairet, M. (1992). Ramiz Sadiku: A case study in the industrialisation of Kosovo. *Soviet Studies, 44*(5), 897–912. https://doi.org/10.1080/09668139208412052

Palairet, M. (1993). Mismanaging Innovation: The Yugo Car Enterprise (1962–1992). *Technovation, 13*(3), 117–132. https://doi.org/10.1016/0166-4972(93)90035-T

Peck, J., & Theodore, N. (2007). Variegated capitalism. *Progress in Human Geography, 31*(6), 731–772. https://doi.org/10.1177/0309132507083505

Peck, J., & Zhang, J. (2013). A variety of capitalism … with Chinese characteristics? *Journal of Economic Geography, 13*(3), 357–396. https://doi.org/10.1093/jeg/lbs058

Perović, J. (2007). The Tito-Stalin split: A reassessment in light of new evidence. *Journal of Cold War Studies, 9*(2), 32–63. https://doi.org/10.1162/jcws.2007.9.2.32
Peukert, H. (2001). The Schmoller renaissance. *History of Political Economy, 33*(1), 71–116. https://doi.org/10.1215/00182702-33-1-71
Pezo, O. (1983). *Vojna industrija Jugoslavije*. VIZ.
Pontusson, J. (2005). Varieties and commonalities of capitalism. In D. Coates (Ed.), *Varieties of capitalism, varieties of approaches* (pp. 163–188). Palgrave.
Prevezer, M. (2019). *Varieties of capitalism in history, transition and emergence, new perspectives on institutional development*. Routledge.
Przybylski, P. (1992). *Tatort Politbüro, Band 2*. Rowohlt.
Ramet, R. (Ed.). (1985). *Yugoslavia in the 1980s*. Westview Press.
Ravenhill, J. (2005). Regional trade agreements. In J. Ravenhill (ed.), *Global political economy*. Oxford University Press.
Rehmann, J. (1998). *Max Weber: Modernisierung als passive Revolution. Kontextstudien zu Politik, Philosophie und Religion im Übergang zum Fordismus*. Argument Verlag.
Rolf, S. (2021). *China's Uneven and Combined Development*. Palgrave.
Sacks, S. (1983). *Self-management and efficiency: Large corporations in Yugoslavia*. Routledge.
Sanchez-Sibony, O. (2014). *Red globalization: The political economy of the Soviet Cold War from Stalin to Khrushchev*. Cambridge University Press.
Schierup, C. U. (1990). *Migration, socialism, and the international division of labour: The Yugoslavian experience*. Aldershot.
Schneider, B. R. (2013). *Hierarchical capitalism in Latin America: Business, labor, and the challenges of equitable development*. Cambridge University Press.
Schwartz, H. (2010). *States versus markets: History, geography and the development of the international political economy*. Macmillan.
Scranton, P., & Fridenson, P. (2013). *Reimagining business history*. JHU Press.
Selwyn, B. (2011). Trotsky, Gerschenkron and the political economy of late capitalist development. *Economy and Society, 40*(3), 421–450. https://doi.org/10.1080/03085147.2011.574425
Shabad, G. (1980). Strikes in Yugoslavia: Implications for industrial democracy. *British Journal of Political Science, 10*(3), 293–315. https://doi.org/10.1017/S0007123400002210
Shonfield, A. (1965). *Modern capitalism: The changing balance of public & private power*. Oxford University Press.
Sirc, L. (1979). *Yugoslav economy under self-management*. Macmillan Press.
Spaskovska, L., & Calori, A. (2021). A nonaligned business world: The global socialist enterprise between self-management and transnational capitalism. *Nationalities Papers, 49*(3), 413–427. https://doi.org/10.1017/nps.2020.27
Stankovic, M. J. (2018). Automotive factory 'Crvena Zastava': Yugoslav self-management socialism and challenges for national automobile industry. *The Journal of Transport History, 39*(2), 236–251. https://doi.org/10.1177/0022526618763597
Streeck, W. (2010). *E pluribus unum? Varieties and commonalities of capitalism*. MPIfG Discussion Paper 10/12.
Swain, G., & Swain, N. (1998). *Eastern Europe since 1945* (2nd ed.). Routledge.
Taylor, N. (2014). Theorising capitalist diversity: The uneven and combined development of labour forms. *Capital & Class, 38*(1), 129–141. https://doi.org/10.1177/0309816813513091
Trecker, M. (2020). *Red Money for the Global South: East–South economic relations in the Cold War*.
Unkovski-Korica, V. (2014). Workers' councils in the service of the market: New archival evidence on the origins of self-management in Yugoslavia 1948–1950. *Europe-Asia Studies, 66*(1), 108–134. https://doi.org/10.1080/09668136.2013.855020
Unkovski-Korica, V. (2016). *The economic struggle power in Tito's Yugoslavia*. I.B. Tauris.
Van der Pijl, K. (2005). *Transnational classes and international relations*. Routledge.
Weber, M. (2019). *Economy & society* (K. Tribe, Trans.). Harvard University Press.
Weeks, J. (1997). The law of value and the analysis of underdevelopment. *Historical Materialism, 1*(1), 91–112. https://doi.org/10.1163/156920697100414113

Wehr, I. (2015). Entangled modernity and the study of variegated capitalism: Some suggestions for a postcolonial research agenda. In M. Ebenau (Ed.), *New directions in comparative capitalisms research*. Palgrave.

Witt, M. A. (2010). *China: What variety of capitalism?* INSEAD Working Paper No. 2010/88/EPS. SSRN. https://ssrn.com/abstract=1695940 or https://doi.org/10.2139/ssrn.1695940.

Wolf, M. (2010, September 22). How China must change if it is to sustain its ascent. *Financial Times*, p. 15.

Woodward, S. (1995). *Socialist unemployment: The political economy of Yugoslavia 1945–1990*. Princeton.

World Bank. (1983). *A World Bank country study*. Adjustment Policies and Development Perspectives. http://documents.worldbank.org/curated/en/784961468760753771/pdf/multi-page.pd

Index

Page numbers in **bold** refer to tables and those in *italic* refer to figures.

Ahrens, Joachim 127
Akgöz, Görkem 78
the Anglo-Saxon world 90
anticipated double production volumes 43
Association of German Chambers of Industry and Commerce 89
Augustine, Dolores L. 79
A Worker in a Worker's State: pro-market/pseudo-market policies 75–6; rational calculations 75; SED-leaders 75, 76

Basic organizations of associated labour (BOALs) 28, 29
Bentley, Raymond 8
Betts, P. 5
'Block 6' (Mamutica (the Mammut)) 26
Bockman, Johanna 5
Böll, Heinrich 74
The Bosnian War 111–12
Bretton Woods institutions 95
Brink, Tobias Ten 128
Bukharin, Nikolai 131
Bulatovic, Dimitrije 44
bureaucratic state capitalism 130–2
business history 7–9, 106–7

Calori, A. 5, 141
Calvinism 124
capitalism 129
capitalist market competition 129
Carr, E. H. 132
casino speculation mentality 123
Chandler, A. D. 1, 3
The Chandlerian method 2
Chinese state capitalism 123
Coates, David 126, 127
comparative capitalism 122, 126–7
comparative political economy 124
competition and exploitation 123
contractual management 45
coordinated market economy (CME) 7, 126
Cop, Mate 23–4
corporatism 130–1
Croatian spring 28
Crouch, Colin 125

Dayton Peace Agreement (1995) 113
decentralisation and deregulation 77–8
Despotovic, Vlado 24
diversity of planning regimes 124–6
Dore, R. 125

East German 'Association of Entrepreneurs 100–1
East German 'entrepreneurship' 93–4
economic co-operation 6
Eriksen, Jesper 124
Etzerodt, Søren 124
export-oriented companies 109

factories for production of factories 20
'failed' negotiations 115
Fava, Valentina 2, 3
financial investment 41
Fordism 2
Frost, Adam K. 3–4, 20

German Democratic Republic (GDR) function 8; East German industry 57; Hartmann, external representative of AME 64–5; historical roots 60–1; innovative process 57–9; Jena, Carl Zeiss 66–8; microelectronics program 61–4; technology transfer and secret police 65–6
Germuska, Pál 6
Gerth, Karl 4
globalisation 107
Görlich, Paul (1905–1986) 60
Granick, David 2
Great Leap Forward (1958) 4

Hall, Peter A. 6, 126
Haraszti, Miklós 74
Harris, N. 132
Hartmann, Matthias Falter (1908–1985) 60–3
Hartmann, Werner (1912–1988) 60

hidden champions 90
high party functionaries 81
Hilferding, Rudolf 131
Holt, Knut 59
homers 75
Hübner, P. 80, 82, 83
hydraulic sliding formwork 24

Iandolo, Alessandro 5
import-substitution industrialisation (ISI) 130–1
Industrogradnja Zagreb (1966–1980): becoming large industrial system 23–7, **26**; business history 19; case of *Uljanik* 19; company papers 19; counter-reform and atomisation of 1970s 27–32, *30*; large business structures 19; marketisation and birth 20–3; socio-economic framework 18
Institute of World Economics of the Hungarian Academy of Sciences 126
institutionalism method 124
international community 114
international experts 114

Jarausch, Konrad 77
Jelinic, Grga 24
Jena, Carl Zeiss 60, 66–8, 79–82
Jünemann, Patrick 127

Keynesianism 130–1
Kopstein, J. 75, 77, 82, 83
Kortum, Herbert (1907–1979) 60
Kosmet Šper 40–1, 43
Kragh, M. 2
Krneta, Nikola 22–3
Kulikov, Volodymyr 2, 3

Labour Communities (LC) 31–2
LaFalce, John J. 96
Lampland, Martha 77
League of Communists 49
Lenin, V. I. 132
liberal market economy (LME) 7, 126
Lindenberger, T. 77, 78
Luft, Christa 89, 95–6, 98

Macrakis, Kristie 59
Maier, Helmut 6
Manchester capitalism 123
Mark, J. 5, 133
Marx, C. 126
Marxists 128
Marx, Karl 123
Mcnally, Christopher 127
Mirkovic, Đuro 19
Mittelstand 89–90, 93
modernization 107
Modrow government 90, 99
Modrow, Hans 95
municipal commission 43

neo-American model 125
New Economic System (NES) 79
New International Economic Order 108
Newly Industrialising Countries (NICs) 132
Nimon, Fazli 47
non-aligned movement (NAM): Belgrade in 1961 108; developing and newly de-colonised countries 108; economists and researchers 109; Energoinvest's managers 111; engineers and experts 110; export-oriented companies 109; fierce capitalist competitor 110; Global South 110; UNCTAD 108; workers' councils 111; Yugoslav Federal Council for International Technical Cooperation 108–9
non-alignment 106–7

objective factors 42
"objective" strategic decisions 47
October revolution (1917) 1
Office of the High Representative (OHR) 113
old 'Zeissianers' 79
Oreškovic, Mirko 19
Osnovna organizacija udruženog rada (OOuR) 28

Peck, J. 128
People's republic of china 3
Polanyians 126, 128
Pontusson, Jonas 127
Prevezer, Martha 126
private economy 97–8
property reforms 96–7

reformed socialism 95–6
Reitmayer, M. 126
research and development (R&D) *see* German Democratic Republic (GDR) function
reunification 95
Rhine model 125
Rolf, Steven 130
Romano, Angela 5
Romero, Federico 5
Roscher, Wilhelm 123–4
Rupprecht, Tobias 133

sales of plywood 42
Sanchez-Sibony, Oscar 5
Schäffle, Albert 124
Schiefer, Mark 59
Schmoller, Gustav 124
Schulz, Ulrike 58
Scranton, Philip 4, 77, 82
Seidman Michael 75
self-management 20
self-management agreement (SMA) 29
self-managing community of interest for housing (SCIH) 27
Shonfield, A. 124, 125

shopfloor 82–4
shop managers 47
Small and Medium Enterprises (SMEs) 113
socialist fordism 77–8
socialist globalisation 106–7
Socialist Unity Party 58, 89–91
Socialist Yugoslavia: first post-war decade 39; General Agreement on Tariffs and Trade 39; *Kosmet Šper* 40; market reforms and regional development 40; professionalization of management 44–6; rise and fall of 41–4; socio-economic conditions 40; *see also* "subjective" production relations
social market economy 100
Sombart, Werner 124
Soskice, David 6, 126
Soviet atomic bomb program 60
Soviet-style/Soviet-derived systems 2
Spaskovska, L. 5, 141
Stalinism 130–1
state capitalism: soviet-style 132–3; *see also* variegated capitalism
state-influenced market economy (SME) 126
state owned enterprises (SOEs) 131
State Planning Commission 58
stock market capitalism 126
Stokes, Raymond 78
Streeck, Wolfgang 125
subjective factors 42
"subjective" production relations: description 46; peasant-worker 49–51; production planning 46; shifting understandings of skill 47–9
Suvin, Darko 22

Taylor, Nick 127
technoscience and high tech fields 60
timber production 41
Tito, Josip Broz 108
totalitarian command-and-control system 2

Ulbricht, Walter 58, 91–2
uneven and combined development (UCD) 123, 127–30
US Joint Publications Research Service (1957–1995) 4

variegated capitalism: dilemmas of globalisation (1961–1975) 139–43; GDR and Yugoslavia 134; geopolitical and geo-economic competition 134; global shocks and unravelling of state capitalism (1975–1991) 143–7; national capitalisms (1945–1961) 134–9; periodisation phases 134
variegation 127–8
Varieties of Capitalism (VoC) paradigm 6, 122

wage differentiation 48
Wagner, Adolf 124
war economies 130–1
Washington Consensus 125
Weber, Max 124
Wehr, Ingrid 128
welfare capitalism 126
welfare dictatorship 77
Welskopp, Thomas 58
Wenzel, Bernd 63
The West Berlin congress 89
Wood Institute in Zagreb 43
World Bank document 145

Yányshev-Nésterova, Irina 5
Yudanov, Andrei 3, 94
Yugoslav companies 107–8
Yugoslav Federal Council for International Technical Cooperation 108–9

Zeiss-employees 80–1
Zhang, J. 128

FSC
www.fsc.org
MIX
Papier | Fördert
gute Waldnutzung
FSC® C083411

Kolibri 360 GmbH
Ferdinand-Jühlke-Straße 7
99095 Erfurt, Deutschland
produktsicherheit@kolibri360.de